Infrastructures of Freedom

jovis

Infrastructures of Freedom

Stephanie Briers

jovis

Public Light and Everynight Life on a Southern City's Margins

Acknowledgements

I begin my acknowledgements with
Prof. Dr. Christian Schmid and Prof. Dr. Sophie
Oldfield for shaping this research with me.
Thanks to all the professors in the Urban Research
Incubator (URI) at the Institute for Science
Technology and Policy (ISTP) at ETH Zurich, for
ensuring strong collaborations within the group,
notably Prof. Hubert Klumpner.

To the rest of the URI group – Samuel Lloyd,
Christian Joubert, Michael Walczak, David Kretzer,
David Kostenwein and Yael Borofsky— thank you
for the reviews and many good research discussions. To the rest of the team at ISTP, it has been a
pleasure to be part of the institute, a special thank
you to Dietmar Huber. To Sophie's students at
the African Centre for Cities, our online meetings
every two weeks and writing sessions kept me going during the pandemic.

The project team deserves a massive thank you.
Together, we managed to install more than
700 lights in PJS Informal Settlement. What
started as a big dream became a reality because
of the team. Firstly, thank you to my project partners, Yael Borofsky and Prof. Dr. Isabel Guenther.
Without your collaboration, the project would
have remained on paper. To the PJS Informal
Settlement community, especially the leaders,
thank you for trusting me, welcoming me into
your community and being patient when the
project was delayed. Thank you to the local survey team and local installation teams for working
very hard to make this project happen. Thank
you, especially to the maintenance team, you
were absolutely central in keeping this project
on track. Yamkela Rongwana, Sibongile Mvumvu,
Jennifer Qongo, Thabile Tsitsa, Anele Dekada
and Mandilakhe Weni, thank you for giving your
all to this project. Thank you to Thabisa Mfubesi
and Xolelwa Maha, two of the most powerful
woman I have met. You were the first to welcome
me into PJS, and you remained by my side
throughout the project, always ready for the next
challenge. Pam, thank you for all the sleepovers
in PJS. Keyaam Dutoit, thank you for stepping in
when we could not be there to install the second
phase of lights due to the pandemic — always
with utmost professionalism.

Thanks to the film team, Ilzé Myburgh, Sandiswa
Tshefu, Bulelani Mvotho, Mveliso Jevu, Götz
Froeschke, Mandisi Sindo, Hangula Lukas and
Nasi Tautona, for making the research results into
a beautiful short film, accessible to all.

Social Justice Coalition, thank you for offering a
home base in Khayelitsha, for endorsing our research and supporting us in our funding applications. To the City of Cape Town, thank you for
approving our research and also endorsing it as
useful to the development of new public lighting
solutions in self-built communities.

On a personal note, I would like to thank the late
Sally, and thereafter Nadya, for getting me through
the toughest moments during my research. Thank
you to my friends who accompanied me throughout this process, particularly Amy, Carolina and
Angelica. Thank you to my entire family for
believing in me and letting me do my research,
even when it meant putting myself in a potentially
dangerous situation. Greg, thank you for always
offering to help during my fieldwork. Wianelle,
thank you for sacrificing so much time to make my
PhD a success. Thank you, Lucas Lerchs, for being
my pillar of strength, partner and collaborator.

Thank you to the funders of this research:
Zumtobel Group, ETH for Development (ETH4D),
the ISTP and the Department of Architecture,
Chair of Sociology at ETH Zurich. Thank you to
the funders of this publication: the Department
of Architecture, Chair of Sociology at ETH Zurich,
and the Swiss National Science Foundation.

Foreword

by Christian Schmid and Sophie Oldfield

In *Infrastructures of Freedom: Public Light and Everynight Life on a Southern City's Margins*, Stephanie Briers demonstrates the ways in which darkness and a lack of public lighting mark the boundaries that work to exclude residents and settlements materially and routinely from the city and from rights to citizenship. She shows the ways in which access to public lighting, in contrast, can work to blur these boundaries, arguing that: lighting as infrastructures of freedom can liberate everynight life from debilitating darkness.

This is a critical and original book. Through in-depth, multi-dimensional, qualitative research and the piloting of an experimental solar lighting project, Briers makes visible literally and figuratively the realities of everynight life, and the impact that solar public lighting can make in PJS Informal Settlement (PJS) and in settlements surrounding it in Khayelitsha, Cape Town. To make this argument, the book tracks the realities and limits, the dangers and fears resident face, their everynight life in the shadows of highly insufficient apartheid-era high-mast lighting. These realities, Briers conceptualises as nightlife lived 'trapped by darkness'. Pivoted on the piloting of solar lighting in the settlement, Briers demonstrates the ways in which solar lights—placed above front doors and in alleyways—'free the night', shifting fundamentally the material and emotive possibilities for life at night in the settlement. In short, public lighting is an infrastructure that shapes freedom and citizenship—and its corollary, exclusion—in South African cities

and in similar contexts elsewhere on the margins of southern cities.

In this book, Stephanie Briers demonstrates compellingly the imperative of interweaving technical approaches to public lighting with social scientific work on the social and material realities of everynight life in settlements. The research that underpins this book is truly exceptional. Briers draws on a creative and rigorous mix of qualitative interviews, focus group and theatre-based workshops, large scale survey work, visualisation, and mapping, as well as a participatory experimental piloting of solar lighting itself. Visually rich, *Infrastructures of Freedom* combines powerfully rendered and effective mapping at multiple scales, from the city, across Khayelitsha, and within PJS itself. It draws readers into its argument through evocative photography, which share powerfully the physical and social spaces of the settlement in the light of day and the darkness of night, before and after the solar lighting installation. It draws on participatory photo methods, through which participants themselves share the precise spaces of darkness in the settlement and these hard lived realities. It shares Briers' own journey as a researcher, creating, navigating, and participating with residents in the research process. These empathic, insightful, and sensitive observations are combined with a strong analytical perspective, making this a work of outstanding scholarship.

The piloting of solar lighting is the pivot on which the book and its argument build. Briers shares the effective and meaningful co-production of this public lighting intervention, which she implemented with her colleague Yael Borofsky from the Institute of Science, Technology and Policy (ISTP) at ETH Zurich and which built on careful collaboration with community leaders, the Social Justice Coalition, a Cape Town-based NGO, and the City of Cape Town. Designing, coordinating, implementing, and managing the lighting project was extremely complex. It required persistence, ambition, savvy, as well as the capacity and energy to push ahead a multi-layered collaboration with community, NGO, City, and solar lighting industry stakeholders. It built on Briers' technical and social understanding of lighting, rooted in the empirical realities of the settlement's material and social organisation. Against many odds—including the start of the COVID-19 pandemic—the project was implemented successfully with the local leadership, who Stephanie involved in the design, coordination and management of the placing and monitoring, and maintenance of solar lights.

Through the analysis of the co-produced solar light intervention, the book powerfully shares and theorises the impact of the project, demonstrating the ways it is a local lighting solution built 'within the settlement', as opposed to 'from above', the problem of most public lighting approaches. Here, Briers demonstrates concretely the ways in which technical interventions in public lighting operate in a literal 'blindsight'. She moves beyond critique by demonstrating in practice how projects can be reworked to root in a rigorous reading of the social and material logics of lived realities in self-built communities. The book documents and reflects on the pilot project, tracking the technical dimensions on which the project was built and developed, from virtual reality testing to the monitoring

and mapping of community resources, household surveys, and the placing of solar lights. It shares the layers of experimentation, the failures, and the creative ways obstacles were overcome. In this careful discussion and reflection, Briers shows how settlement leaders and the local solar light maintenance team, with participating residents, fundamentally shaped the project, grounding the lighting experimentation and solution in their own work and knowledge of the realities of life in the settlement. This inclusive and participatory approach to the lighting project played an important role for its success: after the conclusion of the project, the newly installed public lighting has become both an individual and a collective "ownership" of light and thus is understood as contributing to the collective good. In that sense, this book is also a practical guide for the planning and implementation of infrastructure projects in underserviced neighbourhoods. Indeed, this project has already become an exemplar for the City of Cape Town and its planning of solar lighting elsewhere in the city.

In short, *Infrastructures of Freedom* is a 'must read'. It brings into 'light' the possibilities that solar-driven public lighting can offer to families and settlements insufficiently serviced on the margins of southern cities. It addresses a significant gap in work on lighting, integrating a body of architectural and engineering research into lighting as technical intervention with qualitative, phenomenological, social-theoretical work on light and its criticality for urban life. It builds with settlement residents, leaders, the City and NGOs in an ethical and collaborative way, placing this expertise and lived experience—embodied, material, and performative knowledge—at the heart of its analysis.

Completed as a PhD in ISTP at ETH Zurich, this book also documents a path-breaking transdisciplinary research project. It provides an architectural doctoral work, combining empirical (social) research with the practical realisation of an architectural project and concrete proposals for politics and planning. It has been a pleasure and privilege to work with Stephanie Briers as her PhD advisors, to be advocates for her, and supporters of this ambitious, important, and rigorous research. We hope readers enjoy this beautifully crafted, critical argument for paying attention to everynight life, for imagining the ways that infrastructure might create freedom, and for engaging with human-centred, as well as technical, solutions to public lighting in southern cities.

Christian Schmid
Department of Architecture, ETH Zurich

Sophie Oldfield
Department of City and Regional Planning, Cornell University
African Centre for Cities, University of Cape Town

Introduction

How does a lack of adequate public lighting infrastructure play out in everynight life? And what does it mean to confront darkness on a nightly basis in self-built communities, from walking through dark, narrow pathways, to the inability to recognise someone as a friend or a foe or feeling lonely and trapped because of darkness?

Everyday life in 'informal settlements'[1] or self-built communities in Cape Town and across the globe is challenging, from meeting one's basic sanitation needs to accessing opportunities and living a dignified life. In these communities, everynight life comes with additional challenges that go far beyond the daily challenges. Darkness is an everyday feature that contributes to and exacerbates daily struggles. Nightlife is shaped by fear that prevents people from venturing out to meet even their most basic needs. For many residents in self-built communities, commuting hours are long. They spend the daylight hours at work, and leave and return home in the dark. Darkness forms a large part of their domestic experience.

Khayelitsha is an apartheid-planned township[2] located on the outskirts of Cape Town. It is the second largest township in South Africa with a high rate of informality. Cape Town is a city well known for its historical inequality (UN-Habitat, 2012); an inequality also reflected in the City's public lighting infrastructure and racial demography (Maps 1 and 2). Khayelitsha and its self-built communities have a history of darkness and inadequate public lighting. It is therefore an appropriate context to address the lived realities of darkness and everynight life.

There are currently two main public lighting modes in Cape Town: 30–40 metre tall high-mast lights that cast light in a 175–200-metre radius, and pole-mounted streetlights (City of Cape Town Memorandum, 2013). Khayelitsha is predominantly lit with high-mast lighting, first implemented by the apartheid government exclusively in townships. For many, high-mast lights symbolise apartheid, setting areas like Khayelitsha apart from the rest of the city and intensifying inequality between areas that the apartheid government racially segregated. Technically, high-mast lights do not provide even lighting in densely built-up areas with narrow pathways, but instead cast dark shadows. In many self-built communities, darkness and the complete lack of public lighting is even more problematic than insufficient high-mast lighting. Widespread, planned power outages are increasingly frequent in South Africa, leaving whole neighbourhoods in the dark and further exacerbating public lighting problems. Living in the dark shadows of high-mast lighting or in total darkness exacerbates daily struggles in self-built communities, and compromises a sense of dignified living. It brings about feelings of being forgotten by the state.

---

1   The term 'informal settlements' relates directly to the terminology that is most commonly and colloquially used by South Africans, including residents of self-built communities. I also use this term to relate directly to the South African policy landscape, where the term is also used to refer to neighbourhoods that are self-constructed.

2   Neighbourhoods designated for black migrant labourers during apartheid were referred to as townships and are still colloquially referred to as townships. Thus, the term township is connotated to neighbourhoods that have a predominantly black population.

With this lived reality in mind, and because of the increased necessity to go outside at nighttime to access basic services, public lighting in self-built communities should be prioritised over all neighbourhoods in cities. In self-built communities, the public realm is an extension of one's home and accessing the public realm safely and comfortably at night is a very important component to meet basic needs with dignity. However, darkness hinders this vital need to access services, essentially trapping people indoors, and restricting opportunities and community life. Not acknowledging the nighttime in everyday life neglects a major component that brings about much stress in daily life. Nighttime stresses move far beyond the technical means to access services and opportunities, raising many abstract and concrete concerns, from not being able to go to the toilet at night to feeling lonely or forgotten.

Within the research context, the main keywords I use in the literature are infrastructure and everyday life, darkness and light, and informality. My research is built on the existing argument that infrastructure articulates citizenship through everyday lived infrastructure (Graham and McFarlane, 2015). Yet, the impact that darkness has on infrastructural citizenship (Lemanski, 2019) and the everynight experiences of light or darkness are topics that are absent in the discourse of infrastructure and everyday life, particularly in self-built communities. To refocus everyday experiences on the night, I develop the terminology everynight life, which I use and build on throughout the thesis. I also use urban lighting literature to frame the everyday experiences around lighting infrastructure specifically.

The most prominent literature on urban lighting is on the link between light and the reduction in crime or fear of crime (David P. Farrington and Brandon C. Welsh, 2002, 2008; Chalfin et al., 2021; Painter, 1991b, 1996, 1994). Public lighting has also been linked to more pedestrian activity and greater confidence walking alone at night, improving nighttime access to basic services and promoting a willingness to spend time outside at night in public space (Nasar and Bokharaei, 2017; Painter, 1996). Previous research on public lighting and crime has focused on the Global North, where informality is not a major part of the urban landscape. I build on the light and crime debate with empirical evidence from Khayelitsha's self-built communities, where lighting conditions are poor and crime and fear of crime are rife. The light-crime debate also disregards everyday experiences of fear of crime and the consequences crime has on daily life, focusing mainly on the correlation between improved light and reduced crime.

Social relations and public life also play a part in nighttime experiences. Lighting can contribute to increased sociability by creating an attractive nighttime atmosphere (Bordonaro, Entwistle and Slater, 2018). I draw on authors like Edensor (2012) to build the argument that it is not about whether there is light or no light, but rather about the type of urban lighting and the atmospheric quality generated by lighting which improves everynight life. Fear of crime may increase with the addition of high-mast lighting or decrease with the addition of other lighting solutions as more people enjoy spending time outside, making people feel safer. In summary, this research builds on, and also addresses the gaps identified in, three bodies of research and lies at the intersection of the research (Figure 3). It addresses the impact

Map 1   Streetlights in yellow and high-mast lighting in red in the Cape Town metropolitan area

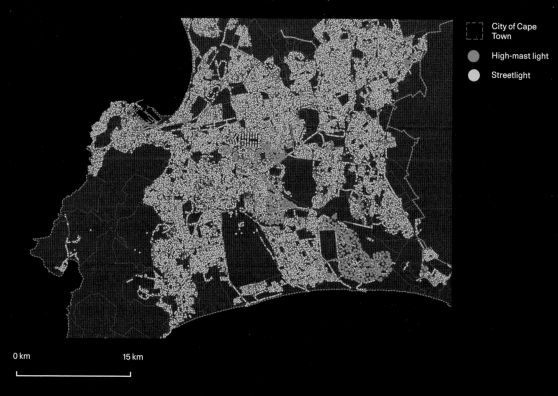

City of Cape
Town

High-mast light

Streetlight

0 km   15 km

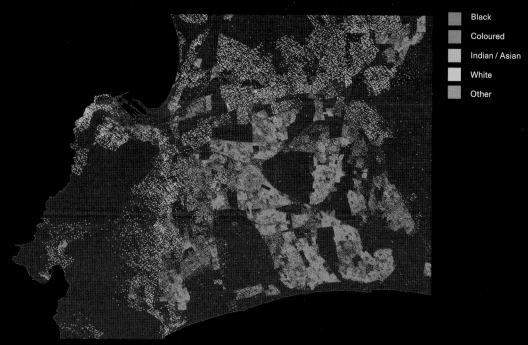

Black

Coloured

Indian / Asian

White

Other

Map 2   Racial dot map of Cape Town, with red representing black Africans

that both public lighting infrastructure and darkness have on everynight life in self-built communities, from fear of crime to freely leaving one's home to socialise with a friend.

To understand life in the dark and how to improve everynight life, this action research project first co-produces empirical data on nighttime experiences. This requires a highly visual and mixed methods approach. Visuals are central to communicating nighttime ethnography, something that text alone cannot do. Second, I acknowledge and explore the power of lighting from within a self-built community, both in the process and technical solution, by co-producing wall-mounted solar lighting with residents from PJS Informal Settlement (PJS) in Khayelitsha as an alternative public lighting solution to current top-down high-mast lighting. Simon and Pieterse (2017) refer to the importance of simultaneous experimentation in everyday life and the interaction with the policy and governance world as a 'double approach'. This research takes on a triple approach, where the research ultimately also advances theoretical discourse, as displayed in Figure 4. In structuring this research as an action research project, the theoretical, experimental, and legislative can intersect. I deal simultaneously with empirical work on everynight life in self-built communities, the theoretical discourse on infrastructural citizenship, and public lighting policy in self-built communities. The evidence base from this project is vital to make policy recommendations on public lighting and infrastructure that are specific to self-built communities, to achieve lighting solutions that are feasible, resilient, and scalable. Within this context, this book aims to contribute to discussions around everyday infrastructural experiences, focusing on the role of public lighting infrastructure and darkness in everynight life in self-built communities.

I examine the development of Cape Town's segregated lightscape to develop an understanding of everynight life and the impact of light and darkness in Khayelitsha's self-built communities. I specifically look at the planning logics that drove the implementation of high-mast lighting and the road that led to this techno-political mode of segregative development in the late-apartheid era. From this point, I look at the current policies that allow the continuous deployment of high-mast lighting in townships and self-built communities. The next step moves from policy to on-the-ground experiences to demonstrate what is entailed in a life lived in the shadows of such inadequate lighting. I investigate several self-built communities in Khayelitsha and their lived realities with high-mast lighting to argue for the need for new public lighting solutions in self-built communities. I then move to study darkness specifically, to understand the daily practices and perceptions that develop as a result of a life lived in darkness. Understanding the impact of inadequate lighting and darkness in self-built communities forms the basis of the argument for more effective and co-produced public lighting, which follows. Here, I demonstrate how co-producing human-scaled public lighting from within a self-built community could drastically improve everynight life in self-built communities. Finally, I turn this lighting debate into an infrastructural one. Here, I build on existing scholars to contribute concrete evidence and means to articulate citizenship demonstrated through the public lighting project, drawing conclusions on how infrastructure can effectively articulate citizenship in everyday and everynight life.

First, discourses on public lighting often focus on the correlation between light and reduced crime or fear of crime. Khayelitsha, where violent crime is rife, is no exception. Understanding the link between lighting and crime could contribute valuable knowledge in the fight against this endemic social issue. I conclude that a holistic approach, such as suggested by third-generation crime prevention through environmental design (CPTED) theory, needs to be taken in this light-crime discourse. Here, everyday lived experiences should be related to the impact that light has on crime reduction. I use another body of literature on lighting and its effects on social patterns and practices to understand the everyday lived experiences of lighting. When thinking through light and everynight life, an important component to consider is the effect of light on the nighttime atmosphere. I conclude that urban lighting in self-built communities should shift from the technocratic to focus on lighting for everyday life, where the human is at the centre of lighting infrastructure.

Fig 1   Relative position of the research

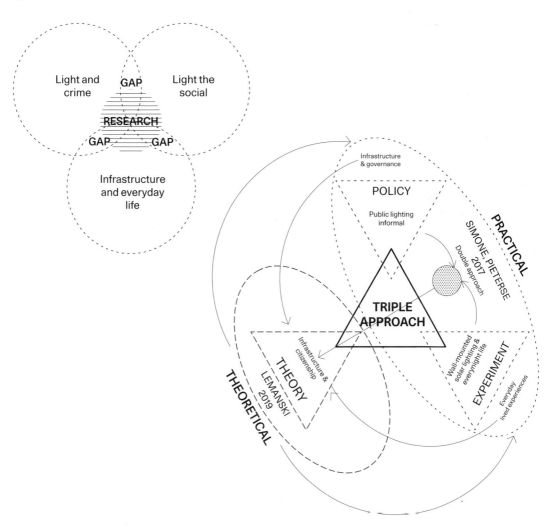

Fig 2   Triple approach addressing theory, policy and everyday lived experiences through an action research project

For this reason, I turn to the literature on lived infrastructure (Graham and McFarlane, 2015), where scholars highlight how the presence and everyday use of infrastructure affects, and is affected by, citizens' identity and practices (Wafer, 2012; Lemanski, 2019; McFarlane, 2019; Graham and McFarlane, 2015; von Schnitzler, 2016, 2019; Pesa, 2019). In this discourse, existing infrastructure has primarily been studied. It lacks a way forward for infrastructure to successfully articulate citizenship, notably in self-built communities where notions of full citizenship (Millstein, 2020) are more complex. This research takes the opportunity to study the everynight experiences of public lighting infrastructure, recognising what such infrastructure may mean in articulating citizenship in self-built communities in democratic South Africa (Millstein, 2020 Wafer, 2012, p. 233; Bond and Dugard, 2008; Desai, 2002; Parnell and Pieterse, 2010; Swilling, 2006; von Schnitzler, 2008; Lemanski, 2020).

Overview of Chapters

The summary below outlines each chapter to introduce the structure of the book and its key methods. The eight chapters in the book each build on the previous chapters. Collectively, they contribute to achieving an understanding of everynight life in self-built communities and the impact of co-producing public lighting infrastructure.

The first chapter establishes public lighting infrastructure as an important tool for addressing fear of crime, developing a more positive social environment and even articulating citizenship.

Building on the first chapter's discussions on infrastructure, citizenship, and urban lighting, Chapter 2 situates the case study in Cape Town's segregated lightscape. The chapter builds the argument for Khayelitsha as the appropriate case study to investigate the impact of public lighting, everynight life and citizenship, due to the complex history that led up to its development. I also elaborate on Khayelitsha's urban planning and the relevance of informality as a symbol of resistance to forced removals. Finally, democratic South Africa is discussed, and the presence of high-mast lighting is questioned as a symbol of apartheid infrastructure and unequal provision of effective public lighting infrastructure.

Following the establishment of the broader case study, Chapter 3 develops the research project, situating the research in specific self-built communities, firstly to investigate darkness in Khayelitsha's self-built communities and then to co-produce lighting in PJS. The chapter establishes the research as transdisciplinary action research facilitated through a highly visual mixed methods approach. The chapter explains the necessity of the methods and how they are able to answer the research question on everynight life and the impact of public lighting in self-built communities. The chapter ends with a discussion about lessons learned beyond the questions that govern this research.

Chapter 4 investigates the lived experiences of public lighting policies elaborated in Chapter 2, strengthening the argument for more effective public lighting in self-built communities. As the first empirical chapter, I prove that high-mast lighting is not effective in lighting self-built communities, and show how its ineffectiveness is experienced in various ways in everynight life. I do this by looking at lighting in self-built communities at a community level, followed by individual experiences of public lighting in PJS.

I conclude with a public lighting preference study to understand whether individuals prefer lighting solutions other than high-mast lighting. The chapter uses a mixed method and highly visual approach to capture life in the shadows of high-mast lighting.

The second empirical chapter, Chapter 5, presents darkness and its impact on everynight life in self-built communities in Khayelitsha. The chapter develops the argument that darkness is experienced as being trapped in one's everynight life, where darkness amplifies the fear of crime is amplified and prevents people from venturing out at night. This fear of the dark affects social relations at night. Nighttime social conflict seems to thrive in the dark. The second section presents everynight practices, including social activities, walking practices at night and the impact of darkness on accessing basic services. The final section elaborates on nighttime perceptions, highlighting the negative perceptions people have of nighttime in self-built communities, lacking dignity in everynight life to feeling forgotten by the state, to name a few. This chapter demonstrates how darkness and lack of adequate public lighting in self-built communities exacerbate the already challenging everyday struggles.

The final empirical chapter presents an alternative public lighting solution to address the issues around darkness and inadequate public lighting. This chapter presents the importance of co-producing public lighting from within, and tests the impact of wall-mounted solar lighting in PJS. Furthermore, it reveals the change in PJS after the community lived with their new public lighting for six months. People had more courage to use the toilet at night, some began to greet strangers, and many reported feeling free in their everynight life. Ultimately,

this chapter argues that a decentralised, co-produced lighting solution drastically improved everynight life in PJS, and that the solution can be used as a model for other self-built communities.

The book concludes with a synthesis of the research into a discussion around everyday, and, importantly, everynight experiences of infrastructure. I use public lighting to reinforce the need for alternative modes of infrastructure provision in self-built communities. Darkness is established as a boundary to a fulfilled everynight life, and the need for adequate public lighting is emphasised for the final time. The specific conditions of the lighting are synthesised, necessitating co-production, decentralisation, and blurring the boundaries of infrastructure and everynight life. Thereafter, I theorise the findings of this research in dialogue with literature on infrastructure and citizenship to establish the importance of infrastructure to facilitate self-determination.

In rapidly expanding self-built communities in the Global South, the provision of safe, resilient, and free access to urban life at night remains a complicated and understudied topic. This research seeks to understand the impact that darkness and public lighting have on everynight life in self-built communities. There is a lack of research on everynight life and lived experiences of public lighting infrastructure generally and, most notably, in self-built communities. This knowledge is particularly important in understanding everyday experiences more holistically and how infrastructure provision can contribute to a full sense of citizenship in self-built communities.

Reading through Light and Beyond

Chapter 1

Light is far more than 'infrastructure' in a narrow sense of technological networks but encompasses a range of developments including material and symbolic dimensions to state formation, the coevolutionary dynamics of different modes of governmentality, and the delineation of distinctive forms of public culture ranging from the mundane to the spectacular. (Gandy, 2017)

This research aims to understand the impact of public lighting on everynight life in self-built communities—a topic understudied in academia and undervalued by policymakers. Currently, the discourse on light predominantly focuses on light as a crime deterrent, or on the fear of crime. An emerging body of research from geographers, sociologists and anthropologists investigates nightlife and lighting. However, these discourses seem to stand alone and focus on highly regulated formal urban environments, while the context of self-built communities is missing.

Chapter summary: This chapter critically assesses two overarching research bodies: urban lighting and urban studies/infrastructure planning in self-built communities (Figure 1). It highlights the gaps, strengths and weaknesses, looking particularly at the relationship between the two. The review is thematically structured, beginning with research on urban lighting. The first section evaluates the research on light and crime, while the second evaluates research on light and the social or lighting for everyday life. The third section reviews research on urban studies and planning practices in self-built communities through the lens of public lighting. The chapter concludes by presenting the gaps and strengths that will guide the research to better understand the impact of public lighting on everynight life in self-built communities.

The rise of illumination in the nineteenth century was central to man's conquest of nature in cities (Nye, 2019, p. 2), transforming nighttime urban spaces practically, aesthetically and commercially. Though illumination may be strongly linked to liberalism, in the book *American Illuminations,* Nye (ibid.) points out that Europe's first public lighting was not intended to host public activity. Rather, it was used for safety and security, preventing crimes and keeping pedestrians safe, and to enhance dignity of central locations as a mechanism to show state pride and power. As a result, many Europeans were resistant to illumination efforts, even smashing lanterns, feeling that the development of lighting networks served as a visible manifestation of burgeoning state power (Gandy, 2017).

Illumination symbolised the importance of technological advancement and modernity to colonised spaces. It also marked the rigorous spatial distinctions that colonisers sought to impose by designing "dual cities" (Gandy 2017a) organised into native

quarters and European cantonments. The former was generally consigned to darkness (Frasch 2012; Winther 2008), while the latter was typified by rationalised systems of pervasive illumination. These colonial inequities produced a legacy that continues to shape lighting inequality today (Edensor, 2017). Gandy (2017a) also speaks of lighting discrimination in the late nineteenth century and demonstrates how gaslight networks supplied white neighbourhoods in Washington, while predominantly African-American areas relied on oil lamps or had no lighting. Gandy also mentions how elite areas were lit differently. In poorer neighbourhoods, lighting was used for social control.

Otter (2008) criticises the frequent categorisation of lighting into two historical paradigms: the "disciplinary", embodied through the architectural panopticon, and the "spectacular", embodied through the human flaneur, where the disciplinary paradigm "implies a cruel, cold, fixed gaze" and the spectacular, "a more playful, empowered and mobile one." Otter argues that "the visual dimensions of space were … engineered with neither coercion nor seduction in mind." He attempts to replace these two paradigms with a more supple, broader range of terms that recast the political history of light and vision as part of a material history of Western liberalism. However, Otter does not clearly differentiate between state and individual illumination efforts. More human-scale lighting, which served as self-expression, was installed by people rather than by the state, representing a degree of resistance to the state's efforts to make the city resemble great expositions through lighting displays (Nye, 2019). Depending on the illumination design(er), lighting

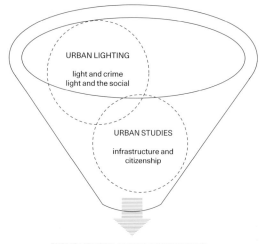

URBAN LIGHTING

light and crime
light and the social

URBAN STUDIES

infrastructure and citizenship

PUBLIC LIGHTING AND EVERYNIGHT LIFE IN SELF-BUILT COMMUNITIES

Fig 1　　Synthesis of research from urban studies and public lighting

served as a political tool, a tool of resistance and a tool to create a spectacle.

In the twentieth century, state control was still expressed through illumination. Today, centralised illumination, such as high-mast lighting in South Africa or the sodium illumination of East Berlin, still mark the emergent forms of the symbolic power of the 1980s (Neumann, 2002) and still stand in strong contrast against other forms of illumination consciously deployed to project freedom (Edensor, 2017). The rise of master-planning lighting in the twentieth century changed urban lighting from a more practical focus, such as energy efficiency after the 1970s energy crises and vehicular traffic, to creating hierarchy and legibility of space for the city dweller.

Zielinska-Dabkowska (2018) provides a very useful overview of the development of lighting master-planning in the twentieth and twenty-first centuries. In the 1990s, French cities began to value lighting design from a cultural point of view, highlighting heritage, different public spaces and walking routes. With time, this focus on lighting heritage changed to using less light and establishing hierarchies in the city, improving the ability to navigate the city at night and "generating a stronger identity" (ibid.). From here, a move towards legibility at night, inspired by Lynch's (1960) theories on legibility, began to develop. Spatial elements affecting the way people perceive the city by day are highlighted with lighting by night, allowing people to organise the city to make the surroundings familiar and easier to navigate.

Colour temperatures began to play a role in the distinction of urban elements and legibility, with the invention of new lighting technologies and approaches spurred on by the energy crises of the 1970s (Zielinska-Dabkowska, 2018). Warm low lighting was used for more human-scale elements, and cool white, brighter and higher-level lighting was used for modern elements, highways, and greenery. Now the city was legible in terms of where to add light and also what colour and height the lighting should be, according to the different urban elements (ibid.). In the twenty-first century, lighting designers focused on people moving through the city, called "journey through the site" (ibid.). Light is used to improve the experience of moving from one place to another by enhancing visual connections with lighting. From about 2010, with a greater focus on the negative impact humans have on ecology, darkness became a focus not only ecologically but also with regard to the rich atmospheres created when playing with light and dark (Dunn and Edensor, 2020;

Edensor, 2013, 2017). Preserving dark spaces and only lighting specific spaces with appropriate levels of lighting became increasingly valued (Zielinska-Dabkowska, 2018).

Lighting is not only about crime

Throughout the development of different lighting approaches, lighting as a deterrent for crime has remained an aim and a widely researched topic. Light is also used to enhance safety, mobility, surveillance, create intimacy and style in domestic space, selectively highlight buildings to reinforce state and corporate power, promote festivity and generally expand the city's uses at night (Edensor, 2012, p. 1106).

By the 1900s, lighting was widely regarded as a tool to prevent crime and expand the public realm (Nye, 2019, pp. 5–6). Many researchers have tried to directly and quantitatively correlate increased public lighting with reduced crime incidents. Atkins et al. did one of the earliest and seminal studies on lighting and crime reduction in 1991. They concluded that although the public welcomed street lighting as reassuring, the area-wide introduction of new street lighting did not reduce reported crime (Atkins, Husain and Storey, 1991). Ramsay and Newton (1991) also concluded that lighting alone had little effect on crime reduction, but it did reduce fear of crime. In the same year, Painter (1991b) evaluated a UK-based re-lighting project and found a twenty-seven per cent reduction in crime. Though she concludes that lighting statistically reduces crime, Painter's conclusions are criticised for following a common formula—having small sample sizes and not enough time between baseline and endline surveys (Atkins, Husain and Storey, 1991).

Farrington and Welsh (2002, 2008) reviewed difference-in-difference[1] studies on crime and lighting correlations. They review thirteen studies that meet their criteria of evaluation (ibid, p. 9). Although some areas experience an increase in crime, the pooled results reveal a twenty-one per cent reduction in crime incidents. Farrington and Welsh recognise two reasons why lighting interventions may be effective. The first, which is quite reductive, involves increased surveillance at nighttime, or the feeling of being watched, and can only affect nighttime crime statistics. The second involves informal

---

1   An experimental approach comparing the changes in outcomes over time between a population where an intervention took place (treatment group) and a population where no intervention took place (comparison group)

social control due to increased pride in the community and more effective use of space. This factor would effectively reduce crime by day and night. The second reasoning takes a more holistic view on reducing crime and highlights the importance of community participation in efforts to reduce crime.

Adding to this, many communities fear that neighbourhood improvements may lead to gentrification and eviction (Atkinson, 2004). While many accept that environmental improvement increases pride and care and reduces crime, this can only be true if the community welcomes the environmental change. To ensure long-term improvements, including reductions in crime, community involvement and fostering acceptance throughout the project is vital. In their evaluations, Welsh and Farrington do not address the nature of the implementation process and whether it was participatory.

In a more recent study (Chalfin et al., 2021), a large-scale randomised control trial in several New York City social housing complexes proved that street lighting reduced outdoor nighttime index crimes by thirty-five per cent. The experiment installed several temporary, generator-powered, security flood-lights of 600,000 lumens about ten metres off the ground. These extraordinarily bright lights bothered many residents (WNYC, 2014). A high-mast light, for example, emits 660,000 lumens but is forty metres off the ground. If you blast 600,000 lumens into an area, crime may reduce, but how might this very intense lighting affect public space's general quality and pleasantness? Interviewees in the reports on the New York project also requested participation. Some welcomed the lights but wanted the city to consult on what other neighbourhood improvements were needed (ibid.). Newspaper reports also mentioned the lighting experiment combined with increased police surveillance, and interviewees spoke more about the increased police in their neighbourhood than the new lighting (ibid.). In 2017, after testing temporary lights, permanent lighting was installed without apparent effects on crime statistics. Some housing complexes only experienced a 0.1 per cent drop in crime incidents (Brooklyn Eagle, 2018). These reports on the re-lighting project (ibid.; Bittle and Craven, 2018; WNYC, 2014) clearly show the complex task of evaluating lighting and crime reduction.

Although this evidence is useful, the intervention's reductive nature does not holistically consider what reduced crime means for everynight life, how the atmospheric quality of the lighting intervention affects people, the importance of the implementation process (participatory, co-designed, local employment) for community acceptance and the longevity of such infrastructure. The danger of such a reductive conclusion is that government may think that simply installing streetlights will solve crime problems. The community may not care for the lights, which may aggravate crime or social tensions in the area.

Studying the direct correlation between improved lighting and crime reduction is unnecessary and almost impossible in the context of self-built communities. Painter (1996) points out how counter-intuitive it seems to challenge the proposition that people feel safe in well-lit areas. However, Painter (1991b, ibid., 1994) consistently tries to prove the correlation between reduced crime and lighting. She does conclude very well that policymakers should link community safety strategies to public intuition that lighting makes people feel safer. She encourages policymakers to consult communities and create well-informed policies to reduce fear in urban streets (Painter, 1996, p. 201).

Pease (1999) comes to the same conclusion in his review of street lighting and crime reduction evaluations. He states that bathing an area in light to reduce crime is "crude" and that we should think "laterally", not "literally" about lighting and crime reduction. He concludes that we should liberate the crime-lighting debate (implying that it is stuck) by changing the research focus from "does or doesn't it work" to "how can I flexibly and imaginatively incorporate lighting in crime reduction strategy and tactics?" (ibid.). Twenty-two years later, researchers still seem determined to prove that light reduces crime, as seen in the New York study. Researchers should take Pease's lateral thinking one step further, beyond crime and fear of crime, and study the link between lighting and everynight life, including feelings of freedom, safety and productive use of public space.

Gandy (2017) (among others) argues against the quantitative discourse due to the complex relationship between light and safety. Questions of contrast between light and dark, illumination patterns, and social and cultural milieu need to be considered when assessing the impact light has on safety (ibid.). The emphasis on quantitative dimensions does not acknowledge the important qualitative effects of light on perceptions of safety, derived from colour, glow, warmth and other perceived (emphasis added) differences (Gandy 2017). However, Gandy's writing is not empirically grounded and calls for investigation. Through qualitative methods, it may be more productive to explore the impact re-lighting has on fear of crime and everyday life and whether residents change their nighttime practices, rather than only looking at light and crime incidents. For example, a study in Spain on the impact of colour temperature on perceived safety showed that the whiter the light, the safer people felt (Peña-García, Hurtado and Aguilar-Luzón, 2015).

Lighting for reassurance

In studying the relationship between light and crime, many feel that understanding fear of crime is more useful (Atkins et al., 1991). This section looks at what heightens the fear of crime and how urban lighting can appropriately address these elements and reduce fear of crime in public spaces. Unwin (2018) highlights the importance of understanding the definitions of fear of crime in interviews on the topic, as outlined by Farral et al. (1997): The authors describe a scale of fear ranging from a "diffused set of concerns" such as expressive opinions and attitudes towards crime and society to an "immediate sense of threat" such as experiencing fear in an actual situation. Unwin (2018) remarks that public lighting is unlikely to diminish fears that reside at either extreme of the scale (expressive and experiential) but can reduce fear of crime that resides somewhere in between, such as feeling the precautionary need to take a different path at night.

Earlier research generally refers to spatial and social elements that contribute to fear of crime. Spatial elements include openness, nooks and crannies, for example. Bonnie et al. (1992) define these elements as prospect (can I see far?), refuge (can a criminal hide and surprise me?) and escape (am I able to easily escape if I am confronted?). The appearance of disorder, coined by Wilson and Kelling (1982) as the "broken window theory", can also contribute to fear of crime, especially in unfamiliar areas. Well-designed urban lighting that is uniform, bright and overhead (Nasar and Bokharaei, 2017) addresses the spatial elements of fear by increasing prospect, diminishing potential refuge areas by making them visible and highlighting possible escape routes. Lighting can also give the appearance of a well-maintained area, with infrastructure investment, though at the same time, it may also reveal more disorder (Unwin, 2018).

Social elements of fear of crime include perceived social safety, defined as the perception of being protected against danger through human action (Boomsma and Steg, 2014), i.e. "eyes on the street" (Jacobs, 1992), or caring eyes on the street (Mihinjac and Saville, 2019), the reputation of an area and presence of people (good and bad). The degree of community connectedness may increase fear of crime

because stories of crime incidents spread more. Prieto, Curiel and Bishop (2017, p. 5) outline three contributors to fear of crime: a personal experience of crime, time passed (fading memory), and interaction with someone who has experienced crime. They write "fear is contagious, and the impact of an interaction might depend on the closeness between the individuals or the strength of their ideas" (ibid.).

Lighting addresses social elements of fear, signifying life on the street and helping to assess the degree of perceived social safety by identifying if people present are trustworthy or not (Boomsma and Steg, 2014). Boomsma and Steg (ibid.) found that perceived social safety mediated how much light people find acceptable in an area. In other words, people find lower levels of lighting more acceptable when their perception of social safety is greater. Their study found that people, especially women, felt less safe in lower lighting areas with a high degree of entrapment (no escape) (ibid.).

Sometimes the spatial and social are intertwined. For example, pedestrians feel reassured when there are street-facing windows, because of the perception of more eyes on the street; or more orderly appearance, signifying greater care for an area (Unwin, 2018). Re-lighting may increase neighbourhood pride, which may in turn increase incident reporting as residents maintain their neighbourhood more actively. Additionally, crime and anti-social behaviour are more visible, possibly resulting in increased reporting (ibid.).

The psychological impact of specific kinds of public lighting should be considered when assessing fear of crime (Nasar and Bokharaei, 2017). Lighting is linked to more pedestrian activity, greater confidence in walking alone at night and a sense that an area is cared for (ibid.; Painter 1994, 1996), although not indicating the specific qualities of the lighting may be misleading (high-pressure sodium vapour floodlights versus LED streetlights) (Boyce et al., 2000). Nasar and Bokharaei (2017) highlight three lighting components: bright light, uniform light and overhead light. Lighting that meets these three criteria gives the impression that a space is exciting, appealing and safe (Nasar and Bokharaei, 2017), attracting more people. This study links to the importance of lighting atmosphere, addressed later in this chapter.

The type of lighting and different light qualities needed to reduce fear of crime also depend on different material cultures. For example, cool or white light could be perceived as inviting in some cultures and uninviting in others. Much research deals with lighting and perception of safety, but how a change in lighting changes nighttime practices is under-studied. Additionally, while researchers conclude that lighting reduces fear of crime by addressing the social and spatial elements contributing to that fear, to date no study discusses the effects of improved lighting in the more complex context of self-built communities.

Fortunately, more crime studies are focusing on a holistic approach to reducing fear of crime. Lighting and crime reduction fall directly under the theory of crime prevention through environmental design (CPTED), first defined by Jeffery in the 1970s as improving urban environments through architectural and planning interventions, which reduces crime opportunities and fear of crime and improves quality of life (Jeffery, 1971). CPTED theory tries to address elements of fear of crime holistically. Lighting is part of an integral approach to increasing night-time reassurance and should not be studied as a stand-alone element to deduce direct correlations.

First-generation CPTED focuses primarily on reducing crime through environmental manipulation, with aspects like beautification being only a by-product of the intervention (Mihinjac and Saville, 2019). Second-generation CPTED expands on the first, acknowledging that more eyes on the street, social gatherings and positive events in spaces are likely to reduce crime and/or fear of crime (Armitage, 2016).

Gibson's (2016) thesis, *Third Generation CPTED? Rethinking the Basis for Crime Prevention Strategies*, explores improving the sustainability of CPTED interventions by focusing on the social characteristics impacting their effectiveness. Her focus is on improved communication, collaboration and enhancing social context with robust methods. Third-generation CPTED, defined by Mihinjac and Saville (2019), takes Gibson's (2016) social focus one step further to fulfil the higher Maslowian needs (Maslow and Frager, 1987; Mcleod, 2018) of self-esteem, self-actualising and transcendence (Mihinjac and Saville, 2019). Mihinjac and Saville couple the revised needs with liveability or quality of life indices in a neighbourhood. They classify neighbourhoods in a Neighbourhood Liveability Hierarchy, which has three neighbourhood categories—basic, moderate and advanced. Their classifications are made according to the ability to meet Maslow's needs **(Figure 2)**. In this system, Mihinjac and Saville correlate neighbourhood liveability with the three different generations of CPTED interventions. A basic-level neighbourhood would correlate with first-generation interventions, a moderate-level with second-generation and an advanced-level would have elements of third-generation CPTED (according to their Maslowian definition of third-generation CPTED) (ibid.).

This categorisation is oversimplified. It assumes that there is a direct correlation between formal CPTED

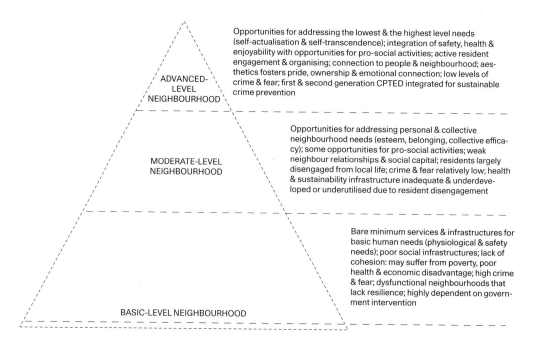

Opportunities for addressing the lowest & the highest level needs (self-actualisation & self-transcendence); integration of safety, health & enjoyability with opportunities for pro-social activities; active resident engagement & organising; connection to people & neighbourhood; aesthetics fosters pride, ownership & emotional connection; low levels of crime & fear; first & second generation CPTED integrated for sustainable crime prevention

ADVANCED-LEVEL NEIGHBOURHOOD

Opportunities for addressing personal & collective neighbourhood needs (esteem, belonging, collective efficacy); some opportunities for pro-social activities; weak neighbour relationships & social capital; residents largely disengaged from local life; crime & fear relatively low; health & sustainability infrastructure inadequate & underdeveloped or underutilised due to resident disengagement

MODERATE-LEVEL NEIGHBOURHOOD

Bare minimum services & infrastructures for basic human needs (physiological & safety needs); poor social infrastructures; lack of cohesion: may suffer from poverty, poor health & economic disadvantage; high crime & fear; dysfunctional neighbourhoods that lack resilience; highly dependent on government intervention

BASIC-LEVEL NEIGHBOURHOOD

Fig 2 Third-generation Crime Prevention Through Environmental Upgrading

interventions and the degree of social cohesion in a neighbourhood. In other words, a basic-level neigh-bourhood has first-generation CPTED, which does not pay attention to the social ecology and assumes it has poor social cohesion and social infrastructure because it has poor CPTED interventions.

In self-built communities, there is often strong so-cial cohesion and resilient informal social infra-structure, even though the neighbourhood receives bare-minimum basic infrastructure (Vertigans and Gibson, 2020). Categorising basic neighbour-hoods as dysfunctional does not acknowledge the existing modes of and potentials for self-actualis-ation. The desire to self-actualise—a third-gener-ation CPTED goal—is independent of the degree of formal intervention in a neighbourhood. By not recognising this ability to self-actualise, the com-munity is disempowered. The goal of self-actual-isation in third-generation CPTED may be unsuc-cessful because it does not come from within the community but is instead imposed through exter-nal intervention.

Although third-generation CPTED contains all the correct concepts for creating liveable neighbour-hoods, focussing on crime prevention and address-ing various needs from the social to the self, over-simplifying neighbourhoods and their potentials leaves a gap. Self-built communities are all about self-actualisation, so the inherent dynamics need to be integrated into CPTED interventions. A common struggle for housing and basic services often gen-erates major community and individual social cohe-sion and transcendence (Brown-Luthango, Reyes and Gubevu, 2017). Planning with self-built commu-nities is discussed later in this chapter.

A holistic view on light and crime reduction

Attempting to deduce the direct correlation be-tween lighting and reduced crime incidents is dif-ficult, expensive and may be unnecessary. It also misses other vital aspects that lighting may ad-dress, such as reducing fear of crime, increasing re-assurance and improving everyday life. Holistically addressing fear of crime as suggested by CPTED theory is a step in the right direction, where inter-ventions focus on improved quality of life and not only crime reduction. First- and second-generation CPTED interventions have been studied through structured surveys and controlled experiments, though these have been criticised for not studying the long-term sustainability of such interventions (Gibson, 2016). Third-generation CPTED advances the theory, focusing on liveability and a willingness

to participate in street life and pro-social activi-ties that do not merely depend on preventing crime (Mihinjac and Saville, 2019).

To date, third-generation CPTED is theoretical and lacks empirical grounding. When considering no-tions of liveability, suggested by Mihinjac and Saville (ibid.), it may also be useful to include more qualita-tive and ethnographic evaluations of CPTED inter-ventions. Studying a public lighting intervention and how everyday practices and perceptions change af-ter the intervention is implemented will strengthen third-generation CPTED theory, highlighting the psychosocial implications of such interventions. The next section elaborates on the important social component of lighting, which should be integrated into the discourse on light and crime.

Lighting up social patterns and practices

This section looks at four aspects of human-cen-tred public lighting research into social patterns and practices related to light. First, different con-texts have different relations with the materiality of the lumen, which affects their experiences of light in various ways. Secondly, "affective atmospheres" (Gandy, 2017b) of lighting, as studied in anthropol-ogy, geography and architecture, affects the way people experience space. Thirdly, lighting "the so-cial" (Slater and Entwistle, 2016) focuses on us-ing intense social research to design lighting that activates outdoor social space. Finally, according to Davoudian (2019), lighting for everyday life has been an area of significant interest in recent years, to understand the needs and experiences of peo-ple and how those can be addressed through evi-dence-based public lighting design.

According to Bille and Sørensen (2007), the archi-tectural discourse on light is focused more on how to light (original emphasis) but does not focus on the social question of why people want light to illumi-nate in certain ways. They refer to this idea of why to light as the anthropology of luminosity:

> The anthropology of luminosity is also about the element of the light source itself: The materiality of the lumen. Therefore, questions concerning how light is used in relation to social identity are also questions of what role different modes of light (bright light, dim light and so on) have, what types of light (sunshine, electrical, gas, candle-light) are used to do what, why, and how this is socially manifested and experienced. (Bille and Sørensen, 2007)

Different contexts have different relations with the materiality of the lumen, depending on past experiences. To a European, a candle is romantic and cosy; but it is a symbol of danger, risk and poverty to a low-income resident of a self-built community. Bille (2015) speaks of light in Danish culture as a material to stage atmospheres representing a sense of community through creating hygge or cosiness. The use of this lighting indoors shows the distinct associations and sensitivities Danish culture has with different kinds of light. Many Danish households are light-filled and allow visibility, intentionally not drawing curtains at night to signify openness and connection to the surrounding neighbours (ibid.).

Kumar (2015) explores how culture affects the materiality of light in Indian villages, finding that light placed outdoors has a critical role in establishing and reinforcing honour. Light signifies hospitality and celebrates religious beliefs among Hindus. The conclusion is that light has both material and non-material properties as it interacts with culture (ibid.). Different colour temperatures in the lumen also have different material associations. A study in London suggested that white light is considered harsh and intended to support the effectiveness of CCTV cameras (Sloane, Slater and Entwistle, 2016). In other countries, white light is considered more modern and a symbol of wealth (Kumar, 2015). While few authors speak of light's material culture, there is no research that highlights that of public lighting in South African self-built communities, or anywhere in the world, and the different associations with various types of public lighting, such as high-mast lighting versus LED street lighting. Such different lighting solutions create vastly different atmospheres, provoking different responses from residents.

A growing body of qualitative research sees the importance of understanding the urban atmosphere. Probably the simplest to start with is Gandy's (2017b) definition of atmosphere as a space with "prevailing affective characteristics". Thibaud (2011) has worked extensively on ambience or urban atmospheres, defining it as "space-time qualified from a sensory perspective. It involves a socio-aesthetic approach that enables us to grasp everyday urban atmospheres". Thibaud (ibid.) and Edensor (2012) both move towards a more dynamic notion of atmosphere, and Edensor explores how the creation of these atmospheres is not passive, where a pervasive quality of atmospheres embodies people. People, in turn, further contribute to the atmosphere. With many ideas and no strict understandings of "atmosphere", Thibaud highlights the multidisciplinary focus, with anthropologists, geographers and sociologists

(among others) beginning to look at atmosphere as a collection of qualitative aspects of sensing the urban environment.

More researchers consider lighting as a key contributor to nocturnal urban atmospheres. Cultural geographer Jürgen Hasse (2012) studies the affective qualities of light phenomenologically, offering an alternative to the dominant technical discourses. Hasse's (ibid.) interest lies in the sensory experiences of light, rooted in its history as a powerful architectural tool (Bille and Sørensen, 2007). Levels of light and colour create a composition of qualitative spatial and temporal tuning to the nighttime atmosphere (Anderson and Wylie, cited by Edensor, 2012). These different lighting qualities impact elements in space, producing particular illuminated landscapes with complex relations between light and dark space, influencing how individuals understand, and feel when moving through, space (ibid.). These nocturnal atmospheres can evoke strong feelings and potential action in place (Duff, 2010). Therefore, the atmosphere generated by lighting contributes greatly to the degree of social interaction in public space (Slater, 2018; Bille and Sørensen, 2007; Gandy, 2017; Edensor, 2012; Hasse, 2012).

Edensor attempts to ground notions of atmosphere and effect of illumination in the production of sociable space in Blackpool (Figure 3), England. He focuses on lighting as a crucial ingredient in the atmospheric qualities of nocturnal space (Edensor, 2012). An eclectic mix of lighting (neon, lasers, floodlights—to name a few) fills six miles of beachfront, highlights landmarks and invigorates space (ibid.) He finds that when interviewees describe memories of a festive environment, lighting conditions form a big part of their memory. Although Edensor (ibid.) studied illumination in festive environments, he states that the role of illumination in generating an atmosphere in more mundane environments is equally available for exploration.

Numerous accounts from the nineteenth century highlight the effect light had on the senses and the experience of space. Then, the public heavily opposed illumination, largely sparked by the Arclight's excessive light (Figure 4). It is not surprising that the Arclight was heavily used during World War I to facilitate attacks at night (Gandy, 2017). Below are some reflections cited by various authors.

> Arclight experiments have only succeeded in blinding the bypassers, and projecting long shadows behind them (Higgs, 1879, cited by Otter, 2008)

... a lamp for a nightmare... a horror to heighten horror (Stevenson, 1878, cited by Gandy, 2017)

... a light as this should shine only on murders and public crime, or along the corridors of lunatic asylums, a horror to heighten horror (Stevenson, 1878, cited by Nye, 2019, p. 9)

Lighting can contribute to positive (Figures 3 and 6) and negative atmospheres (Figures 4 and 5), though there is a gap in the earlier research on the latter. In certain cultures, lighting with negative associations may contribute to negative nocturnal atmospheres, presenting an area for potential further research. Lighting designers regard atmosphere as "an aesthetic property of privileged social spaces" such as heritage and commercial centres, while more mundane spaces, such as housing estates, are not sufficiently valued to merit lighting that contributes to a positive atmosphere (Entwistle and Slater, 2019). The literature follows the same route. So far, most literature refers to interior spaces (Bille, 2015), festive environments (Edensor, 2012) and historic investigations around public responses to atmospheres generated by lighting in the nineteenth century (Gandy, 2017; Nye, 2019). As Edensor (2012) points out, the atmosphere generated by lighting in more ordinary environments is under-investigated. The mundane urban, particularly the self-built urban environment, is not discussed or empirically studied.

As discussed earlier, atmosphere generated by lighting contributes to the degree of social interaction in public space (Slater, 2018; Bille and Sørensen, 2007; Gandy, 2017; Edensor, 2012; Hasse, 2012). Therefore, it is important to "recognize the designer's performativity as a producer of 'the social'" (Entwistle and Slater, 2019). Entwistle and Slater criticise literature on lighting and sociology for not acknowledging the designer's role in performing the social or creating the previously absent social. Most research suggests that the social peaks already exist and must be complemented, highlighted or respected, but the designer also plays a role in creating the social. This methodological research calls for more evidence-based lighting design. Social research findings define the societal needs and diverse realities that lighting choices engage with, rather than guide aesthetic design choices (Bordonaro, Entwistle and Slater, 2018).

"Configuring Light", a project in Colombia, uses this researched rationale in its lighting design projects (ibid.; Entwistle and Slater, 2019). The organisation emphasises the lack of research on how light behaves in space and the damage it can do, diminishing or destroying the nocturnal street life designers seek to illuminate, if using an imposed set of standards generated from algorithmic protocols (Slater and Entwistle, 2018). Entwistle and Slater (under review) categorise the "socialness of light" in three forms: lighting that shapes social space; light as a material with different socio-cultural relations; and finally, social issues related to light, such as crime or light pollution. Understanding the various types of socialness through sociological research, the designer acknowledges diverse people and their practices and activates public life in various senses.

Bordonaro et al. (2018) highlight four overarching issues to consider when designing human-centred public lighting: diversity of actors, different practices, the different meaning of places and various connections to other spaces. Understanding these four issues allows the lighting designer to know what to light according to what different people value in urban space. Bordonaro et al. (ibid.) do this through a fluid, ethnographic approach. Finally, Bordonaro et al. highlight the importance for designers not to hide behind standards to legitimise their decisions, claiming that, in reality, designers know "that choosing and applying a standard for a unique place requires careful understanding and interpretation."

"Configuring Light" focused on the idea that nighttime design is a discipline on its own, with its own set of problems and solutions. "The project was premised on looking for small scale design interventions rather than big and pervasive infrastructure — small designs that could be rolled out iteratively across a neighbourhood" (Slater and Entwistle, 2018). Community engagement with consultation and customisation formed a key part of the project. People in the area could choose lighting variations and mount them at a human scale (ibid.). In this project, the relationship between public and private "civic and domestic energy had to be treated as one integrated system, as a single and integral ecology" (ibid.). They found that socially activating the nighttime spaces using light increased the "meaningful legibility of these spaces and the possibilities of social interaction and encounter". Social research is required to understand people's different maps and movements as a basis for lighting (Bordonaro, Entwistle and Slater, 2018).

Although the use of rigorous social science methods is vital in designing human-centred lighting, "the social" is perhaps too narrow and over-emphasises the collective public realm, not acknowledging

Fig 4   Nighttime atmosphere of the Arclight "moonlight tower"

Fig 5   Nighttime atmosphere: high-mast lighting in a self-built community, South Africa

Fig 6   Nighttime atmosphere: Tanzanian self-built community by night

the more mundane daily practices and experiences shaped by public light and darkness. Light as a part of people's daily lives is of growing research interest—how lighting enables people to move around their neighbourhood or their city daily, allowing them to see themselves and their neighbourhood (Davoudian, 2018). Shaw (2014) emphasises the importance of connecting public lighting policy with understandings of day-to-day lived experiences of infrastructure, "generating the knowledge required to make choices regarding new technologies and innovative practices".

Ebbensgaard (2016) studied the co-production of the nocturnal urban realm through planning practices and design; and everyday routine practices of elderly people in Newham, London. The borough replaced streetlights with brighter, whiter LED lights, a change which the government, with a certain "technological determinism", thought would increase nighttime activities and eyes on the street. Ebbensgaard takes a phenomenological view and ethnographic approach to researching the everyday experiences of public light. He concludes that instead of a prescriptive approach to lighting, designers, planners and policymakers should consider how residents' everyday practices shape and co-create urban environments. By acknowledging this, lighting solutions will complement specific conditions rather than adhering to regulations that do not necessarily result in "good lighting" (ibid). This study is a useful starting point to investigate how darkness and public lighting affect daily practices and mundane routines in self-built communities. This major gap in the literature is of significant interest. People living in self-built communities have to carry out many routine activities outside their homes which often require walking, such as accessing water and using sanitation facilities.

Lighting everynight life

Light is more than just infrastructure. It encompasses a range of material and symbolic developments attributed to state and community formation and the delineation of distinctive forms of public culture (Gandy, 2017). The material culture of lighting needs to be understood for specific contexts. Lighting can create atmospheres conducive to positive social activities. Using rigorous social science methods is key in understanding this "social" and responding appropriately to it or creating new forms. In addition to the collective social, individual, mundane, daily realities need to be considered in lighting design, including how everyday life co-creates nocturnal atmospheres. Researchers call for more

attention to these socialities and mundanities using an ethnographic approach, which should inform evidence-based lighting policy.

Research on light for everyday life refers to a qualitative or ethnographic study of the impact lighting has on practical everyday experiences, such as accessing public transport, how people feel when walking outside at night and how much more time they are voluntarily willing to spend outside at night as a result of improved urban lighting. This is especially relevant for self-built communities in South Africa, where shared public services require venturing out on foot after dark. When questioning the presence of high-mast lighting in today's society, it is important to consider the qualitative effects the lighting has on everyday lived experiences where light, more than a medium, evokes agency (Bille and Sørensen, 2007).

While research on human-centred lighting is a growing field, to the best of my knowledge, none focuses on human-centred lighting in self-built communities. Instead, much research on the atmospheric and social aspects of light focuses on the twentieth century, when electric light was first widely introduced to cities.

Lighting infrastructure, citizenship and self-built communities

In the opening sentence of the book *Urban Lighting for People*, Davoudian (2018) introduces urban lighting in the developing world, stating that even in developing countries "street lighting is now considered a basic infrastructure". The context within which street lighting in "developing countries" is positioned is "lighting for everyday life", as discussed in the previous section. Davoudian states that the intention of the book is to raise "basic issues regarding how people interact with urban spaces", and emphasises that "urban space must be carefully analysed for both daytime and nighttime use by people according to their day-to-day lives". However, throughout the book, all the contexts that contributors write about are in the Global North, in so-called "developed" countries. It is precisely this gap of the "developing", not to mention informality or self-built communities, that this research tries to address (ibid).

It is not surprising that the British Museum named a solar-powered LED light intended for people in rural Africa and Asia as the final artefact in their 2010 exhibition "A History of the World in 100 Objects" (Cross, 2013). When imagining lighting in the poorer, especially African, context, one imagines a rural so-lar lighting project where people are given a Little Sun (Elliason, 2016). However, these projects fo-cus mainly indoors, providing light for individuals to improve studying or conducting focused tasks, and do not look at the collective. The 2011 Foroba Yelen project did address the collective compo-nent of lighting, aiming "to facilitate the genera-tion of new businesses, support education and help maintain the cultural practices of festivals and cer-emonies" with a portable solar light comparable to a streetlight, as shown in **Figure 7** (Hall, Konate and Kulkarni, 2012). While their study found that the in-troduction of portable lights increased widespread activities to enhance the quality of life in unelec-trified villages (ibid.), such lighting would present problems in denser urban self-built communities. The portable solar light is still a task light, though it does facilitate public tasks such as ceremonies. It does not support the more mundane flow of ur-ban nightlife such as pedestrian mobility—a vital component of daily life, especially in urban environ-ments where walking in the dark is a stressful task.

The NGO project "Litre of Light" looks at alternative lighting solutions for grid-deprived communities. It teaches communities such as in Bangalore to build cheap solar-powered streetlights made from a wa-ter bottle, a PVC pipe, a solar panel and a battery (Pareek, 2015). While the Foroba Yelen and Litre of Light projects focus on outdoor lighting, encourag-ing intense community participation in the design and use of the light, the government is not included in the implementation, nor is scalability of the solu-tion discussed as a viable option. In urban lighting solutions, where the government has the mandate to provide infrastructure, scalability and a degree of regulation is required, coupled with intense com-munity engagement to ensure successful adoption and longevity of infrastructure.

However, planning norms and standards for in-frastructure provision, such as public lighting, in South Africa's self-built communities do not move beyond the technocratic, where infrastruc-ture only becomes visible when it fails (Star, 1999). Unfortunately, such technocratic modes of light-ing and planning in self-built communities spread to other areas. Other African cities look to South Africa as an example when considering public light-ing in self-built communities, implementing high-mast lighting regardless of its clear shortcomings. "Adopt-a-Light", a Kenyan high-mast lighting com-pany, worked with the City of Nairobi to install high-mast lights in as many as seven self-built commu-nities since 2005. The founder won a UN-Habitat Business Award in 2009. In her application for the

award, she noted that South Africa was a source of inspiration.

This is a continuation of the 1970s and 80s infra-structure planning, where planning theory was shaped by a reaction to technocracy and positivism (Fainstein, 2000). Collier et al. (2016) describe tradi-tional infrastructure planners as experts who sup-posedly know the public interest, define the needs that infrastructure is designed to meet and define the attributed values according to which the infra-structure is assessed. In his review of the Lagos master plan, Gandy (2007) explains this planning mode as technocratic policymaking, where ra-tional planning attempts to control and shape the so-called "undisciplined population" through tech-nical specifications preconceived by experts. This outdated planning mode assumes that a collective public exists, where needs are similar and where an expert represents one common voice. Planning the-ory has shifted from this centralised approach, but its outcomes are still ingrained in South African cit-ies and planning policies. New theories increasingly focus on achieving widespread improvement in the quality of life in a context dominated by a global cap-italist political economy (Fainstein, 2000). Although this shift has taken place, Harrison (2014) sees plan-ning theory primarily as being shaped by anti-real-ist ontology that will struggle to engage with the real world unless there is an ontological shift. Sanyal (2002) further probes if it is necessary to produce planning theory if it produces no results in practice. A survey revealed that practitioners considered planning theory to be of little practical use.

Focusing on the theory that tries to offer a more appealing prospect of the future, Fainstein (2000) defines three dominant models in current plan-ning theory. These are the "Communicative", "New Urbanism" and "Just-City" models. In the Communicative model, the planner mediates be-tween stakeholders, allowing people to shape their environment. New Urbanists espouse a pictur-esque ideal of planning, involving an urban form that creates neighbourliness, a sense of community, in-tegration and aesthetic satisfaction. The Just-City model is concerned with well-being relying on a more decentralised form of welfare provision than the state-centred model of the bureaucratic welfare state. The Communicative model and the Just-City model are more relevant in self-built communities, where there is a need to mobilise a previously ex-cluded public. Although the Communicative model is well intended, critics say that planners become subjective interpreters, leaving a gap between rhetoric and action. The Just-City model better ad-dresses the need for action, particularly the radical

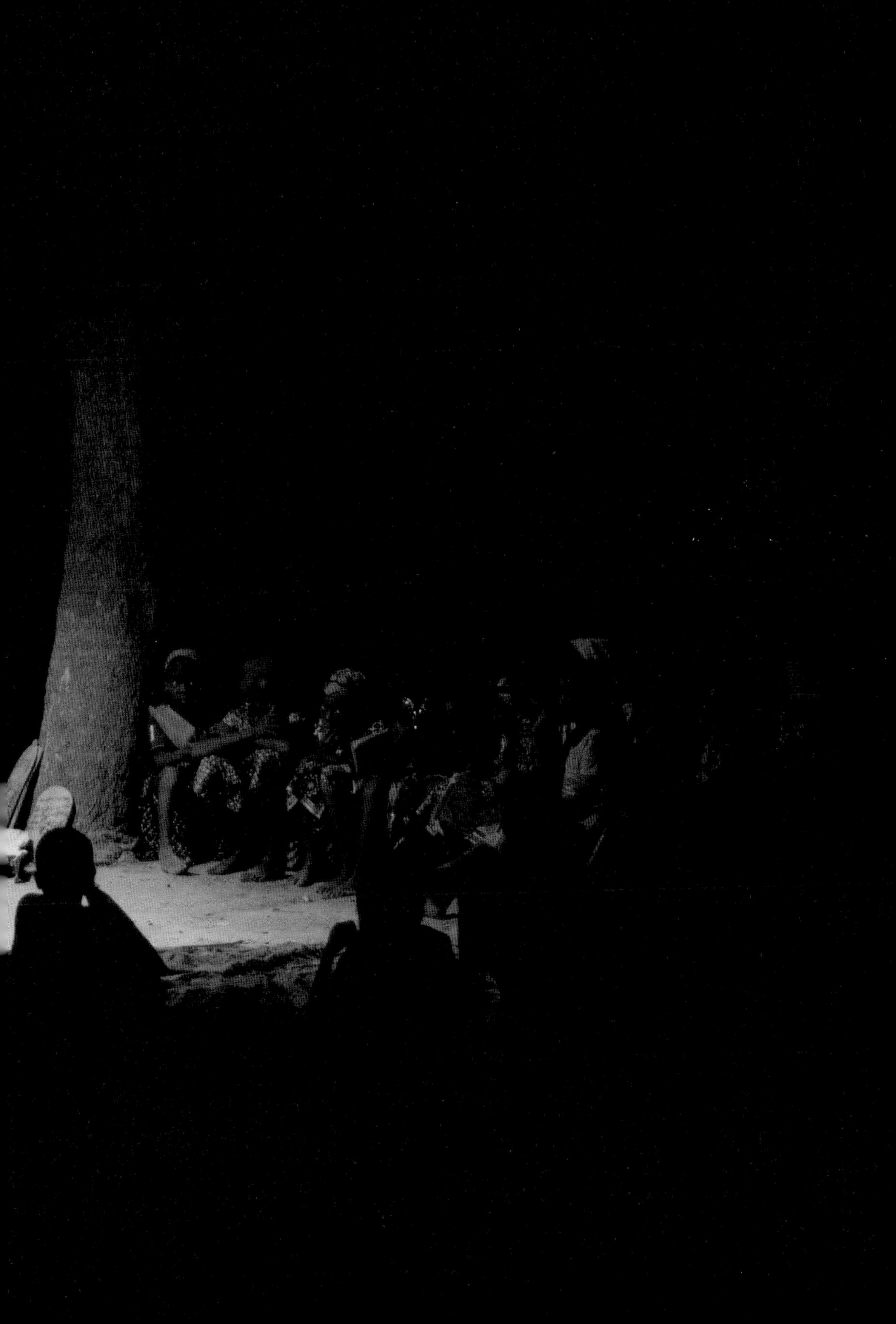

democrat branch of the model. Here, more radical participation occurs where it is believed that social change can only come from power exercised by the previously powerless (ibid.).

In South Africa, participation often happens without a planner's involvement, in the form of service delivery protests. Miraftab (2009) refers to this as "insurgent planning", where citizens create "invented" space of participation through direct action as self-activity, challenging the status quo and resisting dominant power structures and advocating social change (Miraftab and Wills, 2005). According to Sinwell (2010), preferred participation in South Africa has become protest and resistance, evident in the high numbers of protests in South Africa.

A Southern turn in planning theory began to see events such as protest action as a quest to focus on transgressive politics and insurgency that produce counter-hegemonic practices (Harrison, 2014). Watson (2013) refers to insurgent planning as one approach that deals with contexts characterised by "stubborn realities". Political, social and spatial contestation characterise these "polarised" contexts, filled with antagonism and opposition (Bollens, 2012 cited by Watson, 2013). Watson poses new assumptions that need to be made, defying current planning theory:

> Weak and corrupt states where state information is taking a suspect; unequal and divided 'civil society'; community organisations engaging with state through activist means rather than through dialogue or collaborative processes; citizenship based on rights but not responsibility; NGOs and social networks who serve their own interests; decision-making dominated by 'power' and little consensus; processes driven by different and often conflicting rationalities that shape expectations and outcomes; planning professionals are under direct challenge, where communities will want to take control of knowledge and idea production.

These proposed assumptions point to the obvious sensitivities of working in environments where insurgent planning might be practised. Insurgent planners such as Miraftab (2009) warn that although insurgent planning identifies the importance of ordinary citizens shaping their lives and is often empowering and done positively, disruptive actions may not always have correct motives.

To respond to the often antagonistic environment in which the insurgent planner operates, Watson (2013) considers the next step for insurgent planners as co-production, forming a "basis for action-oriented thinking at the state-civil society interface". Watson counters her proposed assumption for insurgent planners of "citizenship, based on rights but not responsibility", acknowledging a growing movement towards poor urban communities empowering themselves through processes of self-enumeration, mapping and presenting specific demands to the state (ibid.). The idea of the "community" contributing information has been turned into an empowerment strategy. Collier et al. (2016) suggest that what is needed is creating a complex ecology of knowledge producers, including technical experts, designers, planners and local experts (residents). This arrangement sees expert authority next to the public voice, in what Michael Callon (2009) refers to as a "hybrid forum" and creates an invited space for participation (Miraftab and Mills, 2005).

Harrison (2014) introduces speculative realism as a planning theory that can counter the more dogmatic approach Southern theory has taken. The theory was first formed to identify approaches that speculate "on the nature of reality beyond human cognition". Speculative realism links rationalism and naturalism, forming a relationship between conceptual thinking and non-conceptual reality. The "realism" here acknowledges "the power of consciousness, language and history in shaping our sense of reality" (ibid.). The planner speculates, hypothesises and proposes tentative formulations open to adjustments and clarification. The primary advantage of speculative realism in the context of self-built communities is to allow the planner to engage more flexibly, aligning to what Yiftachel (2009) refers to as "grey space", where spaces are neither formal nor informal, legal or illegal, and form "pseudo-permanent margins of today's urban regions" (ibid.).

There are various obstacles to moving with agility through the disciplinary bounds of planning in the "stubborn realities" of South Africa. Simone and Pieterse (2017) write about the paradoxes of urban environments in Africa. Cities have become venues for countervailing tendencies. A rights-based constitution might well have given rise to insurgent citizens. Apartheid planning theories of the past still bind the present into a spatially segregated society. They propose a dynamic solution of urban politics and programmatic interventions operating simultaneously through acupuncture or pilot interventions at a neighbourhood level that inform policy interventions at a municipal level and vice versa (ibid). This double (original emphasis) approach is appropriate where conventional rules of planning and regulatory frameworks are not adequate for the lived urban realities (ibid.). A double view affirms the importance of simultaneous experiments at the level of everyday life and in the worlds of policy and official governance. This is where one can attach value to experimenting with pilot projects, testing new solutions speculatively and, through this dynamic process, informing policy at a municipal or national level. With the double approach, Simon and Pieterse (ibid) speak of a practice that transpires through experimentation, pedagogy, failure, exchange and persistence, much like that proposed by speculative realism.

Infrastructure and citizenship

During apartheid, infrastructure, specifically housing, was often the only representation of the apartheid government in apartheid-planned townships, where the state was otherwise absent. Von Schnitzler (2016) argues that infrastructure became both the source of struggle and the terrain of protest for township inhabitants to make their voices heard. Referenced here, infrastructure includes all forms of techno-political work comprising socio-technical assemblages of materiality, discursive, fiscal, and organisational (ibid.). When considering infrastructure as a mode through which people experience the state, what does statehood's material form look like in today's democracies?

In the democratic context of post-apartheid South Africa, Wafer (2012), among others (Bond and Dugard, 2008; Desai, 2002; Parnell and Pieterse, 2010; Swilling and Annecke, 2006; von Schnitzler, 2008; Lemanski, 2020), discusses the importance of infrastructure and its capacity to articulate citizenship. The democratic government adopted an infrastructure-centric mode of extending citizenship (Wafer 2012), mainly through housing and, more recently, free basic services. Millstein (2020) argues that people associate formal housing with becoming recognised as "proper urban citizens" or "to becoming free". Self-built communities are still associated with being temporary and not recognised wholly as a citizen. However, providing a free standalone house for all South African citizens who qualify[2] is not possible. Consequently, the government is increasingly moving towards incrementally upgrading self-built communities and qualifying "housing" as a shelter, even if self-built, with adequate access to basic services (taps, toilets, refuse removal, electricity). How, then, does basic service infrastructure shape the embodied and subjective encounters (Wafer, 2012) with infrastructure to represent citizenship in a democratic country? McFarlane and Rutherfore (2008) refer to new forms of citizenship, where people use infrastructure as the basis of asserting new forms and challenging existing colonial forms (such as citizenship through legal documentation). When actively participating in everyday life through the infrastructural terrain, what Shaw (2014) refers to as "lived infrastructure", a form of infrastructural citizenship (Lemanski, 2020) emerges.

However, government departments distinguish between service delivery and social development, the former being a technical-administrative task and the latter involving resident participation (Chipkin, 2003). This separation negates the possibility of services functioning as a conduit for a sense of citizenship. Instead, services represented through infrastructure become purely technical modes of delivering needs defined by technical experts rather than by residents themselves.

Importantly, Chipkin (ibid.) refers to basic service delivery as not only how (design, implementation and maintenance) services are provided but also "what services are delivered that will assist residents in sustaining and improving their material needs and quality of life". Haque et al. (2021) emphasise the importance of working with social capital and social norms when designing infrastructure, re-framing the techno-centric role of infrastructure to a more human-centric role, where government puts people at the centre of the design process. Focusing on the "how" rather than what services are provided, Collier et al. (2016) call for collectively re-framing the purpose of infrastructure to a multifunctional role, attending to the various ways infrastructure shapes everyday life and the attributed values according to which these infrastructures may be assessed. Relating back to lighting infrastructure, Ebbensgaard (2016) speaks of this consideration of social practices as the core difference between performative lighting design and prescriptive lighting planning. The latter takes the outcome of technological change as the starting point (ibid.).

When putting societal needs at the centre of infrastructure, it is useful to refer to what Simone (2004) refers to as "people as infrastructure", acknowledging the dynamic nature of societal needs. Simone explores how the intersection of social encounters makes for new, unexpected spaces of economic and cultural operations. In Johannesburg, the decaying city centre creates a void or provision that facilitates

---

2   If a household collectively earns R3,500 or less per month, they qualify for a free house

these social intersections. Provisionality is about self-conception, a co-production of space, where space becomes a social product (Lefebvre, 1991), creating new forms of citizenship through a sense of belonging to and ownership of space. Simone (ibid.) concludes that policymakers must consider both regulation and provisionality in their policies.

Lefebvre (ibid.) refers to space as a social product where conceived space (infrastructure), perceived space (people's values) and produced space (the everyday lived experience) are in constant interaction. Reconceptualising infrastructure from a technical solution for a technical need to a technical solution for a societal need is necessary to transform space into a social product that represents a sense of citizenship and belonging. Graham and McFarlane (2015) highlight the lack of empirical research into the nature of politics and lived experiences through the lens of everyday infrastructural experiences. People's relationship to infrastructure, exemplified in writings such as *Infrastructural Citizenship* (Lemanski, 2020) and *Lived Infrastructure* (Shaw, 2014, p. 2240), also introduces important concepts of the lived experiences of infrastructure and the power of infrastructure to articulate citizenship. However, to date, these concepts are theoretical and lack empirical studies. Furthermore, planning practices in post-apartheid South Africa are still technocratically oriented, though planning theory has advanced to include concepts of participation, needs and values. To date, there is no empirical study on lived experiences of public lighting infrastructure in self-built communities. Shaw (ibid.) suggests "detailed explorations of public lighting technologies and the everyday use of infrastructure", particularly the policy implications of such studies. Shaw (ibid.) identified this gap in research. Exploring this gap in self-built communities fills a further gap.

Holistic lighting infrastructure for self-built communities

This review looked at understanding and planning human-centred public lighting in urban environments. The first two sections focused on the potentials and impact of light in particular. On the one hand are those who study lighting's impact on reducing crime, fear of crime and insecurity; on the other hand, those who write about the nighttime urban atmospheres and the potential for light to activate space in everyday life.

From the first branch, exploring the nexus between light and crime, the review found that most of the research focuses on direct correlations between light and crime, showing that lighting can reduce crime. Some are increasingly discrediting direct correlations between light and crime by criticising their simplistic nature. Instead of studying the reduction in actual incidents of crime, some look at reducing the fear of crime through urban lighting, also investigating the factors that generate fear and how lighting can address these factors. Situational crime prevention, or CPTED, looks at crime prevention even more holistically, especially third-generation CPTED. Mihinjac and Saville (2019) highlight that CPTED interventions should meet various Maslowian needs, which goes beyond lighting and crime or fear of crime. What is particularly important in CPTED theory is the need for self-actualisation at night, in which urban lighting appears to be a key enabler. In this sense, this research is in line with third-generation CPTED that looks at how fear of crime affects psychosocial and societal well-being. How does lighting perform in this context, to reduce the fear of crime and improve quality of life by creating a more positive nighttime atmosphere through public lighting? However, the research on third-generation CPTED is very new. It lacks empirical evidence, especially in informal environments where this research is based and where the need for self-actualisation and the reduction of fear of crime are everyday struggles.

The second branch of the research qualitatively studies the impact of public lighting on social patterns and everyday practices. The literature emphasises the importance of lighting and people in space, collectively defining the nocturnal urban atmosphere. This research, therefore, highlights the importance of designing and developing lighting models that place people at the centre. Scholars use advanced social science methods to understand the different material cultures related to light, enabling lighting to address the specific needs of people by understanding their daily practices. Although the research points to the importance of human-centric lighting, it focuses on a domestic scale of outdoor lighting rather than studying the larger scale of public lighting infrastructure. Additionally, there is none focused on the impact of public lighting on the life of residents in self-built communities. Most of the research is geographically focused on North American and European cities, where there are very few self-built communities. This research contributes to raising questions about the role of light at night in other cultures and urban contexts. Therefore, it is important for this research to empirically establish whether public lighting can create an atmosphere that transforms self-built communities into more productive social spaces that offer more opportunities and better day-to-day nighttime experiences.

Regarding the larger-scale infrastructural discussions, this review focused on the relationship between planning practices, infrastructure and citizenship. Patel (2008) suggests that while previously excluded groups have increased access to services, past historical patterns continue, as services remain remedial in their approach and infrastructure is seen as a technical service with little focus on social development. Furthermore, planning theory in the Global South does not pay sufficient attention to creating a "master narrative" (Star, 1999), understood as the symbol and value that infrastructure represents for citizens living in self-built communities. Today, a technocratic infrastructural logic is embedded within planning policies and practice in post-apartheid South Africa. New high-mast lighting interventions merely reinforce the apartheid-era logic of infrastructure provision. This is discussed in Chapter 2.

The lack of consideration of infrastructure and its relation to users' everyday lives has often resulted in a physical rejection of infrastructure through vandalism, neglect and service delivery protests. The government's general response is to adopt a more technocratic planning approach and lay down vandal-proof and inaccessible public infrastructure, instead of understanding user needs and responding with a more appropriate solution. This research aims to break the separation between technical service and social development and points to creating scalable infrastructure, where people and lighting infrastructure can create nocturnal atmospheres conducive to social upliftment. In this sense, this research on South African self-built communities aims to highlight the impact everyone at their domestic scale has on the larger-scale public infrastructure network.

The relationship between people and public lighting infrastructure in self-built communities has not been investigated. The potential for infrastructure in general to articulate citizenship is a theoretical discussion that needs empirical backing. The multiple narratives of public lighting infrastructure need further investigation to understand what public light means to people rather than what it means to the state (Star, 1999). Consequently, by embedding a valued narrative that represents collective and individual interests while still maintaining the scalability of the infrastructure, it is possible to create an infrastructure that resembles citizenship. When it comes to the design, implementation and maintenance of public lighting infrastructure, the impact

of actively involving citizens in the development of their city by participating in the project design is under-researched.

The siloed nature of the three research strands (light and crime; lighting, social patterns and everyday practices; and infrastructure and citizenship) also presents a major gap. These works should be viewed together to form a holistic view on the impact of public lighting infrastructure on everynight life in self-built communities. This research aims to address and integrate these three major gaps by studying the impact of alternative public lighting solutions on everyday life in a post-apartheid self-built community in Cape Town, while critically engaging in planning practice through an applied research project.

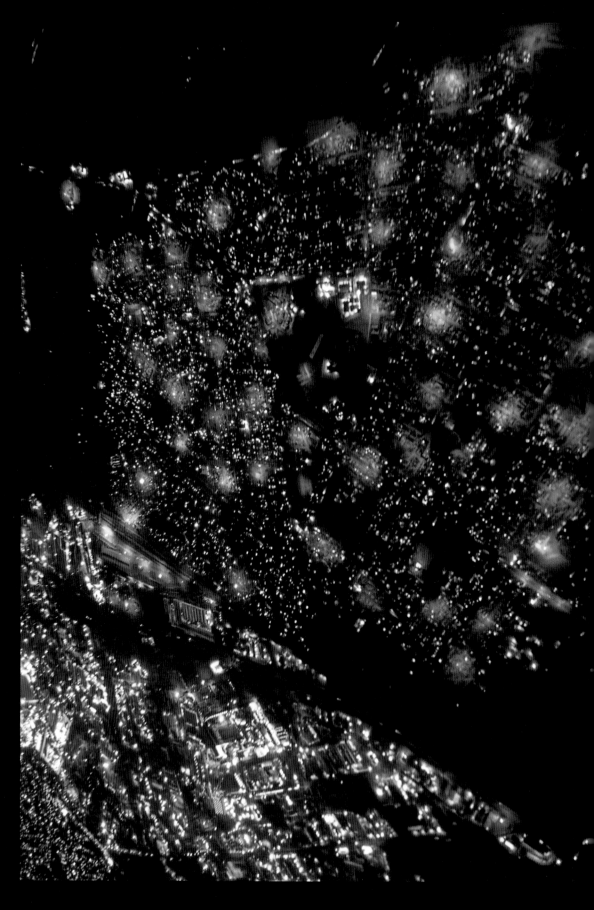

Cape Town's Segregated Lightscape

Chapter 2

The provision of unequal and inadequate urban lighting is a long-standing issue in South African cities, originating from a history of race-based seg-regative planning. Cape Town is the quintessential apartheid city. The Group Areas Act planning deter-mined which races could live where and still reflects in its lightscape today (Maps 1 and 2), twenty-seven years after apartheid was abolished. From a satel-lite view (Figure 1), Khayelitsha, an apartheid-planned township[1] designated for black people, stands out clearly, with a different lighting texture com-pared with the surrounding neighbourhoods. On the ground, this texture reflects a juxtaposed light-scape of yellow-orange light and pitch-black shad-ows as the forty-metre-tall floodlights hover over the community below (Figure 2). How did this contrast-ing lightscape come to be, and why are high-mast lights still being implemented by the government today, despite their clear inadequacy and negative symbolism?

Chapter summary:	This chapter explores Cape Town's segregative plan-ning through its urban lightscape, considers the devel-opment of Khayelitsha and its self-built communities as a symbol of apartheid resistance, and expands on the logic behind the implementation of high-mast light-ing in townships. It presents the case study and situ-ates the theoretical discourse from Chapter 1 into the South African context, beginning with a brief history of Cape Town's race-based segregation, and grounding the exploration of the development of race-based pub-lic lighting infrastructure in the second section of the chapter. The final section discusses the shift to democ-racy and the contemporary conditions in self-built com-munities[2], as well as the fight for more effective public lighting.

The narrative of this chapter follows the narrative of self-built communities in Cape Town. During apart-heid, the city's self-built communities were a sym-bol of resistance, with persistent migration of black populations, especially women, to Cape Town—an area where black people were not allowed to live. This persistence eventually led to the development of Khayelitsha, envisioned as a consolidation plan after the apartheid government realised that Cape Town would have to accept black populations as part of the city. Today, self-built communities sym-bolise the lack of affordable housing and unequal access to opportunities for all. Cape Town faces a crisis, with new communities being established

daily. The gap between serviced and unserviced citizens is expanding—a growing inequality[3] that comes from a history of segregation and unequal treatment of racial groups. Change has been slow during the twenty-seven years since apartheid's demise, and the cracks of inadequate infrastruc-ture in self-built communities are in the public eye. Ineffective public lighting and the government's continuous deployment of high-mast lighting is the latest crack and demands rethinking.

The materialisation of township lightscapes

In South Africa, the historical role of infrastructure had two faces—the conduit of oppressive regimes for the non-white population and an enabler for the white population. Otter (2008) also defines lighting with two historical paradigms, the disciplinary and the spectacular, where "the former implies a cruel, cold, fixed gaze, the latter a more playful, empow-ered and mobile one". Many believe that high-mast lighting was first installed as disciplinary lighting by the apartheid government. Today, this lighting type still serves townships with a predominantly black population. The lack of concrete evidence of high-mast lighting's origin requires a more nuanced un-derstanding of its meaning today. This section fol-lows Wiezman et al.'s (2010) theory, termed Forensic Architecture, using "clues and traces" to analyse high-mast lighting as a materialisation of the apart-heid government's response to opposition between 1946 and 1990. Today, spatial evidence (ibid.) sug-gests that high-mast lighting has racial associa-tions that have not changed in more than two dec-ades post-apartheid. Advocacy campaigns have used this spatial evidence to build a case against the City of Cape Town (CoCT) for more effective public lighting in areas previously designated by the 1950s Group Areas Act (Social Justice Coalition, 2018). This evidence, presented along with proof of budget allocations for public lighting, shows that the City is unfairly and unequally spending its re-sources in areas based on racial demographics. By looking at the materialisation of high-mast lighting and its presence in contemporary South Africa, one can understand that activists use high-mast light-ing's "performance as an object" in the "forum" or debate (Weizman et al., 2010, p. 60) on equal access to services for all citizens of South Africa. A broader

---

1   In the South African context, the term 'township' is com-monly understood to refer to the underdeveloped, usual-ly urban, residential areas that during apartheid were re-served for non-whites who lived near or worked in areas that were designated 'white only'.

2   The City of Cape Town officially refers to self-built commu-nities as "informal settlements", and this chapter uses the term for contextual purposes. The term includes a range of self-built communities—some of these are officially rec-ognised by the City after a process of a land survey, while others are not recognised, either because they are newly established or because recognising the self-built communi-ty obliges the City to provide free basic services.

---

3   UN-Habitat's City Prosperity Initiative (CPI) index finds Cape Town to be one of the most unequal cities in the world. CPI is similar to the GINI coefficient but includes other in-dicators such as productivity, infrastructure development, quality of life, equity and social inclusion and environmen-tal sustainability (UN-Habitat, 2012).

Map 1   Apartheid government's Cape Town Group Areas Act plan for the City of Cape Town

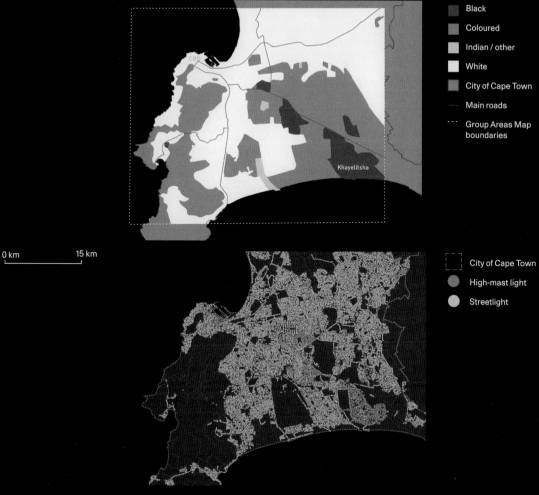

Black

Coloured

Indian / other

White

City of Cape Town

Main roads

Group Areas Map
boundaries

0 km   15 km

City of Cape Town

High-mast light

Streetlight

Map 2   Streetlights in yellow and high-mast lighting in red in the Cape Town metropolitan area

Fig 1   Aerial view of Cape Town at night, with Khayelitsha still demarcated with high-mast lighting

Fig 2   Night march against ineffective public lighting in Khayelitsha in 2019

— 2021 population estimate 60.58 million
(StatsSA, 2020)
— High inequality spurred on by apartheid
— Racially segregated

— 2021 population estimate 4.68 million
(StatsSA, 2019)
— Very unequal (City Prosperity Index)
— Racially segregated
— 2019: 635 self-built communities

— 2021 population estimate 447 120
(Population Data, Western Cape gov., 2020)
— Predominantly black population
— Apartheid planned township with pockets
of self-built communities
— 218 high-mast lights

Fig 3   Overview and scale of research location

historical look into urban planning and infrastructure provision follows to understand the current unequal provision of lighting infrastructure. I look at the development of Cape Town through colonial and apartheid rule, alongside the general political landscape of apartheid South Africa, which led to the eventual implementation of high-mast lighting.

Cape Town's long and gradual history establishing its segregative lightscape began under colonial rule in the late 1800s, when British colonies established a grand aesthetic narrative of Englishness through architecture and urban planning. The foundation of Cape Town's racial segregation was the visibility of "unsightliness" as a legitimate cause for excluding or removing people and structures from the cityscape (Coetzer, 2013). An 1865 census shows a significant black African population in the city centre — today around the Woodstock area in **Map 3**. From the late 1800s, requests were formulated for separate residential development based on race. The opportunity to move forward with separate development arose with the Bubonic plague in 1901, when the Ndabeni camp, a temporary camp reserved for black Africans, was created. Within a few weeks, six to seven thousand black Africans were removed from central Cape Town to Ndabeni **(Map 3)**. This gave rise to the first racially segregative act, called the Native Reserve Locations Act of 1902. With this act, the governor gained the power to reserve land as uninhabitable by black Africans, claiming that this was to prevent further outbreaks of the plague. From 1902 onward, various planning acts[4] removed dense "unsightly slums" from the city, creating race-based neighbourhoods using a trimmed down version of Howard's English Garden City Model (Coetzer, 2013). Here the "home" was used to make "others" look visually the same. Because of this merely aesthetic motif, the British paid little attention to infrastructure and service provision (ibid). In this process of creating the "other", people or groups were labelled as non-normative (Gallaher, 2009) and received "other" infrastructures and levels of service delivery.

The gradual process of separate development led to the planning of Langa. Founded in 1923, Langa was one of the earliest planned townships designated for black people, using urban planning and infrastructure to survey and control its population. Shown in **Figure 4**, Langa resembled the general radial patterns of the panoptic prison system

of surveillance (Foucault and Rabinow, 1984) with "powerful arc lamps" planned in the spaces around the compound (Coetzer, 2013). To my knowledge, this is the first time the British government in South Africa used lighting infrastructure for control, where colonial infrastructure became a means of constituting colonial territories as unified, governable spaces (von Schnitzler, 2008).

The apartheid government took over in 1948, strengthening the colonial logic of removing the "native" from the cityscape. Under the apartheid government, Prime Minister Hendrik Verwoerd advocated a theory of separate "nations", distorting liberalism into separate development. This resulted in the rise of the Bantustan homelands — areas of self-governance for black Africans with no infrastructure or services provided from the apartheid government. The apartheid government housed migrant labourers from the Bantustan homelands in utilitarian townships, described by Prime Minister Verwoerd as:

> orderly housing … of proper control, whereby vagrants and parasites who always flourish in slum conditions can be cut out. This scheme to house all workers under control, coordinated with control of influx. (Verwoerd, 12 May 1952, cited by Coetzer, 2013)

Cape Town became increasingly segregated as the Reservation of Separate Amenities Act of 1953 and Group Areas Act of 1950 created featureless townships for black Africans, with no public space to prevent the emergence of a counter-public (von Schnitzler, 2016). Mbembe (2003) calls this "a peculiar spatial institution scientifically planned [through the use of infrastructure] for the purposes of control". **Map 4** and **Figure 5** show the application of the Group Areas Act diagram to Cape Town's segregated plan. Cape Town had particular conditions because there were no mines close by and no cheap labour needed. As a result, no Bantustans were created. The nearest was Ciskei, 1,000 kilometres away. In 1955, the western half of the Cape Province was separated from South Africa with the Eiselen Line, a legislative demarcation, and the Coloured Labour Preferential Policy (CLPP) of 1955 restricted black Africans' presence to the west of this line. Between 1963 and 1967, this line was moved further east, further excluding black Africans west of the line **(Map 5)**.

---

4   Natives Land Act of 1913, The Ordinance and Housing Act of 1920, building regulations set out by the Cape Institute of Architecture in 1920, Native (Urban Areas) Act of 1923, Assisted Housing Scheme of 1922

In the 1960s, nationwide anti-apartheid protests involved vandalising infrastructure which symbolised the apartheid government. Despite protests, by the

Map 3   The development of racially segregated Cape Town

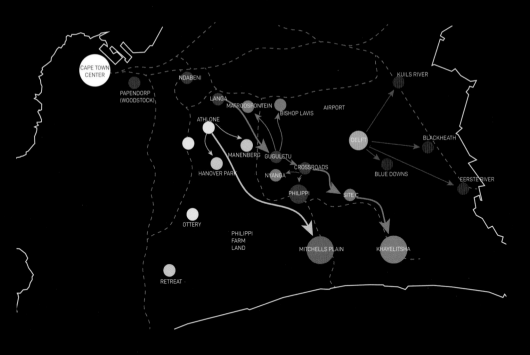

Fig 4   Diagrammatic plan of Langa Township, the first formally planned residential area in South Africa designated for black Africans

Map 4   The application of the Group Areas Act to Cape Town

Fig 5   Group Areas Act Plan of 1956 using infrastructure to enforce race- and class-based segregation

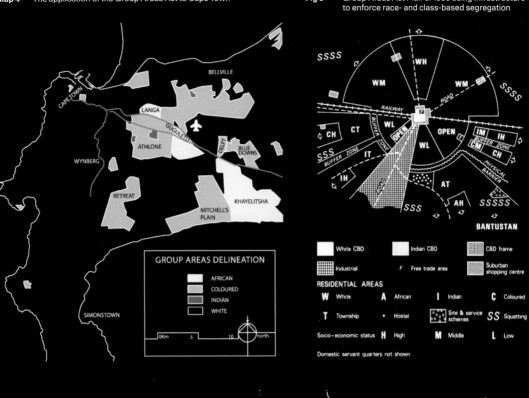

GROUP AREAS DELINEATION

- AFRICAN
- COLOURED
- INDIAN
- WHITE

0 Km   5   10   north

White CBD   Indian CBD   CBD frame

Industrial   F   Free trade area   Suburban shopping centre

RESIDENTIAL AREAS

W   White   A   African   I   Indian   C   Coloured

T   Township   •   Hostel   Site & service schemes   SS   Squatting

Socio-economic status   H   High   M   Middle   L   Low

Domestic servant quarters not shown

1   GOODWOOD
2   KUILSRIVER
3   BELLVILLE
4   STELLENBOSCH
5   WELLINGTON
6   SOMERSET WEST
7   STRAND

EISELEN LINE 1955

WESTERN CAPE AFRICAN LABOUR REPLACEMENT LINE 1963

COLOURED LABOUR PREFERENCE AREA 1967

0   25   50   75   100   150
Km

COLOURED LABOUR PREFERENCE AREA

Map 5   Red lines indicating the Eiselen Line, the Western Cape African Labour Preference Area that restricted all working black Africans to the east (right) of the respective line

mid-1960s, the apartheid government imposed the General Law Amendment Act of 1962 (Sabotage Act[5]) to control infrastructure vandalism, imprisoning many political activists. The country's apparent stability attracted increased foreign investment, leading to significant economic growth and an influx of black migrant labourers. Cape Town's labour demand also increased. More black Africans sought work there, despite the CLPP which restricted black people from legally working in Cape Town. Acts like the Bantu Labour Act of 1964 and the Black (Natives) Laws Amendment Act of 1952 reinforced the CLPP, resulting in many forced removals of black Africans, especially women and children, who were sent back to their homelands or settled in controlled camps in Nyanga West (Gugulethu) (Cole, 2013).

The increase in the urban black population seeking work and the international financial crisis of the 1970s made it difficult to cross-subsidise infrastructure and services in black townships. Self-sufficiency within the townships was therefore the focus from the early 1970s, and the Bantu Affairs Administration Boards (BAAB) took over township administration in 1973 (von Schnitzler, 2016). The BAAB resorted to rent and service charges to pay for basic service delivery in the absence of a tax base. During the 1970s, more women were "deported" from Cape Town after being identified as black African under the BAAB screening process. The women were fighting persistently for their right to stay in the city. The BAAB instructed that they settle on land at the crossroads of Landsdown Road and the N2 National Highway, creating Crossroads (eventually known as Old Crossroads) (Cole, 2013). The government was slowly beginning to lose control of South African cities as an exclusively "white space".

After the 1976 Soweto Uprising[6], a more reformist approach to governing the black urban population emerged. The apartheid government increased infrastructure investments and rents were raised (von Schnitzler, 2016). In parallel with the growing unrest in South Africa, the forced removals throughout Cape Town in 1974–1978 caused the Crossroads squatter settlements to mushroom (Figure 6). The government planned to destroy the settlements

to prevent them becoming political hotspots. However, after papers explaining the government's brutal and inhumane plan to invade Crossroads were leaked, Dr Piet Koornhof took over as the Minister of Development and Cooperation. Under the international spotlight, Dr Koornhof began a reformist approach, carefully negotiating with the "squatters" in Crossroads and making a deal to house them formally. However, many Crossroads residents realised that legislation would not allow them to stay in the formal neighbourhood named New Crossroads. This led to internal conflicts over the approach to resistance and whether or not people would agree to work with the government.

Meanwhile, the reformist approach and outward stable appearance backfired as the rent increases resulted in public protests, rental boycotts and walkouts. These protests formed an anti-apartheid movement that took infrastructure as both the terrain and object of struggle through vandalising infrastructure (von Schnitzler, 2016). Internal unrest and disagreements over approaches to government resistance resulted in public protests in many townships, similar to what happened in Crossroads. The government used the internal conflict to their advantage, referring to the tension and resistance as a "total onslaught" and responded with the Total National Strategy (Cock and Nathan, 1989). The Total Strategy was a distinctly military and securocratic approach to governing the black population in the early 1980s, and the government integrated urban infrastructure into the larger counter-insurgency project (von Schnitzler, 2016). The Total Strategy blurred lines between defence and civil spending (Orbann, 1984). The military used infrastructure as part of the counter-insurgency, yet the infrastructure was classified as civil spending (Cock and Nathan, 1989). The blurring of civil and defence spending supported the two ideologies of governance in late apartheid—the Reformists and the Securocrats. The Securocrats believed in a greater militant approach to control, and the Reformists believed in "winning the hearts and minds" of the black urban population through infrastructure interventions (Boraine, 2019).

Back in Cape Town, aligned with the Total Strategy, the government took advantage of internal conflicts in Crossroads and subsequently cancelled the planned phase 2 of New Crossroads. Instead, they announced the development of Khayelitsha in 1983 (Surplus People Project South Africa, 1984). Khayelitsha was a solution to the state's "apartheid problems". The vision was to screen all black Africans, send all illegals back to Bantustans, and

---

5   The Sabotage Act was defined "as a wrongful and wilful act to inflict injuries, obstruct or tamper with the supply of light, water, power or fuel and the postal and telephone services". It also included interference with the free movement of traffic or jeopardising the safety of the state in any way.

6   The 1976 Soweto Uprising was a youth protest against the use of Afrikaans as the language of instruction in black schools. The peaceful protest drew international attention when police took violent action against the protesters, killing hundreds of youth, among them, eleven year old Hector Pieterson.

move all "legals" to a single, controlled neighbour-hood far from the city, ultimately creating the perfect apartheid city. Khayelitsha's planning is notable because it was founded in the late apartheid years, in 1983, during the Total Strategy, which took on a very technical form of social engineering engrained into the infrastructure of everyday life. The detailed planning concept of Khayelitsha is discussed later in this chapter.

The unrest and violent protests continued to grow across South Africa. In 1984, the South African Defence Force deployed military troops to the townships (Nathan, 1989), attempting to regain control of the protesting urban black population. Some black communities were "placed under virtual military occupation and were lit up by spotlights placed on hills" (Daily Dispatch, 8.10.1984). It was at this point that the government began to investigate the installation of high-mast lighting across townships.

The Draft Guide Plan for the Cape Metropolitan Area in 1983 assessed the advantages and disadvantages of electricity provision options (and with that public lighting) in townships (Guide Plan Committee for the Cape Metropolitan Area, 1983). Their main criteria were affordability, security lighting and tamper-proof infrastructure (Table 1). According to their evaluation criteria, high-mast lighting appeared most advantageous. They evaluated the lighting as moderately expensive but providing a high level of security lighting (according to

their definition of security lighting) and little chance of tampering. From this point onwards, many tender submissions and calls to tender for the installation of high-mast lighting across South Africa occurred (Western Cape Development Board, 1986, 1987a, 1987b, 1987c).

By 1986, the government imposed a series of states of emergency which gave the South African Police (SAP) and the South African Defence Force (SADF) with extraordinary powers to suppress uprisings in townships. Military surveillance in the townships increased, with curfews implemented from 21:00 to 04:00 to prevent political gatherings taking place under the veil of darkness. Night curfews meant that the government dominated private life too, with nighttime activity ultimately banned for the black population for a major part of the 1980s (Truth and Reconciliation Commission, 1998a), and nighttime urban life became a dangerous encounter (Drewett, 2019, p. 133). The military equipped vehicles with floodlights, and soldiers carried powerful flashlights to increase the ease of surveillance in townships during the dark curfew hours.

> Hundreds of heavily armed troops threw tight cordons around ... townships under cover of dark last night, acting under the Emergency Regulations proclaimed yesterday. The troops carried rifles with fixed bayonets (Truth and Reconciliation Commission, 1998b)

Provision	Characteristics	Advantages	Disadvantages
Not provided	No installation of mains electricity within project site. Residents make their own provision for heating, light, cooking and power. Communal facilities such as schools may use generators.	F No capital costs for agencies except for communal facilities V Opportunity for local business development	• Inconvenient S No security lighting possible • Unreliable alternatives F High maintenance costs for communal facilities • High costs for occupants • Woodlots may be needed • Coal yards may be needed
High-mast lighting	Light an area of 125m radius	F Relatively few masts needed V Not easily illegally tapped V Basically vandal-proof S Maximum security of erven (private property) and streets	F Moderately expensive
Street lighting	Lighting for security on streets and footpaths	S Provides partial security	F Expensive V Can be illegally tapped V Can be vandalised
Full connection	An intermediate form of provision is not necessary since additional capital costs are not high. Plot occupants can obtain connection when they can afford it.	• Convenient S Level of security lighting F Can be varied as funds permit F Lower electricity costs for households	F High costs depending on mains equipment required

F financial S security V vandalism

Table 1 Guidance on electricity supply options for townships in the Cape Metropolitan Area by the Ministry of Community Development

By November 1985, an extreme environment of repression existed … There were twenty-four hour foot patrols, and searchlights swept the streets at night. (Truth and Reconciliation Commission, 1998b)

However, citizens continued to gather in the dark in the form of "candlelight protest" (Figure 7), a mode of peaceful protest which valued darkness as a means of circumventing bans on gathering and curfews.

The State of Emergency prohibited up to a hundred organisations from holding meetings… political protest adopted more varied forms such as candlelight protests… The Divisional Commissioner of Police for the Western Cape, Brigadier Chris Swart, said that the candlelight protests were not innocent but "deliberate tactics aimed at stirring people's emotions, which leads them to violent acts". (Truth and Reconcilliation Commission, 1998b)

By early 1987, the military troops withdrew from townships as protests subsided, with restrictions placed on the country in a national state of emergency, and the apartheid government had regained control of the urban black population. With South Africa calmer, a second rise in the reformist approach to governance launched a counter-revolutionary strategy, with techno-political schemes aimed at recasting civil society's foundations through infrastructure upgrades (Cock and Nathan, 1989). This reformist programme, called "Winning Hearts and Minds" (WHAM), which focused infrastructure upgrading on "oil spot"[7] townships, was coordinated by the National Security Management System (Cock and Nathan, 1989). Contrary to the name, most residents distrusted the upgrading programmes because of its connection with military action in townships (Boraine, 1989). Even though the WHAM programme aligned with the reformist approach, a strong securocratic influence in apartheid governance remained, which shaped the nature of WHAM interventions. The reformist logic of late apartheid governance was coupled with a securocratic logic in the infrastructure's materiality (Boraine, 2019).

High-mast lighting suited this combination of securocratic and reformist infrastructure. The provision of public lighting came in the form of virtually indestructible floodlights casting deep yellow light over unelectrified households (von Schnitzler, 2008). High-mast lighting was placed on the periphery, near township entrances rather than in central, public locations, as shown in Khayelitsha's lighting plan (Map 6) (Cook, 1986). The positioning of the lights raises the question whether planners considered the military or community in the decision to implement high-mast lighting.

Many scholars (Dlamini, 2008; Hornberger, 2008; Wainright, 2014; Veck, 2000; von Schnitzler, 2008) believe that high-mast lights enabled police and military surveillance, and some claim that high-mast lights allowed easy helicopter surveillance at night (Wainwright, 2014). During the high-mast lighting installation period, a series of states of emergency between 1985 and 1990 banned black people from venturing outside between 21:00 and 04:00 and also restricted organisational capacity (i.e. public gatherings) (Truth and Reconciliation Commission, 1998). This raises the question of who the high-mast lights were intended to serve, given the fact that the general black population in South Africa were not permitted to gather in public or venture out after dark. With the presence of high-mast lighting, groups could no longer gather under the veil of darkness in candlelight protests as before. Regardless of whether the apartheid government used the high-mast lights for easier surveillance, one can speculate that within the context of apartheid, the atmospheric quality shaped by high-mast lights created a prison-like atmosphere and instilled a psychological feeling among residents in the townships of being watched (Figure 8).

High-mast floodlights encroached on a material, spatial and atmospheric level as the military cast spotlights on the civilian arena (Cock, 1989). Events and documents between 1984 and the demise of apartheid in 1994, as well as interviews with apartheid history experts, show how the deployment of high-mast lighting was in line with the ideology of the Securocrats and the Reformists. On one hand, the lighting was intended to win over the hearts and minds of black Africans, and on the other hand, the lights were intended to facilitate more effective surveillance by the military and police, in line with the Total Strategy. It could be argued that the public gradually accepted the infrastructural language of high-mast lighting as the norm in townships today. The government is still using the same criteria for the continued deployment of high-mast lighting as in the 1984 guide document for

7   The term "oil spot" refers to "strategic bases" from which the security forces believed they could "regain control" over the black population. By 1989, there were thirty-four designated "oil spot" townships (Boraine, 1989).

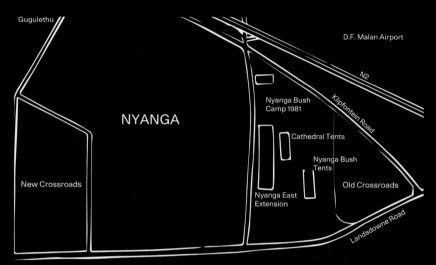

Fig 6   Crossroads complex consisting of various small self-built communities or "squatter camps"

Fig 7   Crossroads residents in candlelight protest

Fig 8   David Goldblatt, *Flushing meadows and lightning masts, Site B, Khayelitsha, Cape Town, 11 October 1987 structures*, 1987
silver gelatin hand print

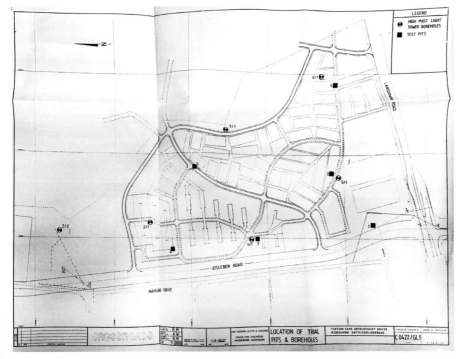

Map 6   High-mast light positions in Crossroads, plan issued by the Western Cape Development Board, 1987

township development—affordability, security and tamperproof.

The next section looks at democratic South Africa's inherited infrastructure and Khayelitsha's apartheid lightscape, analysing policies and technology that continue the deployment of high-mast lighting in townships and self-built communities.

Building democracy and inherited infrastructure

The dawn of democracy in 1994 presented an unimaginable scope of social, political, technical and economic problems for the new ruling party, the African National Congress (ANC). Much work was, and still is, required to redraw the boundary differentiating the new government from the old apartheid government (von Schnitzler, 2016). The ANC inherited both a rapidly deteriorating infrastructure stock that was inappropriate for the needs of the population and legislation that needed complete reworking. Redrawing the infrastructural landscape to represent the new democracy was increasingly challenging because of the techno-political turn during late apartheid, where infrastructure was not only a neutral conduit for service provision but contained deeply embedded questions of citizenship and belonging (von Schnitzler, 2016). New social issues arose from the large influx of people into urban areas and rapidly developing self-built communities that needed infrastructure provision.

The sheer scale of these challenges meant that the ANC prioritised which boundaries needed redrawing, often relying on a "command-and-control" method of "getting the job done quickly" (Bruyns and Graafland, 2012). Understandably, restructuring the political system was the most vital aspect of a new democracy for the ANC (Boraine, 2019). Much focus and energy was devoted to civil society's legal rights, and access to housing became a constitutional right after so many had not had free and equal access to cities and services in apartheid. The government developed several housing schemes where households earning below a certain amount (today R3,500.01, or $195, per household per month) qualify to receive a free house, comprising a top structure serviced with water, electricity and sanitation (Department of Human Settlements, 2020). Though well-intended, this intense focus on housing provision raised many expectations. Today, housing stands as a symbol of democratic South Africa (Millstein, 2020). As a result, the promise of a free house became a politicised tool to gain votes.

The government paid less attention to other infrastructure to spatially undo apartheid. Public lighting was one component that has not been redressed to this day. Given these challenges, it is not surprising that the new government could not rewrite the infrastructural language. Instead, infrastructure was reframed (von Schnitzler, 2016), and the narrative of high-mast floodlights was recast from a technical solution for a political problem to a technical solution for a social problem. In the public eye, high-mast floodlights are a common-sense, quick and efficient solution for lighting townships and self-built communities (Cock, 1989), while the government has rescripted high-mast lighting from apartheid-era infrastructure to a last-resort option that meets citizens' basic needs.

However, since 2017, the CoCT has seen major backlash against public lighting provision in townships with a predominantly black population. This negative attention arose after the Social Justice Coalition (SJC), an NGO focusing on basic service delivery, launched a public lighting campaign that came as a spin-off from their Khayelitsha commission of enquiry into unequal police resources. During their enquiry, they found that police officers often complained about inadequate lighting, resulting in them not being able to do their jobs properly. Since then, several front-page articles have focused on inadequate public lighting and discriminatory public lighting budgets for areas like Khayelitsha (Figure 9).

The other angle of the SJC's argument is the apartheid-era connotation of high-mast lighting. Interestingly, during my research, only one person living in a self-built community raised the connection of high-mast lighting as a symbol of apartheid. The question should be asked whether it matters that high-mast lighting is connected to apartheid if no-one in self-built communities is concerned about it. Outside of townships, almost every South African I discussed my research with proclaimed that "those lights in the townships" reminded them of prison lighting. It is significant that "outsiders" perceive the difference in township lightscapes because it sets townships and self-built communities apart from the rest of the city, as demonstrated in the aerial photograph (Figure 10) of a Johannesburg township illuminated with high-mast lighting. This material difference stigmatises the predominantly black population of a neighbourhood. The government's unequal allocation of technical infrastructure based on an area's demographic structure is highly problematic in post-apartheid South Africa, and several policies enable the continued distribution of high-mast lighting in South African townships.

Fig 9   Cape Argus of March 2019: front-page article on inadequate public lighting allocations for townships

■ LIGHTING

Township left in the dark

Khayelitsha won't get a cent from R62.5m City budget

MARVIN CHARLES
marvin.charles@inl.co.za

THE CITY of Cape Town has R62.5 million to spend on public lighting in the 2019/20 financial year, but none of that money will be spent on Khayelitsha, where a lack of lighting had been highlighted as a risk to safety.

The 2014 commission of inquiry into policing in the township found a lack of adequate street lights contributed to crime in the area.

While there are plans to install more 40m high-mast lights in Khayelitsha, these will only come to fruition in the next five years.

The Social Justice Coalition (SJC), which urged Premier Helen Zille in 2012 to launch the 2014 inquiry, responded.

"There is no reason why Khayelitsha... should not be receiving the lighting that residents elsewhere in the City have on their streets," said SJC co-head of programmes Dalli Weyers.

"The City itself states that the high-mast spotlights aren't effective in their design and management guidelines for a safer city, and yet this is what Khayelitsha has and will continue to receive from the City," he said.

The City said plans were in place to install more high-mast lights, but there were concerns about vandalism and theft of street lights and infrastructure.

"In Site C, vandalism in the area is a massive problem; the protests of last year really had a massive effect on

the lighting in the area as well," said the City Council's mayoral committee member for energy and climate change Phindile Maxiti.

The City also said it had experienced issues such as vandalism, theft, safety of staff and the impact of protests over recent months in the area that had had an effect on the maintenance of existing public lighting. Ward councillor for Site B, Khayelitsha, Thando Mpengezi said: "The City has no proper plan to address the issue of adequate street lighting in the

area. Their budget does not indicate how much they plan on spending in Khayelitsha, even."

Residents remained concerned about their safety. Khayelitsha Development Forum chairperson 'Ndithini Thyhido said: "It's very dark in Khayelitsha and we are concerned that the City is failing in its responsibility to implement the recommendations of the police commission of inquiry."

The SJC said the installation of mast lighting harked back to apartheid when the bare minimum was done to

provide lighting to townships. Weyers said the mast lights cast deep shadows, making it dangerous for residents to move around after dark.

Maxiti said the SJC's claims were unfounded, and the City was working with the group. "That sentiment is not correct. We wrote to the SJC and we invited them to come and meet with us so that we could explain our plan. The one thing they don't understand is that there are very few areas in Khayelitsha that have no lighting."

TAIWAN Informal settlement in Site C, Khayelitsha. | PHANDO JIKELO African News Agency (ANA)

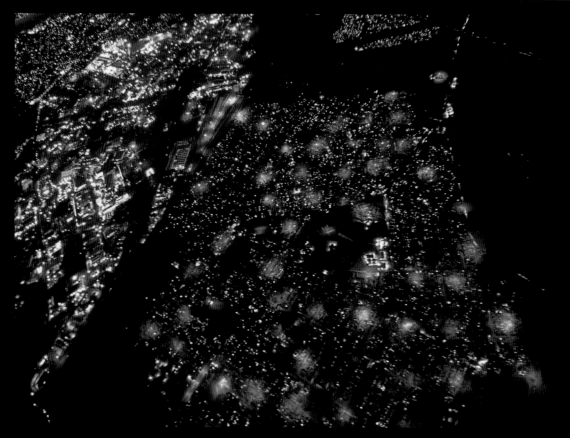

Fig 10   Aerial photograph of a township in Johannesburg, clearly standing out with its high-mast lighting

Yet, despite the CoCT's recommendation against the use of high-mast lights, they continue to be installed (City of Cape Town, 2014; CoCT Energy and Climate Change, 2019). CoCT documents advise avoiding high-mast lights and also to use them to ensure citizens' safety and security where there is no alternative lighting option. The CoCT currently has two public lighting solutions for self-built communities—high-mast lights and streetlights mounted on electricity distribution poles. The technical details are shown in **Figure 11** and shown installed in a self-built community in **Figure 12**. According to a long-standing senior officer at the CoCT, both solutions have their pitfalls, and neither solves the issues of narrow and dark pathways in self-built communities. According to CoCT public lighting data (City of Cape Town Open Data Portal, 2017a) and sub-council meeting minutes (Rowana GL, 2019), high-mast lights are being implemented more than any other lighting solution in self-built communities and townships in the Cape Metropole. The officer's opinion on high-mast lighting was not positive, as he described below:

> High mast lights only produce glare and not illumination. This is totally stupid, and the most important thing in lighting is the variability between light and dark. This has to do with distribution and not with how bright the light is. (Senior officer, expert interview, CoCT Public Lighting Development)

The second solution is streetlights mounted onto electricity distribution poles. This is the CoCT's preferred solution because it saves money by placing a streetlight fitting onto an electricity distribution pole, in collaboration with ESKOM, South Africa's state-owned energy utility, when they electrify an area. This mounting system works because there is not enough space for separate lighting poles in self-built communities. However, when discussing this solution, the officer said that it does not work because the light "falls in the wrong places".

> What we do now, when we electrify a new place, is we put lights on distribution poles, but still, the light is not falling where it needs to.

The public lighting department did an in-depth study of Khayelitsha's public lighting after several public complaints, and SJC demanded answers from the City. The study focused on the central problem, identified as areas lit with high-mast lighting. Residential roads with high-mast lighting were identified as the main challenge. This was where most public requests for streetlights were, even though high-mast lighting serviced the streets. The primary outcome revealed that lighting in many areas in Khayelitsha was poor and below national standards due to the dark shadows that high-mast lighting cast in dense urban environments.

The CoCT's standard for high-mast lighting is that each high-mast light serves a 172–200-metre radius around the light (CoCT Energy and Climate Change, 2019). Consequently, if structures are within a 175-metre radius of the light, residents should receive sufficient lighting. Contrary to what was believed before the CoCT's study, it was found that even inside the coverage area of a high-mast light, lighting quality was not good enough due to dark shadows cast by the light.

> … areas closer to a high-mast structure have immaculate lighting (basically security level lighting). The further one goes away from the high-mast structure within the coverage area; the lighting deteriorates due to shadows being cast onto the road (CoCT Energy and Climate Change, 2019)

Streets at right angles to the high-mast lights had good lighting, and streets perpendicular and at acute angles to high-mast lights were in shadow. The poor uniformity of lighting levels, or the extreme contrast between the high lighting levels in streets at ninety degrees and low lighting levels in streets perpendicular to the high-mast lights, is conducive to very poor lighting conditions (Figures 13 and 14).

In my first interview with the senior officer at the CoCT Public Lighting Development in 2018, he mentioned that the City had a five-year plan to address the lighting issues in Khayelitsha. The plan was to identify gaps in the high-mast lighting plan, and twenty areas were identified where additional high-mast lighting would be installed. The CoCT's decision after the 2019 study was to install an additional thirty-three high-mast lights and add conventional street lighting to twenty-four streets in Khayelitsha, even though the above study points to the need for an alternative lighting solution and the discontinuation of high-mast lighting (CoCT Energy and Climate Change, 2019). Installing more high-mast lighting would not work for two reasons. Firstly, there is not enough space on sidewalks and available land, and secondly, the City's lighting simulation showed that lighting levels did not necessarily improve in the 200-metre radius coverage area with additional high-mast lighting. Over and above this problem is the issue that the entire report does not include self-built communities. It only looks at formal residential roads in Khayelitsha even though the CoCT has

Mast-height : 30 – 40m
Light distribution: 150 – 200m radius
Luminaire technology: high-pressure
sodium vapour
Colour temperature: 2,700 Kelvin
Lumens: 5,624 lm/luminaire
Total lumens/mast: 213,744 lm

40 m

Streetlight : 7m
Light distribution: 7m radius
Luminaire technology: LED
Colour temperature: 4,000 Kelvin
Lumens: 10,000lm/luminaire
Total lumens/mast: 10,000 lm

7 m

Fig 11   Technical details of high-mast lighting and street lighting mounted onto electricity poles

Fig 12   Barcelona Informal Settlement in Khayelitsha, with the two lighting solutions—lights on electricity distribution poles and high-mast lighting

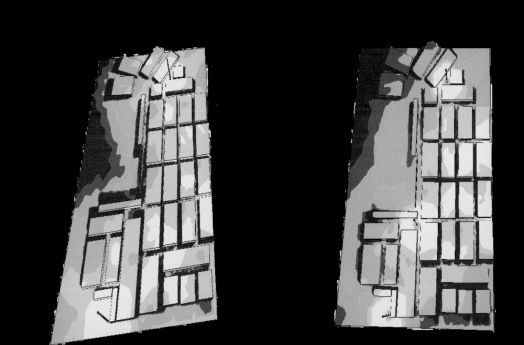

more than 635 self-built communities (CoCT, 2019) and a population estimate of 480,782, or 11.72% living in self-built communities in 2015 (CoCT, 2015).

> Incidentally, the above [referring to the entire study] does not apply to informal settlements and large open areas. Because there are no designated roads, high-mast lighting meets a definite need where conventional streetlights cannot be implemented (CoCT Energy and Climate Change, 2019).

Despite evidence that high-mast lighting is not adequate in dense residential environments, existing policies and a lack of research into alternative technologies perpetuate the continued deployment of high-mast lights. Some policies even prevent the City from implementing any lighting in historically black African townships and self-built communities. Below, I elaborate on several policies currently in place and how they are hindering the improvement of public lighting in self-built communities.

Unfair budget allocation for public lighting remains a significant barrier to improved public lighting. The CoCT did not allocate any of the R62.5 million (approximately $4.5 million) lighting budget for 2019–2020 to Khayelitsha (Charles, 2019), which raises the question of who pays for the deployment of public lighting in Khayelitsha and similar areas with inefficient public lighting. My interviews with the CoCT Public Lighting Department and sub-council meeting minutes indicate that ward councillors in Khayelitsha spend a substantial portion of their ward allocation on public lighting. Meanwhile, wards in higher-income areas spend far less or none of their budget on public lighting because they already have sufficient street lighting. Dalli Weyers, a former researcher at the SJC, points out that while some wards finance public lighting through direct budget allocation, those that do not must decide whether to allocate their limited ward budgets to public lighting or other critical needs (Weyers, 2019). Weyers argues that lower-income, predominantly black wards, spend more of their ward budget on public lighting than other wards, replicating historical inequality. To highlight the severity of the inequality, Weyers compares the lighting in Khayelitsha and a higher-income, predominantly white ward called Rondebosch. Using georeferenced lighting data from the City of Cape Town's Open Data Portal, I analysed the public light distribution in Khayelitsha and the Southern Suburbs, where Rondebosch is located. With an area of 46.7 square kilometres, Khayelitsha has 2,825 streetlights and 218 high-mast lights, while the upper-middle-class Southern Suburbs is simi-

lar in size but has 13,106 streetlights and no high-mast lights (Map 7).

Another downfall of high-mast lighting is their peripheral locations, as seen in PJS, where both high-mast lights are on the edges of the settlement. Light cast from these locations is more uneven and inefficient, and the settlement is only illuminated by half of the light. Peripheral installation is due to two main reasons, land zoning and ownership, and the characteristic high density of self-built communities. The Energy Directorate (EGD), the department that includes Public Lighting Development, is not mandated to provide lighting on property zoned as Community 1: Regional; Community 1: Local; General Business 1, 2, 3 and 4; and General Industrial 1, shown on **Map 8**. There is no zoning category for self-built communities, and so even registered and recognised settlements do not have residential zoning status. They keep the original zoning category in which they are located and many are located in the zoning categories mentioned above.

The CoCT also cannot install lighting or any public infrastructure on privately owned land unless the landowner gives permission, which can be a lengthy process. High-mast lights are therefore often installed on public road reserves, on the edge of private land where a self-built community may be located, and the light shines onto the privately owned land. Peripheral locations are also selected in response to the extreme density in self-built communities. Peripheral locations are also selected to accommodate the required five-square-metre concrete foundation for high-mast lights and to enable necessary access to service the lighting. However, peripheral locations are not always available and households are sometimes displaced to make room for the installation, sowing animosity and distrust. Additionally, the public lighting report refers to informal structures encroaching on formal public pavements, creating a major barrier to installing more street lighting (CoCT Energy and Climate Change, 2019).

Moving away from high-mast lighting by adding more streetlights in Khayelitsha is more challenging than it seems. The CoCT's dual lighting policy does not allow the use of two kinds of lighting in the same area (CoCT Electricity Service, 2013). If an area with high-mast lighting requests street lighting, the CoCT must remove the high-mast lights before installing streetlights. The dual lighting policy is particularly problematic when self-built communities with high-mast lighting are upgraded into formal neighbourhoods with serviceable streets—they often remain stuck with high-mast lighting

Map 7   Public lighting in the Southern Suburbs and Khayelitsha

Public Lighting

● Streetlight

● High-mast light

■ Khayelitsha

■ Southern Suburbs

□ City of Cape Town

Southern Suburbs
Streetlights: 13,106
High-mast lights: 0
Area: 48.7 km^2

Khayelitsha
Streetlights: 2,825
High-mast lights: 218
Area: 46.7 km^2

0 km   5 km

Zones that cannot
receive public lighting

■ Community 1: Local

▩ Community 2: Regional

▦ General Business 1,2,3

■ General Industrial 1

▭ Khayelitsha Wards

— Urban edge

0 km   4 km

0 km   20 km

Map 8   Land use zoning where CoCT is not mandated to provide public lighting

instead of getting streetlights. In areas where high-mast lighting is phased out and replaced by street-lights, the CoCT has to remove the high-mast lights. According to a city official, when the City tried this, the community resisted, and the idea of removing high-mast lighting had to be abandoned. One can only imagine the laborious and costly process of re-moving the 218 high-mast lights in Khayelitsha and the potential socio-political issues that may develop in a context of mistrust of the government as a leg-acy of the apartheid regime.

Beyond the time, infrastructure and specialised la-bour needed to service high-mast lights, a critical is-sue is that the entire community is left in the dark when one high-mast light breaks. During our three years of work in PJS, the two high-mast lights there were often out of order, especially after more fre-quent bouts of loadshedding. According to tech-nicians, electrical surges occur when power is re-stored after load shedding, which often damages lights and electronic equipment. The issue of cen-tralised and grid-dependent infrastructure became more visible during our fieldwork when routine load-shedding started in February 2019 and March 2020. Nationwide, there were 860 hours of loadshedding during 2020 (Calitz and Wright, 2021). It came as no surprise that I received more complaints about high-mast lighting when loadshedding escalated, and people were increasingly interested in solar lighting.

The problems with high-mast lighting continued during 2020, when a group of crime syndicates al-legedly removed five high-mast lights in unelec-trified Siqalo Informal Settlement at enormous cost—around R1,000,000 ($67,000). With the on-going negative coverage of the lack of public light-ing, the City finally focused its attention on alterna-tive lighting options, though only for unelectrifiable settlements. In December 2020, the CoCT Energy and Climate Change Department launched a re-quest for information (RFI) concerning "Innovative Public Lighting Solutions for Informal Settlements with no grid access". The request highlighted many positive attributes and it appeared they had already learned lessons from our work. The City wanted off-grid lighting without grounded poles, community Wi-Fi, and potential Internet of Things (IoT) features, as well as community engagement and acceptance strategies. However, the RFI made clear that sub-missions should be self-financed with the addition of "value-added services". Even though the City is moving towards finding innovative public lighting solutions, it is disappointing that, at the time of writ-ing, there is still no budget allocation for such a proj-ect. We responded to the RFI, teaming up with local solar experts from iShack. We challenged the RFI's

financial model, and the City invited us as the only submission that met the brief. They had many ques-tions and seemed keen to finally change their ap-proach to public lighting. Only time will tell if this en-thusiasm will be sustained and also implemented.

The CoCT faces a problem around public light-ing provision in communities previously disadvan-taged by the apartheid regime. The lack of lighting in Khayelitsha causes a major political problem—public lighting has become a symbol of the City's slowness to change. Existing policies prevent the advancement of new public lighting solutions, and although the City has produced evidence against the use of high-mast lighting, it remains the primary township lighting solution, especially for self-built communities. The public focus on inadequate urban lighting, our interactions with the City and major fi-nancial losses arising from theft of high-mast light-ing have forced the CoCT to rethink its approach to lighting for self-built communities. The neo-liberal approach to lighting these communities without access to grid electricity remains insufficient. While moving towards green, off-grid, decentralised pub-lic lighting is a positive technological move, an ad-equate budget should still be allocated to provide public lighting in self-built communities, which are a permanent feature in Cape Town. This needs to be acknowledged and included in the CoCT's pub-lic lighting policies.

As in the past, today self-built communities stand as a symbol of resistance and right to the city. The next section elaborates on the past and present of Khayelitsha and Cape Town's self-built communi-ties to understand their development and signifi-cance in Cape Town.

Khayelitsha and Cape Town's self-built communities

Developing townships and eradicating self-built communities was a strategy after the 1976 uprising. Initially, development was top-down and heavy-handed, where "oil-spot" areas of national threat were identified and upgraded with security and con-trol in mind. Crossroads was one of these areas. The apartheid government identified 2,100 hectares of undesirable dune and flood-prone land thirty-nine kilometres outside the city to develop Khayelitsha and eradicate Crossroads. This land was not located on the white residential expansion axis and was well contained to prevent further growth. A broad zone of low-income housing for the "coloured" working class, a strip of industrial land and the N2 highway bordered the north and west. The coast bordered the southern edge of Khayelitsha, and to the south-east, South African Defence Force land prevented expansion and ensured control (Map 9).

Khayelitsha was divided into four "towns", and each was divided into four "villages". With no links and focus between villages, this structure discouraged interaction and ensured easier control (Cook, 1986). An enclaved road system gave each town and village a single entrance that could be closed off. Khayelitsha as a whole had only a single entrance. Each village was designed to house 30,000 people. Khayelitsha was intended to house a maximum of 480,000, although the government's prediction was to house approximately 120,000 people. There was no security of tenure, and people could only rent housing space in the area. Included in the plan was land earmarked for educational and social services, a commercial centre, a spinal green heartland and, eventually, a rail link to Cape Town (ibid.)(Map 10). No industry was included (Smith, 2005, p. 126). The 800-square-metre commercial centre consisted of three to four shops, a post office, a mini-market and a bank. Expensive commuting networks linking mainly to working areas discouraged residents from travelling to other places (Cook, 1986). It was already said in 1986 that Khayelitsha's design would restrict residents' way of life and reinforce the inferior position of black Africans in Cape Town (Cook, 1986; Dewar and Watson, 1984; Cole, 1989).

Dewar and Watson (1984) believed that Khayelitsha's negative urban environment would produce many social issues if three components were not considered and included in the urban planning and regulations. First, the lack of security of tenure and the isolated location; second, no provision of opportunities; and third, essential infrastructure does not include the provision of public space.

In 1985, when PW Botha declared a state of emergency in South Africa, the first people removed were taken to Khayelitsha's Site C (Cole, 2013). The prediction then was that it would be home to approximately 120,000 people. By 1985, 150,000 people were living in Khayelitsha, but only 5,000 homes had been built (Towards a Safer Khayelitsha, Commission of Inquiry into Allegations of Police Inefficiency and a Breakdown in Relations between SAPS and the Community in Khayelitsha, 2014). The rest were settled on land waiting for the next "site-and-service" plots to be built. Minimal infrastructure was installed — by 1986 only the main access road into Khayelitsha was tarred, and there were tall high-mast lights on the periphery but not in the centres. Residents received a 25–32-square-metre "core" house on a 160-square-metre plot consisting of a shared tap, toilet, no internal fittings and no electricity. Only schools and hospitals had electricity (Cook, 1986). The BAAB had to approve any expansion to the "core" houses and these had to be built according to local building standards, which made expansion very challenging. Plots in Khayelitsha were thirty-five per cent smaller than officially specified for black residential areas. Eighty-four per cent of houses constructed in phase one measured less than two-thirds compared to standard housing modules used in earlier township schemes. Despite this bare-minimum housing provision, rent was about twenty per cent of a household head's income (Cook, 1986). In reality, Khayelitsha was slow to develop — many people were unhappy about being "tricked" into moving there from Crossroads, which was a well-functioning self-built community. With the demise of apartheid on the horizon, the top-down style of development changed to a negotiated development process, which affected internal dynamics in Khayelitsha. Many people disagreed on whether to enter into any kind of negotiation with the apartheid government (Cole, 2013), resulting in escalating violent internal conflict.

Today, Khayelitsha remains almost intact as the experiment the apartheid government designed. Some believe that close to one million people live there, although the official StatsSA population estimate for 2021 is 447,120. In 2015, an estimated 159,885 people were living in self-built communities (CoCT, 2015). Khayelitsha still identifies with a series of villages. These very densely populated neighbourhoods feature a mix of formal and informal housing, and a unique mixture of *spaza* shops (convenience stores), hair salons, churches, tradesmen and informal traders, among others (Cole, 2013). Khayelitsha is the second biggest township in South Africa, after Soweto in Johannesburg. Service delivery remains a contentious issue — Greater Khayelitsha has been recognised as the centre of service delivery protests in the Western Cape since 2009. In addition to sometimes violent service delivery protests, gang-related violence has escalated. In 2019, this drastic rise in gun violence and gang-related activity resulted in military occupation in Khayelitsha and the Cape Flats.

Khayelitsha's residents also struggle to access basic services daily, despite the government's constitutional mandate to fulfil the right to dignified living through access to basic services, defined as clean drinking water, sanitation, shelter, waste removal and roads (Republic of South Africa, 1996). In StatsSA's most recent household survey, access to basic services in Cape Town looks relatively good, as seen in **Graph 1** (Statistics South Africa, 2018).

Map 9   Location of Khayelitsha on the periphery of Cape Town

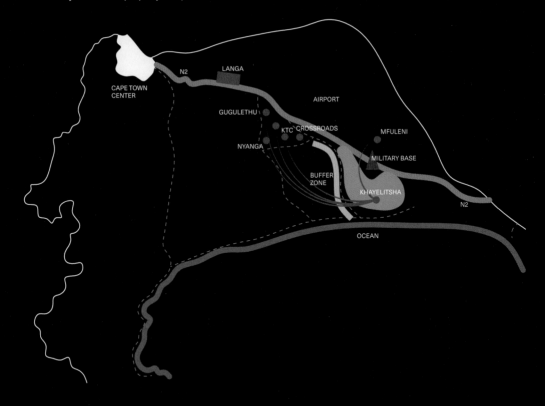

Map 10   Outline plan of Khayelitsha, divided into separate towns and villages

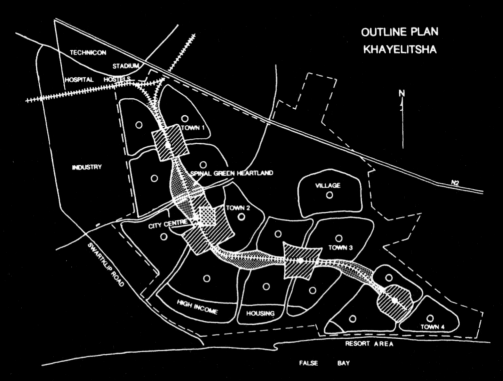

However, this does not consider nighttime access to shared infrastructure in self-built communities where inadequate public lighting exacerbates poor access. Mutyambizi et al. (2020) point out that national statistics conceal the inequality of basic services based on the type of household—formal, informal and traditional. They also show that access to and consumer satisfaction with basic services in self-built communities, is much lower than national statistics suggest (Table 2 and 3) (ibid.). The lowest income quantile (1) are least satisfied with electricity (including access to lighting), followed by sanitation. In self-built communities, dwellings use shared basic services, often centrally located in the settlement, such as communal taps, refuse disposal points and toilets. Therefore, it is important to note that access, especially at night, can look very different in self-built communities than statistics reveal.

Khayelitsha has developed significantly, with an increasingly mixed-use development fostering a more positive urban environment, but apartheid-era infrastructure remains. It is still forty kilometres away from the CBD, and violent crime is rife. Self-built communities in and around the area are here to stay, and are increasing in numbers and size. Between March and August 2020, more than 260 land invasions were recorded (Evans, 2020), and the CoCT demolished nearly 60,000 structures between July and September 2020 (Meyer, 2020). Residents' commutes are still long—many people experience public space only at night and on weekends, a time when fear of crime increases. This emphasises the importance of designing public spaces for nighttime activities even more, especially for dormitory townships and self-built communities located on the periphery of cities. Nocturnal access to shared basic services and opportunities is a significant challenge for residents of self-built communities in Khayelitsha, more than statistics suggest, because nighttime access and the lack of public lighting are not considered. This is an understudied challenge, and one that more effective public lighting could address, which is what this research aims to do.

The post-apartheid lightscape: a layered understanding

In colonial South Africa, particularly in Cape Town, infrastructure was used to separate and control the non-white population. This first occurred largely by removing non-whites from the city centre and creating "orderly" housing outside the city to "civilise the natives" according to British cultural norms. The apartheid government took this much further, incorporating separate development into all aspects of civil society, including infrastructure, in which high-mast lights play a significant part.

Twenty-seven years post apartheid, these lights, with a long legacy of racial division and control, remain in place after the democratic government initially focused on housing provision before redressing apartheid-era infrastructure. Today, the ANC still promises a free house to all who qualify, which

Access to basic services

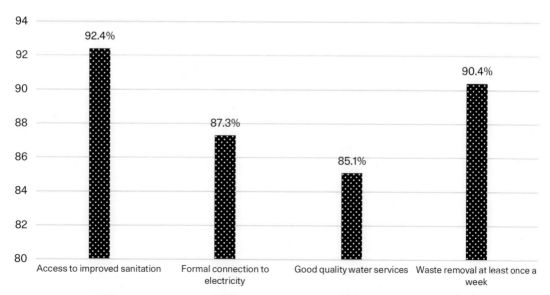

Graph 1 Cape Town's access to basic services. However, nighttime access to shared basic services is not considered here

Table 2 Satisfaction with basic services in self-built communities by wealth quintile (per cent)

Basic Service	Income Quintile					
Water Quality	1	2	3	4	5	Total
Dissatisfied	50.62	37.06	34.96	31.14	22.55	35.53
Neutral	3.25	3.93	8.56	5.05	4.78	5.11
Satisfied	46.13	59	56.47	63.81	72.67	59.35
Sanitation						
Dissatisfied	86.85	69.67	67.29	60.42	55.69	68.24
Neutral	6.3	9.48	11.98	11.97	7.75	9.48
Satisfied	6.85	20.85	20.73	27.61	36.55	22.28
Refuse Removal						
Dissatisfied	72.65	60.41	51.84	44.92	43.94	55
Neutral	13.41	13.88	15.51	12.73	16.65	14.41
Satisfied	13.94	25.71	32.66	42.35	39.41	30.58
Electricity						
Dissatisfied	97.33	93.89	60.23	41.74	23.56	62.21
Neutral	2.06	3.28	9.77	12.32	6.52	6.9
Satisfied	0.61	2.83	30	45.94	69.92	30.89

Note: All estimates are weighted.

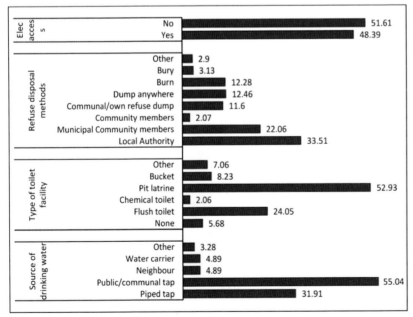

Table 3 Access to basic services in self-built communities in South Africa

remains a symbol of a democratic country (Millstein, 2020), yet is available to so few. Many qualifying households registered on the housing waiting list will wait an average of seventeen or more years before receiving their house (Oldfield and Greyling, 2015). Self-built communities are growing rapidly, presenting many challenges in service delivery by day and night. It is time to focus on providing other forms of infrastructure for self-built communities that may also symbolise the democracy currently so dominantly symbolised by formal housing.

With many living in darkness and apartheid-era high-mast lighting still dominating public lighting in townships and self-built communities, public lighting is one such infrastructure that needs redressing. In May 2017, the SJC launched a campaign calling on the CoCT to provide more effective public lighting in apartheid-planned townships and self-built communities. In 2019, the CoCT launched an investigation into the effectiveness of high-mast lighting. In 2020, the City released an RFI for innovative public lighting solutions for grid-independent self-built communities. Despite these positive prospects, high-mast lighting continues to be justified and deployed, showing an ideological acceptance of the high-mast light in South African townships and self-built communities.

This chapter unfolded the layered past and the presence of high-mast lighting in Khayelitsha's lightscape, a process that requires a multi-dimensional approach to understanding public lighting and its impact on everynight life. Using such a multi-dimensional approach, the next chapter aims to address the inadequacy of high-mast lighting in Khayelitsha's self-built communities by proposing alternative modes of public lighting—both in terms of implementation and technology. The next chapter expands on the specifics of studying public lighting and everynight life in Khayelitsha's self-built communities.

Endeavours of Studying Khayelitsha's Lighting

Chapter 3

Cape Town's lightscape is the materialisation of years and layers of political race-based oppression and inequality. Understanding the layered narrative of high-mast lighting and of Khayelitsha and its self-built communities requires an equally layered approach. Using mixed methods was imperative to get a holistic understanding of everynight life and the impact of public lighting in Khayelitsha's self-built communities. Through visual methods, participants could imagine, draw and photograph their everynight life. This produced data that text cannot capture. An action research approach put knowledge into action, producing an even deeper understanding of the impact that co-producing lighting from within a community has on everynight life.

Chapter summary:	This chapter focuses on this mixed methods, visual and action research approach. It also elaborates on developing the lighting concept, project design, phases and location. The chapter closes with valuable reflections gathered throughout the project.

The academic context largely inspired the layered approach to studying everynight life and light in Khayelitsha, which proved to be vital in developing the research. Being based at the Institute of Science, Technology and Policy (ISTP), a multidisciplinary institute at ETH Zurich that encourages policy-relevant research, meant dealing with real-world problems. Within the ISTP, the research was based in the Urban Research Incubator (URI). The URI group consisted of eight doctoral students from various disciplines[1] and four professors from various departments of ETH Zurich[2]. The research focus of URI was how "policy-makers could leverage science and technology to create safer, more inclusive cities that serve the needs of all citizens" (Urban Research Incubator, 2020). Following the ISTP and URI research goals, this research took on a highly transdisciplinary and action research approach. Transdisciplinary research has the core intent of scientific research contributing to "real-world" societal problems and combines different disciplines of scientific knowledge with non-scientific stakeholders.

I had developed an exciting lighting concept that I wanted to implement and evaluate, but I lacked some disciplinary skills to make such an ambitious project viable, so I collaborated with other academic disciplines within URI and non-scientific collaborators. Polk (2014) highlights three common motivations for transdisciplinarity. The first is the need to contribute to societal problem-solving, which the public lighting aimed to do. Second, transdisciplinary researchers value and need a broad knowledge base to define a problem, often coming from other disciplines. Dr Yael Borofsky was my main academic collaborator and partner in the public lighting implementation, who was also a doctoral researcher based at URI (see Borofsky, 2022 for more detail on Dr. Borofsky's doctoral research). The non-scientific partners were non-governmental organisations (NGOs), government officials and community members, who are introduced later in this chapter. Lastly, Pohl (2014) emphasises the closeness of academics and non-academics to ensure scientific rigour, practical legitimacy and usability of the results. Here the action-research[3] approach assisted in achieving a public lighting project that was relevant on the ground and in academia.

The field research took on a largely ethnographic and qualitative approach to capture the nuanced everyday experiences, which were difficult to capture quantitatively and with text alone. Choosing methods was iterative, addressing gaps in knowledge that required new methods. As a starting point, full immersion was key, alongside some more conventional methods. The methods evolved as the research evolved, becoming more creative and visual to capture the nuanced nighttime experiences. In collaboration with my research partner who led the data collection, quantitative data was gathered to reinforce my qualitative data. Presenting the work to various departments at the City of Cape Town (CoCT) and other important actors in Cape Town, such as NGOs and urban experts, was important to make the research relevant and applicable to the context. The findings were also reviewed in presentations about specific components of the research at seminars and conferences, and additional studies supplemented my knowledge and advanced some research components.

1 Dr. Michael Walczak, architect; Dr. David Kretzer, lighting engineer; Sam Lloyd, public health specialist; Dr. Yael Borofsky, development economist and planner; Dr. David Kostenwein, planner; Dr. Christian Joubert, mechanical engineer; Dr. Stephanie Briers (me), architect and urbanist.
2 Prof. Hubert Klumpner, Chair of Architecture and Urban Design, Department of Architecture; Prof. Dr. Reza Abhari, Laboratory for Energy Conversion, Department of Engineering and Process Engineering; Prof. Dr. Andy Wenger, Centre for Security Studies, Department of Social and Political Sciences; Prof. Dr. Isabel Günther, Development Economics Group, Department of Social and Political Sciences.
3 As defined by the Sage Encyclopaedia of Qualitative Research Methods, "Action research is a flexible research methodology", which "integrates social research with exploratory action to promote development". (Somekh, 2008, p. 4).

Map 1   Areas of engagement in and around Khayelitsha and the intensity of engagement

Level of engagement in
self-built communities

- Primary case study
- High
- Medium
- Low
- None
- Khayelitsha suburb
  boundaries
- Suburb boundaries

Marikana

Sesikhona

CT-Section

OR Tambo

RR-Section

BM-Section

PJS

Site B

Qandu Qandu

Siqalo

SST

Makhaza

Monwabisi Park

Enkanini

Zwelitshe

0 km   4 km

Khayelitsha

PJS Informal Settlement

- 2021 population estimate: 447,120
  (Population Data, Western Cape Gov., 2020)
- Predominantly black
- Apartheid-planned township with
  pockets of self-built communities
- 218 high-mast lights
- High unrest in area

- 768 households
- 2,275 people
- Pocket self-built community
- 30 years old
- Two high-mast lights
- One main dirt road
- Consists of homes and independent shops

Map 2   Facilities, movement network and infrastructure in PJS Informal Settlement (PJS)

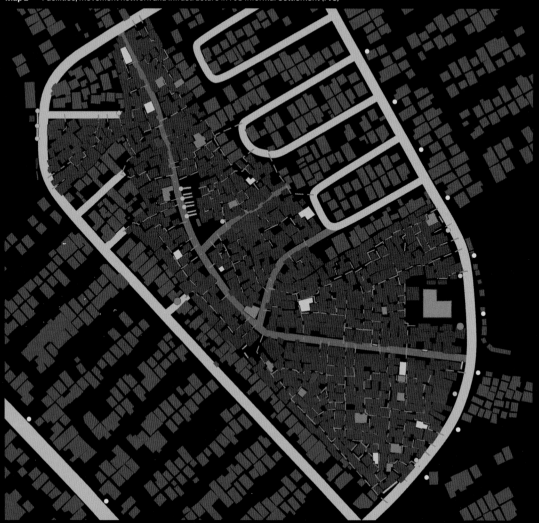

0 m · · · · · · · · · 100 m

Church
Snacks
Spaza shop
Food stall
Other
School
Shebeen
Tailors
Residential
Refuse
Toilets
● Taps
● Public lighting
◉ High-mast lights
　Primary route formal
　Secondary route formal
　Tertiary route formal
　Primary route informal
— — Narrow pathway

Fig 2   Aerial view of PJS Informal Settlement, a "pocket" self-built community surrounded by formal Khayelitsha

Khayelitsha's
self-built communities

To understand the impact of darkness on everyday life, I engaged with fifteen self-built communities in and around Khayelitsha to varying degrees of intensity, as illustrated in **Map 1**. The primary case study was PJS Informal Settlement (PJS), which is described later. All the self-built communities had different levels of service provision and substantially different access to public lighting. Marikana, a settlement with very poor service provision, had no access to public lighting or electricity. It is located on a flood plain, making service delivery more complicated. Everynight life is very tough in Marikana, as explored in Chapters 4 and 5. SST Informal Settlement (SST) had access to high-mast lighting, yet many complained it was too dark and they wanted the surrounding formal neighbourhood's LED streetlights. I did a pilot test with wall-mounted solar lights in SST, but soon realised that crime was a big issue—all the lights were stolen almost immediately. These different areas of engagement shown in the map had different socio-spatial situations and degrees of development, but the common ground was that life at night was difficult; more so in some places, but generally, darkness was an issue for them all.

PJS Informal Settlement and its stakeholders

I met the Social Justice Coalition (SJC), an NGO with a rights-based approach to its work (Social Justice Coalition, 2020), nine months before the first research trip to Cape Town in February 2018. The trip had three goals: finding a site for the intervention, securing our formal collaboration with the SJC and networking in the Cape Town academic environment. We secured a site visit to PJS at the first meeting with SJC. PJS was one of three sites presented to us and met the requirements listed in **Table 1**. Thus, after a site visit and two leadership meetings between February 2018 and April 2018, we agreed to work there.

PJS, also known as Nonqubela, is located in Village 3, Site B or Ward 89, Khayelitsha **(Figure 1)**. It covers five hectares and is surrounded by formal housing **(Figure 2)**. This formation of a self-built community surrounded by formal housing is also known as a "pocket informal settlement".

PJS was established in 1989, when a fenced-off parcel of land belonging to the Department of Education was occupied largely due to the apartheid government's forced removals in Crossroads, KTC, Philippi and Gugulethu. Another group of people migrated from the Eastern Cape to PJS to be with their families. Over thirty years later, the settlement is one of the oldest existing self-built communities in Khayelitsha.

PJS gained access to formal grid electricity in 2009 and has two high-mast lights. The high-mast light in the east was installed in the late 1980s and the second in the southwest in 2009. Residents share approximately 15 public taps—although most residents have an informal tap connection in their houses—and approximately 125 public toilets, located mainly in the centre of the community (Borofsky and Briers, 2019). PJS has no formal roads. Two dirt roads accessible by car form a T-junction (shown in brown on **Map 2**) in the settlement centre. The rest of PJS is only accessible by footpaths. PJS is predominantly residential, with scattered informal social and economic activities. **Map 2** shows PJS's informal facilities, road and footpath network, as well as shared-basic infrastructure.

PJS is home to 2,275 inhabitants, living in 768 structures (153.6 dwellings per hectare). There is a general lack of employment in self-built communities, and although PJS is considered a fairly well-established and "privileged" settlement, the unemployment rate is 40.37%. The reasons people were satisfied living in PJS were mainly because of its central location, with 45.02% of the residents liking PJS, and 42.1% of these residents liked living in PJS because it was close to transport and facilities such as the police station, clinic and shopping mall[4].

---

4   Data collected from our enumeration in March 2019

Approximately 400 households to measure the impact of the intervention at a large scale	A self-built community with contained boundaries that could not expand much
A settlement based in Khayelitsha, due to its history of high-mast lighting	Dense enough settlement to illustrate the inadequate horizontal illuminance of high-mast lighting
Safe enough to do research at night	An established leadership committee willing to engage on the topic
Established relationship with at least one NGO	

Table 1   Criteria for selecting PJS Informal Settlement as the project location

In PJS, 42% of households believe they are on the waiting list for a government-provided house. This belief often caused problems while conducting fieldwork in PJS. Community members wanted to know what we were doing there and immediately asked us if we would bring houses to PJS. When I responded that I was researching lighting, my answer was often met with disappointment or even frustration. Residents would repeatedly say, "We don't want lights, we want a house" or "I want a house, or I want nothing". The preoccupation with housing led to concerns that the lights, when installed, would be vandalised because of frustrations with the housing issue. PJS is an old and very dense self-built community. People living there have been waiting for the settlement to be upgraded to formal housing for many years. It is categorised as B2, meaning it qualifies for emergency basic services (water, sanitation and electricity) because upgrading is not feasible and relocation is not urgent or possible (Parikh et al., 2020). City officials told me that PJS's B2 categorisation was because it was too dense to accommodate everyone on the site, and there is no available land where they can move people to. Politicians constantly use the promise of housing as a tool to get more votes, which means that residents in PJS are continually lured with vague promises. Their frustrations in the face of any other development are not surprising.

A representative from iShack, a non-profit providing solar home kits in self-built communities, told me that the community had destroyed their on-site office because they felt the solar kits prevented them from receiving real development. With the solar kits, the settlement seemed "taken care of", while the government would find other settlements needing more urgent service delivery. Millstein tells a similar story of activist residents in the temporary relocation camp (TRC) in Delft, Cape Town, who were against residents informally upgrading houses because this would be detrimental to their struggle for more permanent housing elsewhere (Millstein, 2020, p. 304).

The politics of waiting for housing often meant that residents did not support developmental projects, such as our solar public lighting. They are tired of waiting for houses, and new lights could diminish the urgency of needing to upgrade a settlement with formal housing. We addressed this challenge by managing people's expectations, largely by working very closely with the leadership, the most important stakeholders in this project.

Stakeholder engagement

The engagement with PJS leaders began in February 2018, on my first visit with the SJC. We developed an intense relationship. Until a few years ago, PJS was under the management of the two wards that had local leadership structures in PJS. However, in 2014, the settlement merged in Ward 89, forcing the leadership committees of the two wards to merge. The approximately eight members of the new merged leadership committee still find it difficult to work together. The leadership is also divided based on political affiliation. The most prominent leadership division is between older, long-standing and new, young leaders. In February 2020, PJS residents elected new leaders after the PJS youth disputed the leadership's decisions to install the public lighting. Since then, we have worked with a large group of officially elected and unofficial leaders.

Leaders in PJS are generally more informed about public lighting and the disadvantages of high-mast lighting, mainly because of interactions between them and the SJC and its public lighting campaign. Some leaders still believe that there should simply be more high-mast lights. Others are aware of the unequal lighting budget allocation and the race-based allocation of high-mast lighting. Another concern is where the CoCT places the lights. They want to know who makes the decisions and whether those decisions will cause tension in the community. Other questions are who would benefit from a job when the lighting is implemented, and whether the CoCT would allocate jobs fairly. These concerns arise from fear of rising tensions, which leaders would have to deal with. Inclusion, dialogue and transparency are essential for leaders of self-built communities.

PJS leaders trusted knowledgeable experts and expected these experts to communicate why the CoCT made certain decisions. They also expected experts to listen to them and take their feedback seriously. One of the leaders related how they managed to get the toilets in PJS fixed. The City did not consult the community when they first installed the toilets, which caused many problems. They overflowed and clogged up, and the community largely abandoned the toilets. Gangsters and drug users started congregating at the toilet facility, and it became a dangerous place. The council would fix the toilets but they continued to break. One day, the leaders decided to stop the truck and would not let it in to fix the toilets. They demanded to speak to the head of sanitation and refused to allow the truck to enter PJS until they had done so. The head of sanitation arrived the next day and leaders voiced their concerns about the toilets. The CoCT rebuilt the toilets according to the leaders' feedback and concerns, and they still work well today. A community leader noted that gangsters no longer use drugs or loiter around the toilets.

Lack of trust is a persistent barrier, exacerbated by ineffective stakeholder engagement. Several residents characterised the CoCT's attempts to involve them as superficial, leaving them feeling unheard and forgotten even when participating in public meetings. That said, our survey results (Graph 1) show that most respondents felt the relationship between PJS and the municipality was one of cooperation and respect.

City officials highlighted the challenges of productively engaging with stakeholders in self-built communities, describing community hostility around inadequate service provision as a major obstacle to developing a better understanding of lighting needs and preferences. The City was a very important stakeholder to ensure the policy impact of the project. We engaged with several departments, but the most relevant was the CoCT Energy Directorate and the Department of Informal Settlements and Backyarders (Figure 3). Public Lighting Development resides within the CoCT Energy Directorate. They are responsible for the rollout of public lighting in the entire metropolis. I engaged with this department extensively from April 2018 to July 2021.

Public Lighting Development expressed considerable concern about who would own the lighting, considering maintenance responsibilities. They felt that this would be complicated with our lighting solution — wall-mounted solar lighting is easy to move —, and the CoCT needs to track its infrastructure. This is discussed in more detail later. In separate interviews, a senior public lighting officer and the director of Public Lighting Development raised this issue. The director said firmly that the City would donate this kind of lighting to a community-based organisation (CBO), but the CBO needed to manage and maintain the lights. Later in this research, Public Lighting Development became more interested in pursuing alternative, grid-independent lighting options for self-built communities but still aimed to enter into a public-private partnership to avoid maintenance and budget issues.

The senior officer was frustrated with the degree to which red tape prevents lighting projects from happening. He said that projects were often suppressed due to red tape surrounding spending budgets, not due to of lack of money. He even mentioned that the City did not always manage to spend its entire allocated budget. Next, I explain the process of rolling out public lighting, and it is clear why budget and responsibility is a major issue.

The CoCT Public Lighting Development's annual budget is approximately R70,000,000 (±$5,000,000). According to expert opinion, this is more than sufficient. It is allocated mainly to maintenance and replacing outdated sodium vapour technology with LED lights. Stringent rules and regulations make installing lights a labour-intensive and time-consuming process. Additionally, once awarded, tenders stay in place for three years. The CoCT needs additional contractors to meet increased public lighting demand. However, the CoCT cannot issue new

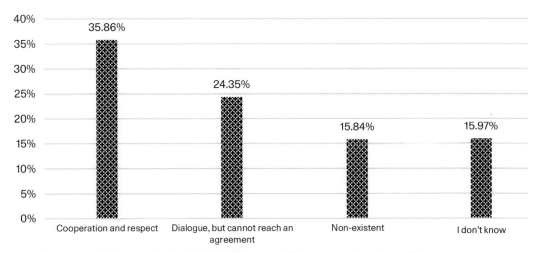

Which option best describes the relationship between PJS Informal Settlement and the municipality?

Graph 1   The relationship between the CoCT and PJS Informal Settlement (PJS) as perceived by residents of PJS

tenders while existing tenders are in place, even though existing contractors do not have the capacity to meet the growing demands.

Public Lighting Development cannot use its allocated budget for new public lighting or lighting an area while simultaneously electrifying it. It must apply for national funding from the Department of Energy (DOE) or the Urban Settlements Development Grant (USDG). If funding is secured, the CoCT must work with ESKOM, the country's energy utility, to electrify and install lighting. ESKOM pays for the pole, and the City pays for the light. It is a time-consuming and difficult process to access this funding, which, when secured, comes with many conditions and constraints[5]. Securing funding for gridded electricity is a huge challenge, added to by the need for community liaison and attending to other restrictions such as settlements located in flood planes or under flight paths. As a result of the constraints, ward councillors often spend their R500,000 (+-$36,000) general annual budget on public lighting provision, rather than on other projects, to counteract the red tape described above.

With all the constraints on grid-dependent public lighting, it makes sense to turn to solar, grid-independent lighting. The City's Sustainable Energy Markets division realised this, and in December 2020, they released a request for information (RFI) for innovative public lighting for grid-independent self-built communities. We received this RFI and submitted our project details as well as proposed improvements. The City responded well, and we were invited to present our research. Our submission emphasised the importance of inter-departmental collaboration, specifically with the Department of Informal Settlements and Backyarders, to consolidate work in self-built communities.

That department was very interested in the public lighting project. However, they felt that public lighting was Public Lighting Development's responsibility, and so chose to observe with interest rather than engage. Their main concern was providing enough taps and toilets, preventing land invasions, and minimising community tensions around basic service provision.

We primarily engaged with the Department of Informal Settlements and Backyarders around community liaison and running the baseline survey, and afterwards officially handed over this survey data to the department. The CoCT and the broader Western Cape Government commonly empower NGOs to conduct enumerations in self-built communities, which are surveys intended to count residents, buildings, and existing services to make it easier for government to assess community needs. Many NGOs expand on these enumerations to include self-report questions about fear of crime, perception of safety, and nighttime activities. Our initial goal was also to work through the Development Action Group (DAG), a Cape Town-based housing-focused NGO, to conduct the survey, but eventually, we played the role of an NGO in PJS as well as in our interactions with the Department of Informal Settlements and Backyarders.

SJC and DAG both worked in PJS. The SJC had a branch[6] in PJS with many leaders as branch members. The branch deals mainly with issues around basic service provision. DAG had worked in PJS for about nine years, mainly on housing provision. Their interaction involved housing development workshops, leadership training programmes and facilitating site visits to PJS by potential funders such as the Bill and Melinda Gates Foundation, who visited PJS in 2019. Early in our research, we saw SJC as research partners because of their public lighting campaign, and DAG as implementation partners for our survey and the lighting intervention. However, DAG's internal priorities shifted and could not continue support the research project.

SJC's main concern with public lighting is to fight crime. They make this obvious connection because the lighting campaign was built around their commission of enquiry into the lack of police resources in Khayelitsha, in which poor public lighting conditions was a constant reference. Their primary complaint is that police cannot patrol areas or enter into a crime scene because of the darkness, and high-mast lighting is not effective. SJC argues that the CoCT continues to install high-mast lighting despite acknowledging its ineffectiveness. They also claim that the continued deployment of high-mast lighting

---

5   DOE do not fund self-built communities. The CoCT fought back on this, and DOE finally agreed to fund a self-built community if it is registered. Therefore, to provide lighting, the City needs to get a surveyor to register the self-built communities officially. DOE will also only fund a settlement if it is not relocated in three years. Lastly, on private land, DOE will only fund one power point, and ESKOM and the City must extend into the land from this point, with the permission of the landowner. DOE is stringent, and it is risky to use their funding for self-built communities because if the CoCT applies for 250 connections, they must meet precisely that number; otherwise, they will struggle to get funding again.

6   Social Justice Coalition had a system of 'branches' in self-built communities in Cape Town. Branch members worked with SJC to solve certain issues that the settlement had, often involving the CoCT.

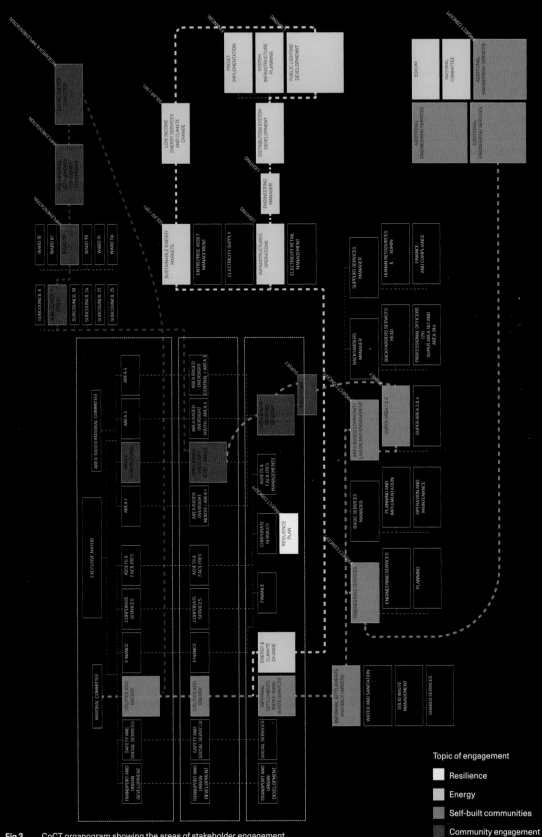

Fig 3 CoCT organogram showing the areas of stakeholder engagement

is race-based discrimination and a continuation of apartheid planning logic.

A large focus of SJC is on budget allocations for public lighting. They question whether the CoCT fairly allocates the public lighting budget among the different wards in Cape Town Municipality. The SJC did an in-depth investigation of public lighting budget allocations, ward allocations and how wards were spending their money. They found that wards in Khayelitsha spend budgets on public lighting and CCTV cameras, while wards in wealthier neighbourhoods often spend budgets on beautification projects. SJC argues the unfairness that Khayelitsha wards have to use their ward allocations to rectify the race-based inequality in infrastructure provision caused by apartheid. This link to apartheid was not important among PJS residents, and it irked the CoCT when this topic was raised in interviews. Despite this, as discussed in Chapter 2, the stigmatising effect of high-mast lighting is significant, and for many "outsiders", it does symbolise apartheid infrastructure.

The academics I engaged with were mainly concerned with the apartheid symbolism of high-mast lighting and the impact public lighting has on daily practices. All academics asked about the rigour with which we would implement and measure the project, engage with community members and encouraged in-depth community involvement. Academics have become more aware and sensitive to extractive research, where academia now places major emphasis on what the community gains from the research rather than how the researcher benefits.

The final stakeholders of the project were practitioners who could make the project practically viable. Practitioners were mostly interested in the technical quality of lighting, taking a very practical approach to the provision of public lighting. They also understood the impact that better lighting had on daily life, often emphasising the difficulties of life in the dark self-built communities. For them, their engagement in the project was almost philanthropic. During the project, I had one long-term interaction with a particular practitioner. We had weekly meetings where I would gradually learn more about the limitations and possibilities of our lighting project and the norms for a lighting engineer in terms of maintenance procedures and choice of lighting infrastructure. I also learned that many practitioners are wary of working with the government due to slow turnarounds in projects, bureaucracy and the risk of corruption.

Engaging with a wide variety of community, City and corporate stakeholders gave me a holistic understanding of the challenges and opportunities inherent in providing public lighting in self-built communities. Without such rich engagement, the project would not have achieved rigour on the ground, in the City or in academia. The next section explains the development and planning around co-producing wall-mounted solar lighting in PJS.

Co-producing public lighting for PJS Informal Settlement

A common first impression of a high-mast light in a self-built community is that it is devoid of human scale, towering forty metres above the community it serves. From the outset of the research in February 2017, I wanted to explore the opposite of high-mast lighting—lighting that is human-scale and adaptable to self-built communities. In a course on evidence-based design later that year, the solution I arrived at was wall-mounted solar lighting, where each household in a self-built community receives their own public light, installed above or close to their front door. The course material was taught through an applied approach, using a sample project of choice to explore concepts of space syntax and spatial cognition (Hölscher, 2017). I chose to explore public lighting in several self-built communities in Cape Town.

During this course, I discovered the *isovist*, a two-dimensional calculation based on "visual obstructions" and voids or "visual vistas". An isovist describes visual information from any given point of observation in a 360-degree field of vision (Bafna, 2003). Using the isovist tool unconventionally, I explored high-mast lighting's horizontal illuminance, or the distribution of light on a horizontal surface. I considered a luminaire as a point of observation, visual obstructions as objects that will cause the light to cast a dark shadow; and visual vistas as openings that allow the light to illuminate within the high-mast light's 200-metre illumination radius (CoCT Energy and Climate Change, 2019). Through this concept, I could see the ineffectiveness of high-mast lighting's horizontal illuminance in densely built-up areas (Figure 4).

The isovist does not consider vertical illuminance and is a simplistic approach, but as an initial exploration, it gave me the idea of wall-mounted lighting as an alternative to high-mast lighting in self-built communities. With a wall-mounted light on each structure, points of observation (lights) and visual vistas would increase and points of obstruction would decrease, resulting in more effective horizontal illuminance, as shown in **Figure 5**.

The concept was more efficient using solar energy. It also offered an opportunity to explore the sense of ownership residents would feel over the light, blurring the boundaries of public infrastructure by mounting a public light onto an individual's house. The final design detail as we installed it can be seen in the technical drawing (Figure 6).

The implementation was planned according to the randomised control trial (RCT)[7] quantitative research design, where some paths would get lights in a first phase and the rest in a second phase. The phased implementation comprised a baseline assessment, a lighting intervention and an endline assessment, broken down into six steps (Table 2) carried out between November 2018 and September 2021.

We worked closely with the PJS leadership and the CoCT to conduct the baseline survey in March 2019, following the Western Cape Informal Settlement Support Programme's (ISSP) enumeration guidelines. The enumeration addressed broad community concerns about development, and the data gathered informed the intervention.

We then worked with the PJS leadership and the ward councillor to develop the intervention, holding community meetings to discuss the project and answer questions. The layout design as seen in **Map 3** blurs the boundary between public and private infrastructure, encouraging a sense of ownership since the solar public light is mounted above or near each household's front door. The lights' placement also ensures that paths are well-lit without creating shadows. The layout design was done with the leadership and with consent of community members. An adult household member had to be present when the light was installed to approve its position.

An awareness campaign using posters, meetings and a WhatsApp service request hotline strengthened acceptance (Figure 7). We trained a local team to install the lights, working in groups of three, with two project leaders conducting supervision and quality control (Figure 8). Households selected to receive a light in phase 1 signed a consent form, received an information pamphlet (Figure 9) and participated in the process by working with the installation team to select a position for the light. Requirements were that the light had to be mounted on the structure, close to the front door, as high as possible, and the light had to shine into the public space/path. It took approximately thirty minutes to install each light.

During installation, we collected cell phone numbers to broadcast messages related to the project (e.g., lockdown plans) on the WhatsApp hotline. In

---

7   Randomised control trial, where a treatment group receives a light and a control group does not receive a light to compare the impact that lighting has at a household level.

Research step		Date	Process
1	Baseline and stakeholder engagement	Nov. 2018 – Dec. 2019	Collected baseline data using both qualitative and quantitative methods and intensive stakeholder involvement (see methods).
2	Phase 1 light installation (283 lights)	March 2020	Implemented 283 wall-mounted solar lights using a local team of fourteen people, divided into four supervised teams.
	Project crisis	March 2020 – Sept. 2020	Lights break, COVID and fixing the lights Within days of implementation, we discovered a manufacturing defect and had to fix all the lights in PJS. Just then, COVID-19 prevented us from working in PJS for three months. All lights fixed by September 2020, and step 3 could commence.
3	Observation and maintenance Planning phase 2 lighting installation	Sept. 2020 – March 2021	Conducted routine checks and maintenance on the lights twice a month. Gathered a set of problems through observations and routine maintenance and used this information in the design of the phase 2 batch of lights.
4	Endline	March 2021 – May 2021	Step 4 began in March 2021, conducting endline data collection using qualitative methods. COVID-related delays prevented me from fully participating in the endline household survey. My research partner led the rollout of the endline survey remotely.
5	Phase 2 light installation (~400 lights)	June 2021 – July 2021	Installed the final ~400 lights on all remaining structures in PJS using a local supervised team. Due to delays, I was not able to participate in this phase.
6	Observation and maintenance Stakeholder involvement	July 2021 – Sept. 2021	Conducted final routine checks and maintenance on the lights twice a month until September 2021. Presented research to stakeholders and submitted policy recommendations.

Table 2   Research steps in implementing the public lighting project in PJS Informal Settlement

Fig 4   Isovist plan of high-mast lighting in a densely populated self-built community

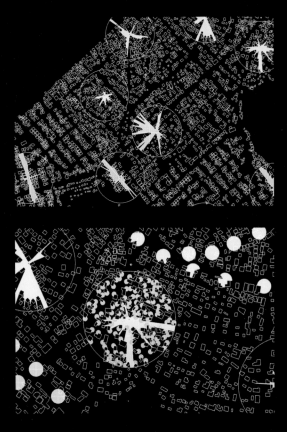

Fig 5   Isovist plan of high-mast lighting compared with wall-mounted lighting in a densely populated self-built community

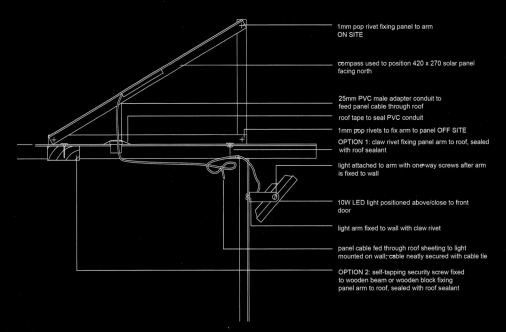

1mm pop rivet fixing panel to arm
ON SITE

compass used to position 420 x 270 solar panel
facing north

25mm PVC male adapter conduit to
feed panel cable through roof

roof tape to seal PVC conduit

1mm pop rivets to fix arm to panel OFF SITE

OPTION 1: claw rivet fixing panel arm to roof, sealed
with roof sealant

light attached to arm with one-way screws after arm
is fixed to wall

10W LED light positioned above/close to front
door

light arm fixed to wall with claw rivet

panel cable fed through roof sheeting to light
mounted on wall; cable neatly secured with cable tie

OPTION 2: self-tapping security screw fixed
to wooden beam or wooden block fixing
panel arm to roof, sealed with roof sealant

Fig 6   Technical drawing of final lighting design as installed in phase 1

Fig 7   Community meeting explaining the lighting installation process

Fig 8   Uniforms and project posters created pride, community awareness and acceptance

Fig 9   Information pamphlet handed out when installing a light

Phase 1 lighting layout

— Pathway

▨ Phase 1 February 2020

▥ Phase 2 May 2021

· Front door

● Phase 1 light position

◉ High-mast light

Map 3   Lighting layout in PJS where each household receives a light above their front door

the enumeration, sixty-five per cent of respondents said they reported problems to the community leadership; only eight said they used the City's SMS reporting service. Although the CoCT's C3 Service Request system could work, a local team would likely remain the primary recipient of fault reports. A local team continues to encourage acceptance, ensures supervision of the project and fosters a sense of urgency in addressing lighting problems.

After finding malfunctions, which are explained later in the chapter, we entered a troubleshooting phase to find the fault. We discovered that the microcontroller unit (MCU) was fusing as it was unprotected from over-voltage. Fixing the MCU issues gave us the opportunity to programme the dimming profile of the MCU, allowing the light to dim and brighten according to the observed traffic and sun pattern. Below is **Table 3** explaining the dimming profile of the modified light.

As explored in Chapter 2, South Africa's and, specific to this research, Cape Town's public lighting largely reflects the race-based segregative policies of the apartheid government. At approximately the same time that I started my research, the issue of public lighting came to the attention of the CoCT, but they were too time-strapped and bureaucratically constrained to explore any alternative solutions. When approaching several departments interested in developing new public lighting solutions for self-built communities, the CoCT responded

enthusiastically, showing how imperative it was to find new and innovative solutions that address the inadequacies of high-mast lighting.

Layered mixed methods

Beyond the highly collaborative public lighting intervention, several other methods were used to develop a rich understanding of the impact of light and dark on everynight life in self-built communities. These methods all served concrete purposes and were adapted and adjusted methods to access data that was lacking. An intense triangulation of methods solidified the findings, often combining highly visual data with interviews and observations. The project spanned forty weeks[8] in Cape Town — ten weeks for project planning and thirty weeks of fieldwork.

Interviews and workshops

Many interviews were conducted in various forms, and photos, walking and virtual reality (VR) workshops were used to facilitate a more fluid discussion. The most conventional form of interviews were household interviews, of which seventeen were conducted at different times in PJS and in SST

---

8   This excludes the final fieldtrip to close the project and present results to the stakeholders.

Dimming profile		Seasons		Explanation
Dimming	Duration	Mid-winter	Mid-summer	
30%	30 min	18:00 – 18:30 Light on Civil twilight	20:20 – 20:50 Light on Civil twilight	When the light switches on, it is still relatively light outside, so brightness is dimmed to 30% to conserve battery. As it gets dark, the lights brightens in 30min intervals
40%	30 min	18:30 – 19:00 Nautical twilight	20:50 – 21:20 Nautical twilight	
50%	30 min	+/-19:00 – 19:30 Astronomical twilight	+/-21:20 – 21:50 Astronomical twilight	
70%	2h	19:30 – 21:30 Night	21:50 – 22:20 Night	The light is brightest at peak pedestrian traffic time in winter, lasting two hours
50%	5h	21:30 – 02:30 Night	22:20 - 03:20 Night	Off-peak pedestrian hours: light switches to 50% to conserve battery
70%	Remaining time	02:30 – 06:20 Night	03:20 – 04:25 Astronomical twilight	The light brightens up again for peak morning pedestrian hours to 70% brightness until civil twilight, when it switches off as the battery is charged
		06:20 – 06:50 Astronomical twilight	04:25 – 05:00 Nautical twilight	
		06:50 – 07:20 Nautical twilight	05:00 – 05:30 Light off	
		07:20 – 07:50 Light off		

Table 3   Dimming profile programming according to pedestrian traffic and sunrise/sunset

while testing the pilot lights. In PJS, seven people were interviewed before the lighting intervention and six after the lights were installed to investigate links between the lighting intervention and possible improved nighttime experiences. Four of the end-line interviewees received a light, two of whom had been interviewed previously.

Each audio-recorded semi-structured interview lasted about thirty minutes. Rough notes taken during the interviews were expanded at the end of each day. The interviews were useful to establish an initial understanding of the impact lighting had on nighttime. However, language barriers, time pressures and the lack of prompting materials made the interviews more complex.

The participatory photo interview was a powerful method, and the impact of darkness immediately struck me after the first round, which consisted of eight interviews. Two more rounds of participatory interviews were done in PJS, but these were not as powerful as the first round, most likely because PJS is a more homogenous and dense environment, and is therefore challenging to photograph. Participatory photo interviews were used to gain insight into individual nighttime experiences in self-built communities. These photographs were used as prompt material, enabling a much deeper discussion. This method involved three phases. The first phase was a workshop where I presented my research on nighttime experiences in self-built communities and asked interviewees how they related to the subject. Participants each received and practised taking photos with a disposable camera. During the second phase, lasting one week, participants took photos to translate and ground their individual experiences. The third phase involved one-on-one interviews, lasting approximately one hour, where participants selected photos they wanted to discuss.

The method was very useful in getting residents to engage with their nighttime experiences. For many, nighttime was something they had not dared explore previously. Many participants chose to take photos during the daytime rather than talking about nighttime out of fear of the night. This presented issues in that the subject matter did not always relate to nighttime experiences, and I tried to frame these photos around the subject in interviews. Secondly, many nighttime photos were illegible because it was so dark. This made the interviews much more difficult. Some interviews were also emotionally challenging, as nighttime experiences raised many traumatic memories, especially for victims of gender-based violence.

Along with the participatory photo interviews, walking interviews facilitated the conversation further because many of the photos in PJS were almost illegible. During these interviews, I asked participants to take me to the places where they took the photos and explain their reasons for taking the shots. Most participants formulated a clear theme that they were trying to represent in the photos. These walks were added to a story map. Walking interviews also helped to map PJS, taking note of the conversations related to the area and situations we encountered. The findings were digitised, recording data on areas of insecurity, social spaces, busy pathways and areas that were very dark at night. Transcribing the recorded interviews was challenging due to all the background noise and sometimes ad-hoc conversation flow. Other interviews were recorded with note-taking and detailed daily field notes. Taking notes while walking proved to be very challenging.

Expert interviews were the final interview method, used mainly during the first two years of the research. These comprised twenty-five interviews with government officials, NGOs, practitioners and academics whose expertise involved urban planning, self-built communities and public lighting. The interview technique mostly involved a presentation on elements of the research relevant to their expertise, followed by feedback from the expert, and concluding with a semi-structured interview. Some experts were interviewed more than once. These interviews followed a meeting format, with a set agenda to guide the discussion. Setting an agenda made interviewees, especially government officials, feel at ease with what to expect, as they often feared facing unexpected contentious topics during the interview. A simple technique of "name-dropping" to support my knowledge of and familiarity with the CoCT organogram[9] convinced interviewees to share many useful policy documents and references to other experts.

Some interviews were recorded, with permission, and others were recorded with interviewer notes. If my research partner was present, that allowed me to focus on developing the conversation while my partner took notes. Opening with a presentation broke the ice and prompted interviewees to answer questions in their feedback session. This left less interviewing to do at the end of the feedback session and allowed the interviewee to feel less pressured in answering question after question. The feedback session also revealed the most impressive or

---

9   I gained this familiarity through stakeholder mapping.

pressing elements of the research for the expert and offered clues about gaps in the research.

I kept in touch with some interviewees and workshop participants throughout the research using WhatsApp. This enabled me to maintain important connections in Khayelitsha while abroad. These contacts included some community members, especially leaders, who provided updates. For PJS residents committed to collaborating on the project, this was reassuring—I was not another researcher who flew in, extracted data and left without benefitting the community with my research. In addition to upholding trust of community members in PJS, I also kept in touch with pilot households in SST, asking them questions about the lights we installed and gaining useful feedback.

WhatsApp Business was also useful in moments of crisis when the lights malfunctioned during the COVID-19 pandemic. I created a WhatsApp hotline to broadcast issues and receive feedback or reports from residents. We distributed flyers and posters around PJS circulating the hotline details. Though the hotline was not very busy, I wanted to pilot this as a more accessible and effective communication platform for the CoCT to explore further.

During the project, several WhatsApp groups were used to coordinate the local field team and to communicate with leaders and other important project members. These groups were a very useful tool for keeping records of the project and incidents that occurred. WhatsApp was an essential tool during the COVID-19 pandemic, when remote fieldwork was necessary. The conversations and discussions were not necessarily interviews but unstructured chats which, over time, offered much insight into the situation on the ground.

Various workshops and focus groups were held to understand collective nighttime experiences and to prompt more interesting discussions. These always involved an exciting mix of methods to engage people for the topic and get them to talk, draw, act and sometimes even sing. One general workshop in November 2018 hosted twenty adult participants to gain an initial, broad overview of nighttime experiences in self-built communities. The workshop was structured around learnings from a course on transdisciplinary methods[10]. After introductions and explanations about the research, participants looked at twenty-two photographs from the first round of photo interviews displayed on the walls. Workshop

participants added keywords or phrases to these photos. Afterwards, participants individually reviewed the keywords and phrases and used stickers to endorse the phrases.

After the photo review, participants were asked to draw their neighbourhoods at night using mental mapping techniques (Bell, 2009). Eleven participants presented their drawings, which sparked a useful discussion on the importance of nighttime and the problems people faced during nighttime in self-built communities. All keywords and mental maps were recorded and presentations were filmed and transcribed. The drawings were compelling in their symbolism and helped to establish some key themes about darkness in self-built communities.

Overall, the workshop offered great insight into the difficulties of speaking about nighttime when so many other problems affect life in self-built communities. The keywording and stickers were very useful in formulating a basis for understanding nighttime experiences. The workshop influenced the idea of looking more deeply into feelings associated with infrastructure in general.

The next interaction was a series of three creative workshops with two youth groups in Khayelitsha, held between June 2019 and December 2019. The other methods had reached saturation and there was value in gaining insights into the more nuanced emotions and perceptions around nighttime in self-built communities, both negative and positive (Morton, 2009). The intention was to creatively explore nighttime experiences in a way to free participants from the constraints of more traditional interview methods.

The first workshop with about twelve male and female participants of the Sakikamva Youth Group took place in PJS at a leader's house, where they held their weekly choir practices. After a singing warm-up, participants wrote keywords, thematically exploring positive and negative dreams and realities of nighttime. Afterwards, several participants gave monologues about their dreams and realities about nighttime. These were recorded. The keywords and monologues were sometimes abstractions of nighttime experiences, giving rise to some theoretical ideas around the importance of feeling free and liberated by light versus feeling trapped by darkness.

The second workshop took place in August 2019 with six members of the Sakikamva Youth Group at SJC offices. The aim was to develop a more concrete narrative around nighttime dreams and realities,

10　https://tdlab.usys.ethz.ch/

using Lefebvre's three modes of production of space—lived space, perceived space and conceived space (Lefebvre, 1991). Participants mapped their neighbourhood (conceived space) and key-worded their daily routines (lived space) and how they felt about nighttime (perceived space). The concept was more challenging to communicate, and in retrospect, other methods should have been used to explore these three modes.

The third workshop was hosted by Mandisi Sindo, a community theatre director, at his shack theatre, called KASI RC (Figure 10). Fifteen youth attended the workshop. We began by looking at photographic prompts and phrases relating to nighttime. Photographs were a combination of my own and photos from the first participatory photo interview. Phrases were taken from transcriptions of previous methods used. We explored each participant's nighttime keywords, sounds, characters and movements. The final task was to write a short play in three groups, and at the end of the workshop, the groups acted out their short stories around nighttime experiences. The group also composed a song on nighttime. The work around nighttime experiences started to take a much more emotive shape, which embodied experiences that are so often difficult to frame in words. The theatre workshops were very useful in getting participants, and me, to think beyond the first nighttime impressions. The tool is also very useful for participatory methods, where participants collaborate with the researching in creating something that tells their story.

By the end of my research and after the lights were installed in PJS, I had a clear idea of the questions I wanted to ask and needed more traditional means to get the conversation going. This was in the form of four conventional focus group interviews for the endline research in PJS. Focus group participants were community elders, the maintenance team working on the project, PJS leadership and the Sakikamva Youth Group. My reasoning was that these groups would be the most important in establishing an understanding of the impact of the public lighting project on everynight life.

Preference Study

Trying to understand people's public lighting preferences in self-built communities by using only interviews and workshops was a difficult component of the research. A more visual method was necessary, presenting imagined scenarios to residents so that they could really compare the differences in public lighting solutions. Working with a colleague, we ran a public lighting preference study, using virtual reality and rendered images, with ninety residents from various self-built communities in Khayelitsha. Participants started with a text-based questionnaire to determine their current public lighting preferences, before exposing them to one of the two visual questionnaires. We also asked them to rate different drivers for their decisions about public lighting preferences, such as vandalism, number of lights, the light installation process, etc.

After the text-based questionnaire, forty-five participants did an image-based questionnaire, and forty-five participants did a virtual reality-based questionnaire. The context of the lighting solution was constant, and the only variant was the combination between lighting type (H shown in Table 4) and the colour temperature (K shown in Table 5). From this, we would begin to deduce which colour temperature, as well as light type, was mostly selected.

Both visual questionnaires concluded with another set of the same text-based questions, asking participants about their public lighting preferences and to measure the change in preference after exposure to the visual questionnaires. This was followed by a feedback section asking participants about their experience related to the visual questionnaires.

The survey was a success but very labour intensive. Before participants took the survey, we had to train them on using the iPads and/or virtual reality (VR) goggles. Each participant took about forty-five minutes to complete the survey, and many felt that the VR questionnaire was too long. Thirteen participants removed the VR goggles and completed the survey with a computer screen because they experienced motion sickness. We also had an issue with

Lighting type				
Code	Light type	Lumens (lm)	Height (m)	Distribution (m)
H1	Wall-mounted light	600	2.5	6-8
H2	High-mast light	120,000	40	200
H3	Streetlight mounted on electricity pole	10,700	7	20

Table 4   H—lighting types used in the preference study

Colour temperature		
Code	Light temperature	Kelvin (K)
K1	Warm	2,000
K2	Neutral	4,000
K3	Cool	6,000

Table 5   K—varying colour temperatures used in the preference study

Fig 10   Theatre workshop about nighttime experiences at KASI RC, performing arts rehabilitation centre

loadshedding, where electricity cuts paused our work for up to two hours, and participants had to wait until the electricity was restored. Regrettably, there was no time to interview anyone after the survey. Fortunately, some participants were filmed while conducting the VR questionnaire, and others talked their way through the videos, with comments such as "that's right" or "this is so bright". Participants also often nodded their heads when they liked a clip or kept relatively quiet when they disliked something. Women tended to change their opinions more before and after the image/VR survey. Most participants found the exercise very useful in making decisions and felt that they learned something about public lighting from the exercise (Table 6).

Perceptions before and after the VR and image survey did not change drastically, except for perceptions of streetlights in the image survey. Although not very significant, the image survey displayed a greater perception change than the virtual reality survey, with an average of 0.38/5 compared with 0.19/5.

To show the CoCT the potential of virtual reality as a tool of participant involvement, we hosted a workshop with the CoCT Energy Department. Eight city officials attended the workshop, comprising a presentation of digital planning tools, running the VR questionnaire on all eight attendees, a feedback session and finally, a presentation of the research on public lighting. The VR experience was a great way to start the conversation about public lighting in self-built communities. Many attendees had never been to a self-built community, so their experience walking through a community virtually gave them a new perspective on the importance of public lighting.

Documenting everynight life in PJS

Documenting who the stakeholders were was probably one of the most important transdisciplinary and action research components. For this

research to make an impact, there was a need to convince the decision-makers of the CoCT as well as on the ground, and, furthermore, to consider their input very carefully. I developed detailed stakeholder maps, mainly of the CoCT, to identify main influencers and with whom we needed to interact. I received the initial CoCT organogram from SJC. From this organogram, I explored the departments I knew were important for our research, namely Public Lighting Development as well as Informal Settlements and Backyarders. This was done through interviews with stakeholders, studying meeting minutes through Advanced Google searches and investigating additional names I found later. Understanding the CoCT organogram was so important in the writing of a policy recommendation which could approach the complicated red tape and bureaucracy with agility. Red tape and bureaucracy often paralyses government, and so it was critically important that the policy recommendation could overcome these factors.

My personal immersion, observation and documentation occurred only in PJS. It started in November 2018 and continued for the duration of the fieldwork. I used various techniques ranging from photography, film, sleepovers and mapping. The first step in mapping PJS was deskwork in Zurich, mapping structures on OpenStreetMaps using high-resolution aerial photographs. DAG's data was added, which included social, economic and physical elements, such as leaders' homes, social groups, churches, danger zones, taps, toilets, flood areas, house numbers, front doors, *shebeens*, tailor shops, hair salons and food outlets.

SJC assisted us with the first fieldwork in PJS in November 2018. They introduced me to two female leaders who were willing to help us. We met at SJC to plan our mapping fieldwork, and I explained why we wanted to map certain details, consulting the printed map in the office and all the mapping done by DAG and other researchers. We asked the leaders to validate the work to establish if the data was reliable.

The first goal was to map out all the physical features in PJS, including the path network, fences, courtyards, front doors, and double storey structures. We walked around, physically marking our movements on a large aerial printout. This was a very laborious process and took three full days to map all the pathways and courtyards in PJS. It was very important to add all the information to OpenStreetMaps as soon as we arrived home, while it was still fresh in our minds. We marked any shops, churches and *shebeens* we had come across.

Did the images help you in making decisions about what lighting you prefer?	Did you learn about public lighting?
Image	Image
4.8/5	4.8/5
VR	VR
4.91/5	4.95/5

Table 6 Feedback on whether VR and images were useful tools in decision-making

We mapped pathways to understand how public lighting affects pedestrian mobility. The pathways were vital for my research partner to design the layout of the RCT[11] and understand where to place the proximity infrared (PIR) sensors[12]. Pathway mapping was useful to contextualise the interviews and understand locations of "danger zones", dark or busy pathways, etc. The path network itself is quite permanent in PJS because of the settlement's age. However, occupants change, and with this, residents form new configurations and "compounds" — residents in specific areas often collectively agree to block off one end of a pathway and secure the other end with a gate, creating a compound of houses. As a result, the surrounding path network adapts too. We needed to check and update the map regularly to create an accurate path network for the randomisation. This attention to detail brought new insight into how people organise themselves as well as the processes that develop when these changes occur.

During the house numbering for the survey, we used an app connected to OpenStreetMaps to map all doors as we numbered them. The door mapping was useful to see how houses form clusters with front doors closely located together. The doors also allowed us to simulate the lighting intervention using virtual reality software designed by a colleague. This was useful to understand whether the light distribution in the settlement would be even and to decide how many lumens each light needed. It was also an incredible communication tool when presenting to important stakeholders, like the CoCT. The doors would also help us keep track of the lights once they were installed.

Related to the doors, courtyards were also mapped to understand how space changed after the lighting intervention and whether more courtyards were created. The courtyards were divided into public and private — private courtyards were fenced. The private courtyards were divided into shared-private if there was more than one front door in the courtyard and private if there was only one front door. When we installed the lights, we mapped whether residents locked their gates at night or not. Initially, courtyards were only important for my research, but we later decided to add forty-eight PIR sensors in a randomly selected number of courtyards to observe

quantitatively if more activity occurs after the lighting intervention.

I maintained the initial social, physical and economic map created by DAG by making notes each time I saw a new shop, *shebeen*, etc. This was combined with the social indicators, small observations, films, interviews and less systematic mapping as a story map on Quantum Geographic Information System (QGIS). Trying to map how many houses had installed lights was a challenge, as many lights were hidden, broken or turned off when the household went to bed.

The map constantly changed throughout the fieldwork, with changes, observations and refinements. At first, I tried to map directly onto OpenStreenMaps on my phone, but it was not easy to map the less defined elements like "danger zones" or "social spaces" on a small cell phone screen. It was also not safe to walk around with an exposed cell phone. Once we had *structure* numbers for the entire area of PJS, mapping became much easier as the structure number could be noted for adding to the digital map later.

Along with mapping, many fieldnotes were generated during my trips to Cape Town. These differed in style — some analytical or descriptive, others keynotes or emotional diary-like entries. The fieldnotes started off being very long and detailed, with the full intention of keeping up the habit, but over time, as fieldwork became increasingly exhausting, the notes become briefer, and sometimes I was unable to write anything at all.

The field-notes helped in various ways, beyond developing the initial research hypothesis. They built a timeline of events when compiling a narrative of action research and tracking iterative use of methods. The notes also recorded the emotions felt during the time and were useful later for critical reflections. Reading the fieldnotes helped to maintain a connection with the research while I was in Zurich, and especially during COVID-19 when only remote research was possible. The fieldnotes were reminders of experiences in Cape Town when I could not be there. Lastly, fieldnotes are important for psychological debriefing after a day's work. The fieldwork was physically and emotionally taxing and using fieldnotes to process these emotions is a constructive coping mechanism. Notably, they were one of the most important but neglected components contributing to the overall development of the research. In hindsight, there should have been a greater emphasis on creating fieldnotes or developing an alternative, more manageable method for making fieldnotes during stressful trips to Cape Town.

---

11   A portion of the pathways were randomly selected to get lights on houses first, and the rest of the pathways would get lights on houses after six months of observation.
12   The sensor records an event when it detects a person's body heat and stops recording when the person has passed. The counters are small, weather-resistant devices fitted with a memory card and Bluetooth that captures the data and transfers it to a server through a cell phone application.

That said, fieldnotes need time spent in the field, and this immersion facilitated an understanding of the everynight experiences and the impact public lighting had on lived realities in self-built communities. Residents often did not articulate their everynight experiences of darkness and public lighting well, perhaps because they did not understand how these experiences would be useful for the research. At times, people were annoyed by the number of questions about their daily routine and at the invasion of their privacy. Physically experiencing and observing daily routines in PJS was useful.

To be able to reflect critically on everynight life in self-built communities, it was important to experience and observe those nighttime realities. I spent ten nights in PJS during my research. I also had an alternative, somewhat political, reason for sleeping over in PJS. Being a white, South African, Afrikaans woman, I had to demonstrate that I was not judgemental of their living conditions and did not consider myself better than them. The leader also wanted me to experience the night to gain insight into nighttime and understand PJS more deeply. My decision to stay overnight meant more than just experiencing nighttime for the leaders; it displayed my trust and commitment to the community.

Sleeping over in PJS was also a strategic tactic to win over the community to create a safe and accessible working environment. Many strangers knew my name, and I even adopted the nickname *Amapara-para*, meaning petty criminal, because of my hustling attitude and nighttime walks in PJS. People would approach me in PJS, asking me, in amazement and excitement, "Did you really sleep over here?" Sleeping over showed the PJS community that I was researching *with* them and not *on* them; we were, in fact, research partners. The final reason for sleeping over was a practical one regarding safety. I needed to observe PJS at night, and the road to leave Khayelitsha after dark was too dangerous.

Because we had so many practical, time-consuming fieldwork tasks in PJS, such as structure numbering and installing the sensors and lights, I had ample time to observe PJS by day. I did not spend much time on structured observation—I quickly recognised that as quite ineffective. Many people would ask what we were doing. Children also got excited, disrupting the flow of everyday life we were trying to observe. However, subtle observation continued while working, which was much more effective. Over a period of three years, I spent many hours in PJS. The place changed a lot—both over time and throughout the day. These observations were recorded as field-notes, photographs, films and rough written notes. Over time, observations developed into a natural understanding of the social dynamics and everyday life in PJS.

Photography was also a useful tool in capturing PJS before and after the public lighting intervention. Photos taken in the field and during the participatory photo interviews were useful prompts during interviews and workshops. This method worked very well and stimulated productive conversations. Photos were also used to narrate stories alongside text, since text alone could not fully portray everynight experiences in self-built communities.

The final and most exciting method for nighttime observation was filming. Throughout the research project, but especially from July 2019, film captured the lived realities and atmospheric quality of high-mast and wall-mounted lighting in PJS. This was done both through short impromptu filming sessions and during four planned nighttime filming sessions in July 2019, December 2019, March 2020 and April 2021, using cell phones, which were more discreet than full camera rigs. It was an ethnographic method, supported by still photographs to capture everynight life as it occurred. Filming soon became a project in itself—in March 2021, in collaboration with several residents in PJS and Khayelitsha, we made a film inspired by the research. The short film called "*Everynight Life*" is based on research results consolidated into the everynight life of a young boy living in PJS (Figures 11 and 12). The film's purpose is to create awareness of the stressful nighttime experiences in dark self-built communities both among residents and among a broader audience. We collaborated with SJC and Stepping Stones, an NGO focusing on teaching film-making to aspiring youth in Khayelitsha.

Collaborative methods

In our collaboration, my research partner used several methods to measure the impact of the lighting intervention quantitatively. Although these methods did not form part of the core of my research, the experience augmented my knowledge of quantitative research, and implementing the methods also served as time spent in the field observing, reflecting and getting to know PJS.

The household survey was probably the most ambitious method of the entire project, which we conducted without partners in the field. The questionnaire was refined and finalised according to the standards set out by the ISSP (Western Cape

Fig 11   Behind the scenes: shooting of *Everynight Life*
in PJS Informal Settlement

Fig 12   Behind the scenes: shooting of *Everynight Life* in PJS Informal Settlement

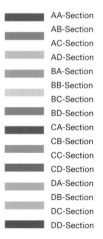

AA-Section
AB-Section
AC-Section
AD-Section
BA-Section
BB-Section
BC-Section
BD-Section
CA-Section
CB-Section
CC-Section
CD-Section
DA-Section
DB-Section
DC-Section
DD-Section

0 m   100 m

Map 4   Map showing the sub-divided sections in PJS Informal Settlement

Department of Human Settlements, 2018). The department hosted a workshop in Cape Town, which other NGOs attended, and lessons from the workshop were incorporated into the questionnaire and into the PJS household numbering survey process. In addition, a translator translated the questionnaire into everyday spoken isiXhosa.

Together with the PJS leadership, we created a new numbering system to ensure that we included all structures during the enumeration. While PJS had a house numbering system, many were duplicated and many houses were not numbered. All structures received a unique code system, created according to what the PJS leadership thought made sense. PJS was divided into four large sections—A, B, C and D section. We divided each section into three smaller sub-sections (e.g., AA, AB, AC, etc.), as shown on **Map 4**. Each structure received a number following its subsection designation, e.g., AA-001, BC-002, etc. We added the structure numbers to OpenStreetMaps to ensure data accessibility.

We began the survey once we received formal approval from the Department of Informal Settlements and Backyarders, to ensure the data would be accepted at the end of the survey. This required extensive negotiation before permission was granted. We used our connections at the CoCT and regularly updated the ward councillor on the survey planning. The survey started the day after approval was given, and two the CoCT field staff members were assigned to "oversee" the process, doing one site visit to assess survey progress.

The PJS leaders chose the team based on competence and equal distribution of people selected in each section of PJS. While we hadn't explicitly asked for women, fourteen young women were trained over three days. The field team comprised three roles: field coordinators, field team leaders (the PJS leadership) and field officers. There were between eight and ten field teams consisting of one field team leader and one to three field officers. Field coordinators were responsible for ensuring that field officers surveyed all structures and resolving any challenges arising.

We conducted the survey in sixteen days over three weeks, working eight hours a day with a very high response rate—764 respondents and two refusals. After data collection, it took eleven months and several meetings with the CoCT for the data to be formally accepted with written confirmation. This was the first time the CoCT had received digital data from another party, which extended the process of integration into their data system.

My research partner was responsible for the survey conducted after the lighting was installed. COVID-19 restrictions meant the endline survey had to be run remotely with a team of local PJS residents. We also implemented PIR sensors[13] in each pathway in PJS to quantitatively measure residents' nighttime walking habits and outdoor activities. The sensors were installed in August 2019, before the lights were installed, to collect baseline data on pedestrian activity. Our field team removed the sensors in June 2019 due to the delay in the lighting installation and a spate of sensor thefts. They were reinstalled after the lights were installed and working. I focussed on mapping the pathways, collaborating on a strategy for delineating pathways and installing the sensors in August 2019. Overseen by my research partner, a team of three local women collected data from the sensors every two weeks. Although sensor technology is an exciting and effective way of capturing data, the conditions in PJS and the unpredictable nature of an applied research project made the sensor project very risky and costly. By the end of the project, most of the sensors had been vandalised or stolen.

I collaborated on the initial light measurements at a household level (one lux measurement at each front door) to assess the lighting conditions before and after the lighting intervention. These measurements were used to show that the CoCT did not provide lighting levels according to standards set out in their policy document and illustrated high-mast lighting's poor lighting uniformity. During July 2019, we visited PJS with a light engineer to advance our knowledge on lux measurements. The military had been deployed to curb gang violence the previous week, and police had their hands full with daily shootings. The engineer agreed to do the measurements if I organised a police escort, and so, together with the leaders, we arrived at the police station the night of the planned visit and implored them to help us. They agreed, and we ran through PJS, taking twenty lighting measurements and quickly leaving Khayelitsha as police got increasingly nervous with our presence. After this, my research partner and I gave a lux metre to our field assistants in PJS and asked them to take measurements at each front door. They only managed to take twenty-nine measurements because of their busy schedules.

Finally, my research partner and I also collaborated on the routine checks after we had installed the

---

13 My research partner and I designed and implemented the sensors in collaboration with an MIT-based startup, called Sensen. The process was led by my research partner, and I played a supporting role.

Fig 13   Mapping PJS Informal Settlement with community leaders

lights. We conducted routine checks and maintenance every two weeks remotely from Zurich with a team of six residents in PJS. We collected data on how many lights were stolen, vandalised, broken or removed for renovations of structures using a service request sheet to enable a more detailed understanding of the post-implementation period of the lighting intervention. With the information collected through routine checks, we were able to understand which issues were common post-implementation and formulate a holistic public lighting recommendation for the CoCT.

Working collaboratively was mostly an enriching experience, but it also came with challenges of different disciplines working in very different ways. As a qualitative researcher, being in the field as often as possible was important for the validity of my results. As a quantitative researcher, this would add variables and potentially prime participants. For this reason, most of our struggles were about how much time we spent in the field and how much we involved the community in our research. At some point in the project, my research partner and my supervisor realised that I was too involved in the quantitative methods and that I needed to step back from this fieldwork. My research partner assumed the task of light measurements, sensor data collection and the second household surveys with a new team of PJS residents, while I observed the process and advised where necessary.

Challenges of co-producing lighting

The next section elaborates on the processes that followed and issues encountered during the design development, data collection and implementation of the project. Engagement with various academic disciplines and non-scientific stakeholders were both unavoidable and key for the project, but these engagements often came with unique challenges.

Collaborating with a local NGO was critically important in developing and implementing the lighting intervention. Finding an NGO with similar research interests that would benefit from the collaboration was also key. SJC launched a public lighting campaign as the research began in 2017. SJC released an article about ineffective public lighting in Khayelitsha and a map showing the distribution of high-mast lighting in Khayelitsha compared with neighbouring Mitchell's Plain (Mtembu, 2017). This striking image and convincing argument from SJC and similarities in the research subject made it clear that a collaboration would benefit both SJC's campaign and my research. NGOs have strong agendas

that can shift with the political climate. Presumably this relates to funding and gaining government attention by either addressing issues in the government's agenda or voicing issues that need urgent attention. This adds a layer of challenges to a long-term research project.

This happened early on, when our survey partner stepped aside at short notice. We attended an enumeration workshop hosted by the Western Province's ISSP and hired two field assistants to proceed with the survey ourselves. Although stressful, this decision enabled us to build confidence in the minds of the ward councillor, the CoCT, PJS residents and other NGOs. We were no longer seen as students but as serious contributors to the development of self-built communities. We also had something everyone wanted: data. This secured the support of the CoCT and other stakeholders and gave us leeway to execute the public lighting project. Working independently, with endorsement from NGOs, benefited the entire project. SJC was one of these NGOs, providing continuous endorsement and sometimes material support throughout the project.

Finding scientific collaborators in the project was also important to ensure scientific rigour. My research partner expressed interest after a presentation I delivered about the project in 2017. This collaboration presented an opportunity to close many disciplinary gaps. The addition of a skilled social scientist to the project added a new dimension of attention to detail, rigour and different viewpoints that pushed the project to a more realistically implementable level. Our supervisors offered their disciplinary expertise as well. Ultimately, disciplines involved included architecture, urban studies, sociology, human geography, planning and development economics. Combining these disciplines ensured that the research was well-considered from many viewpoints. But it was also challenging at times.

Long discussions were required to explore our different vocabularies and respective understanding of scientific research, familiarising each other with our academic disciplines. Sometimes compromises were required, and the research was adjusted to accommodate the other perspectives. At other times, sacrifices were required for the benefit of the project

In order for my research partner to assess the public lighting experiment quantitatively, the lighting project was implemented as an RCT. Initially, approximately one third of the pathways in PJS would be randomly selected to receive lights at their front doors. These pathways were the *treatment group*. The remainder of the houses located on pathways that would not receive lights in the first phase were part of the *control group*. After six months, the remaining houses (control group) would receive lights, too. As an urban researcher, this very scientific terminology— *experiment, treatment* or *control*—was new to me. I was concerned that non-scientific collaborators might see these terms as disconnected from lived realities on the ground. Over time, this discomfort ebbed away, and we agreed to use different vocabularies, depending on whom we were addressing.

A key issue in the collaboration was the degree of engagement in PJS. In urbanism and architecture, extensive fieldwork builds peer credibility. In development economics, when a researcher intervenes in the field, another variable is added to the impact evaluation, and so fieldwork presence is limited. For fear of influencing the RCT's outcome, we needed to agree on when I was permitted to be in the field and when not. Compounding this challenge was the differences in the fields of urbanism and development economics. In the former, participatory planning informs the community about the project in advance, and the community gives feedback and participates in the design and project implementation. In the latter, there was the risk of priming[14] the participants, which meant that we did not announce the intervention until only three weeks before implementation. The community grew frustrated—many were growing tired of seeing us and not being informed on how our research would benefit PJS. That said, there was a benefit to not announcing the project sooner, since many logistical issues delayed the lighting implementation. In that sense we avoided blame for empty promises.

Another collaboration challenge was the relationship between research and activism. As an urbanist, critical or activist research was acceptable, and fellow academics in the field respected advocacy research. In development economics, research grounded in activism risks being too normative[15], and the research outcome could be seen as biased and unreliable. Our partner NGO, SJC, are activists, so this was especially problematic. Our relationship relied on providing research material for their public

lighting campaign. In December 2018, this partnership was threatened as they could not publish our material, and so we needed to revise the conditions of information sharing.

The final issue was the balance of qualitative and quantitative methods. Qualitative methods are often iterative and adapt as new information emerges. Quantitative research needs to be designed, planned and concept-proven, clearly stating the degree of interaction in the field and adhering to the pre-set research plan. The iterative methodology could potentially intervene too much in the field, negatively affecting the rigour of quantitative research. While this issue was never fully resolved, I tried to lessen my fieldwork and shared detailed fieldwork plans.

There were also internal challenges. I was conscious of being a white, Afrikaans South African, who carried the legacy of apartheid prejudice. I only revealed my mother tongue once I gained the trust of the people I worked with. Many residents of PJS associated me with CoCT officials. I repeatedly rejected CoCT affiliations and asserted my role as a student researching nighttime and public lighting. As we did not reveal our public lighting intervention for fear of priming residents according to the RCT design, there was much speculation about our work. People began asking for houses, sometimes aggressively stating that "they wanted a house or nothing at all". When the project was announced, I was nervous that many community members would see the lighting project as an anti-climax, having hoped for housing. Fortunately, this was not the case, and residents were excited about the lighting intervention.

Unexpected real-world problems

Action research presents lessons that go far beyond academic research. In action research, every possibility needs to be considered. Despite best efforts, plans do go awry, and researchers need to adapt to allow the research to evolve. One of our NGO partners left the survey phase after six months of collaboration and preparation, which presented particular challenges but also positive outcomes. Their departure came at short notice, and we had to act very quickly, with little time for proper survey preparation. This makes an important point: project partners need to fully understand the respective priorities at play to ensure a common agenda for the project. Having memorandum of understanding (MOU) should be a mandatory requirement for project partners.

---

14 Priming is a phenomenon in which exposure to one stimulus influences a response to a subsequent stimulus, without conscious guidance or intention. Therefore, if I was in the field all the time, and associated with public lighting, this could cause unexpected influences in the participants' responses to the intervention.
15 Research based on an opinion or subjective values

We encountered further issues, this time relating to the PIR sensors. In August 2019, 117 sensors were installed on pathways and 48 in courtyards or entrance paths. These sensors were monitored every two weeks, and the leaders quickly tackled some early theft and vandalism issues. However, in June 2020, a spate of sensor theft occurred, and the team had to remove all the sensors immediately. Fifty-two pathway sensors and sixteen courtyard sensors were vandalised or stolen by June 2020 — 41.2% of the sensors. It emerged that children were being instructed to break the sensors and remove the memory cards inside them. The leaders recovered some of the cards from the children involved. The lesson learned was that the cost-risk factor of the sensors was too high. We should have piloted the sensors for one or two months before installing so many.

The most critical issue arose when our entire batch of phase 1 lights revealed a manufacturing defect at the start of the global COVID-19 pandemic. When we installed 283 lights in March 2020, the PJS community finally saw our research come to fruition. We had tested fifteen sample lights between November 2018 and January 2020, but in hindsight, we should have tested more extensively. Approximately nine days after we installed the first lights, we started receiving reports of defective lights. We realised that there was a manufacturing defect. Seemingly, the lights we received were not the same as the sample lights we had tested. At the same time, the COVID-19 pandemic was accelerating, and three days after we found the defect in the lights, a nationwide lockdown began in South Africa, one of the strictest globally. We had only two days to unplug the lights from the panels to protect them from further damage, distribute fliers explaining the unfortunate situation and put the entire project on hold until the government eased lockdown restrictions. The project was on hold for four months, and in July 2020, we commenced fieldwork remotely, working with our local team via WhatsApp. We did extensive tests with an engineering student at ETH and finally found a solution to the problem. By September 2020, we had repaired all the lights in PJS, working remotely from Zurich because of COVID-19 travel restrictions. My research partner oversaw the repair work, and we continued to work remotely with our PJS team, a local engineer and the engineering student at ETH. This was an entirely new way of working, and we needed to balance getting the work done without putting our team at risk of catching COVID. The pandemic raised questions about my role as a researcher, the fieldwork process and how it would change post-COVID. A notable positive outcome of remote fieldwork was that the local team was empowered to play a much more active role in our research. By the second phase, we had learned from our mistakes and decided to work with a trusted local lighting engineer who also had long-term relationships with suppliers. We ordered the second phase lights through this local engineer who managed the entire phase 2 installation.

If boundaries are not drawn, an action research project could comprise 20 per cent research and 80 per cent administration. This was very difficult to manage, with ongoing logistical tasks, stakeholder relationships that needed nurturing and employment issues such as contracts, payment, training, etc. Although earning a place through implementing the enumeration in PJS was essential, the associated bureaucracy was both overwhelming and unavoidable. This was distracting and diverted focus on the main objective of the research. By August 2019, I had refocused on completing my PhD and achieving my core research goals. Administration in action research is unavoidable and for an action research PhD, two components are necessary to support it: more time or more assistance. I was fortunate to have a dedicated research partner, with research assistants who lightened the workload and offered significant support during the second half of the project (2020–2021).

This chapter explored studying light and night in Khayelitsha's self-built communities, using a transdisciplinary and action research framework. The research aimed to implement and test a wall-mounted lighting solution in PJS, Khayelitsha, to understand the impact that public lighting has on everynight life. The research used a mixed-method approach of qualitative and quantitative methods between 2017-2021, including interviews, workshops, text, VR and image questionnaires, immersion, as well as randomised control trials. The process of implementing such a project required intense stakeholder engagement as well as an ability to adapt when project developments took unexpected turns. Some of the many challenges experienced throughout the research included restricted working due to a global pandemic, working with different disciplines, failing public lighting prototypes and finding remote solutions for repairs. Action research naturally involves real-world problems. It needs real-world strategies and solutions to address the multiple barriers and unexpected issues that emerge during such a research project.

Everynight Life Screenplay

Stephanie **BRIERS** – Producer and co-director
Ilzé **MYBURGH** – Director and co-producer
Sandiswa **TSHEFU** – Production assistant and sound
Götz **FROESCHKE** – Post-production
Bulelani **MVOTO** – Cinematography
Mveliso **JEVU** – Casting, production assistant
Hangula **LUKAS** – Second camera
Mandisi **SINDO** – Screen-writing consultant

Lizwi is a 12-year-old boy living in a self-built community in Khayelitsha with his mom and little sister. Lizwi is going through a transitional moment in his life where he is no longer a child and wants more freedom to be a teen. However, darkness is holding him back, and each night Lizwi fears going outside.

The film follows the daily struggles of living in darkness without access to public lighting and how the eventual introduction of lighting not only allows Lizwi access everynight life in his neighbourhood but also to transition from childhood to adolescence.

INSIDE LIZWI'S SHACK AT ABOUT 19:00

Lizwi is sitting on the edge of his bed looking out of the window. It's dark outside and difficult to see. He is anxiously awaiting his mother's return from work. We hear familiar township noises outside, including loud music, dogs barking, arguing.

LIZWI voice-over
    What has happened to the light?
    I am desperate on my knees tonight.
    Fighting tears of sadness without joy,
    for you have come to destroy.

HARD CUT TO NEXT SCENE

OUTSIDE, ALLEY WITH HIGH-MAST LIGHT AT ABOUT THE SAME TIME

We see the silhouette of a man, arms waving, speaking passionately, almost violently.

"PREACHER" in isiXhosa:
    As I was saying, some can steal what has
    been given to you.
    Some can take away your brightness,
    your luck.
    And some can take away your star, your
    shine and blessings.
    And you end up walking in the dark with
    no hope.

HARD CUT BACK TO FIRST SHACK

OUTSIDE LIZWI'S SHACK AT ABOUT 20:00

We see Lizwi outside his shack, standing at their gate with a dilapidated fence around their yard, looking down the road anxiously. His mother is still not back yet. He is very worried about her but too scared to cross the perimeter of the fence to go and look for her. In the doorway of the shack, we see his little sister's face in the shadow, peering out at Lizwi standing at the gate.

LIZWI voice-over
    The life I used to know as mine,
    simple, but truthful since my
    childhood time.

HARD CUT BACK TO SECOND SHACK AGAIN

OUTSIDE, ALLEY WITH HIGH-MAST LIGHT AT ABOUT THE SAME TIME

We see the "Preacher" continue his speech. High-mast light outside the house.

"PREACHER" in isiXhosa:
    Let me talk a bit about this darkness.
    To find yourself covered by darkness is
    something that one cannot get used to.
    When you are covered by the dark cloud,
    you feel lonely, you feel rejected, you become confused and at some point you don't
    even see the meaning of life.

Fig 1   Scene: Preacher who has lost hope because of *Darkness*

Fig 2   Scene: Lizwi anxiously waiting at the gate for his mom to come home

Dark clouds create images in your head,
you become scared and don't trust anything around you.
Be scared of evil but face the dark side of it.

CUT TO OUTSIDE OF FIRST SHACK

OUTSIDE LIZWI'S SHACK AT ABOUT 20:30

Lizwi is still standing at the gate waiting for his
mother. He is feeling very scared now.

LIZWI voice-over
    You took my mother to the outside
    And battered her for trying to provide
    For us, me and my sis,
    All living together in a shack,
    Penniless.

With great relief Lizwi sees the lights of a taxi coming around the corner. For a moment, we see
something happening in the dark as the lights of
the taxi shines on it. A man is possibly trying to attack a woman, but the light passes too quickly and
we cannot be sure. The taxi stops not far from the
shack, and Lizwi's mother gets out carrying two
bags of food. They enter the shack together.

INSIDE LIZWI'S SHACK AT ABOUT 21:00

The inside of the shack is lit only by candlelight. We
see the simplicity of the shack. A small table with
four chairs, a double bed standing in one corner, a
small basin to wash oneself and another little table
with a basin for washing the dishes and a little two-
plate stove. The mother lovingly prepares a meal
for her children as they wait anxiously around the
table. While eating she says:

MAMA in isiXhosa:
    Eat and leave some for tomorrow.

They both nod in agreement and start clearing
away the plates after they finished their dinner.
The single candle is moved to the bedside, darken-
ing the other corner of the shack where they just
had dinner. All three of them get into the same bed.
Mama blows out the candle. She cradles the little girl and Lizwi is lying with his back against his
mother, looking out the window at the moon, which
is now the only source of light.

LIZWI voice-over
    The only light we ever knew
    My mother's loving gaze before she blew
    Out the candle for the night
    And we would all fall asleep next her so tight
    Protecting us from you in the street
    Where wild and dangerous people meet
    In the evening you steel our light
    And we become prisoners on the inside.

Fig 3   Scene: Lizwi's nightmare about what happens when *Darkness* is around

Lizwi is falling asleep with the moonlight on his face and he goes into a dream state where he leaves the house and stands at the gate again looking at what is happening on the outside, too scared to venture out into the darkness... We become aware of muffled outside noises entering through the walls of the shack (base of music, laughter of drunk people passing, neighbour's door opening and closing).

OUTSIDE, TOWNSHIP LIFE ABOUT 22:00

We are outside the shack now and experience the nightlife. It is very noisy. We see a young girl walking very fast as if something is chasing her. We see people hanging out at *shebeens* and gang members hanging around at *spaza* shops, watching people as they buy a few essentials. A shot of the toilets in darkness.

LIZWI voice-over
        Because when you are around we do not know
        Where to walk or where to go
        If it is safe for us on the street?
        Avoiding dangerous situations, feeling weak

Still in a dream state, Lizwi walks back inside, closing the gate and locking the door.

LIZWI (CONT.) voice-over
        Without any protection you become

scary, noises turn strange; screams, dogs barking or guns
And we dare not be out on the street to play after a certain time of the day
only *shebeens* stay open when you are here
Creating fights, creating fear.

Fig 4   Scene: Lizwi awake after his nightmare about *Darkness*

INSIDE LIZWI'S SHACK AT ABOUT 03:00

The shack is very quiet on the inside, except for police sirens in the distance. Lizwi wakes up, wanting to go to the bathroom.

LIZWI
        Mama! (in a whispering voice not to wake his sister)

MAMA in isiXhosa
        What? (waking up slowly)

LIZWI in isiXhosa
    My stomach hurts. (rubbing his stomach)

MAMA in isiXhosa
    At this time? (annoyed and surprised) I told
    you not to eat too much.

LIZWI in isiXhosa
    Yes, Mama. (still rubbing his stomach)

MAMA in isiXhosa
    You know we cannot go to the bathroom
    this time of night, my boy.
    It's too dangerous. (turning over and going
    back to sleep)

We see Mama's face staring into the darkness of
the room. She is also scared of the night and what
might happen. Lizwi tries to sleep again, but he
can't and his mom and him both lie awake, backs
facing each other.

LIZWI voice-over
    Returning home you never know
    If you're hiding someone who believes it's
    my time to go
    Or visiting an ablution block late at night
    Walking in utter fear, uncertainty and fright

Pauses as he begins to fall asleep.

LIZWI (CONT.) voice-over
    because someone might be waiting there

opens eyes again...

LIZWI (CONT.) voice-over
    to steal my innocence or make me scared.

INSIDE LIZWI'S SHACK AT ABOUT 05:00

We are greeted by morning sounds. People talking, activity outside, cars/taxi's driving past. Lizwi
wakes up slowly, still tired. He lies in his bed taking in morning sounds and building up strength to
take on the day after another night of bad sleep.
He swings his legs out of bed, gets up and starts
washing his face and getting dressed for school,
looking at his mother and his sister still lying in bed.

OUTSIDE LIZWI'S SHACK AT ABOUT 06:00

We see Lizwi leave for school with his backpack.
Walking through the gate without thinking twice. It
is day now and he is not scared to go out.

LIZWI voice-over
    Everynight life its always the same
    Making us sleep lightly, waking up
    Drained.

Some time passes.

Fig 5   Scene: Lizwi tired in the morning after a restless night, fearful of the dark

OUTSIDE LIZWI'S SHACK AT ABOUT 20:00

Lizwi's mother, his sister and a friend are sitting outside in the better lit courtyard in front of the shack. Lizwi comes out of the shack, closing the door behind him. Nicely dressed. He is looking slightly older and much more confident. Time has passed since we last saw him.

LIZWI
        See you later.

MAMA
        Enjoy, my boy!

Lizwi approaches the gate. For a moment he pauses but then steps out confidently into the street.

OUTSIDE, FIRE BARREL AT ABOUT 20:30

Lizwi arrives at the fire, his friends don't see him until he speaks. They look up to hear him say:

LIZWI
        It must be clear, (pause) this is a free coun-
        try, not a fear country.

Fig 6   Scene: Lizwi and his friends confronting *Darkness*

SHOT OF LIZWI AS HIS FRIENDS ARE LOOKING AT HIM AS HE SPEAKS.

FRIEND 1
        Dear Darkness, go away and bring back
        the light

FRIEND 2
        Take away our fear of the night

We see them standing next to the barrel with fire, warming their hands. They are playful and in a good mood. We see them chatting away, making jokes and laughing.

Fig 7   Scene: Lizwi and his friends enjoying nighttime, no longer afraid of *Darkness*

Fig 8   Scene: Lizwi walking home at night with lights visible in the pathways

LIZWI voice-over
      Take away our fear of the night
      Bring back the light so that we can see
      So that we can walk around and just be
      Happy and full of joy
      Just growing up like normal girls and boys
      Who play with our friends and go to sleep
      when we are tired
      Or stand around a bin, warming our hands
      against the fire
      Telling stories of happy memories of this
      day
      How we were free, how we laughed, how
      we played.

                                                              THE END

Camera zooms out to a long shot showing some
lights in the background and people walking in the
pathway.

Life in the Shadows of Area Lighting

Chapter 4

Until now, we have discussed high-mast lighting at a high level. This chapter introduces the daily experiences of high-mast lighting. What are the lived experiences of high-mast lighting? Would people prefer a different public lighting solution for their neighbourhood? This section aims to ascertain how people perceive, experience and talk about access to public lighting on the ground in Khayelitsha's self-built communities.

For many living in dense self-built communities, high-mast lighting is an apartheid-era infrastructure that has no place in democratic South Africa. Nor is it technically efficient. As described in Chapter 2, high-mast lighting aims to light very large areas with a single forty-metre tall light. Each self-built community will have one or two high-mast lights for their entire neighbourhood. This is the primary problem. Its scale is simply out of context when compared with the scale of houses and pathways, or more pertinently, the scale of the human beings it aims to service. Lights are placed at the periphery of settlements where there is sufficient space. Light shines from *above*, and not *within* the settlement. This physical distance of the light creates a mental distance for people living with this lighting. There is no sense of ownership over the light, resulting in an array of other problems, such as the lack of fault reports when a light breaks. It's clear that high-mast lighting is not only technically insufficient, and the lived experiences of people on the ground clearly reflect its insufficiency.

Chapter summary: The term 'area lighting' already points to the necessity of understanding this lighting at a larger scale. This chapter begins by understanding high-mast lighting at a neighbourhood scale using household survey data in PJS and a public lighting preference study with participants from various self-built communities in Khayelitsha. Data is also used from a nighttime workshop, photography, maps and lighting measurements done in a small section of PJS. Individual perspectives on lighting follow this section, using household interviews, photographs and observations in PJS. Finally, individual preferences are explored mainly using data from a virtual reality public lighting preference study conducted in Khayelitsha. In conclusion, the chapter synthesises the main learnings on living with high-mast lighting in daily life.

That light in the distance?

Some survey respondents and interviewees in PJS did not consider the high-mast lighting closest to them, located on their periphery, as public lighting infrastructure meant for *their* neighbourhood. They said they did not have public lighting because "that light belongs to another neighbourhood". Although people receive coverage from the high-mast light, they do not feel that the light *belongs* to their settlement as it is not located centrally or on their

land. This comment first came to my attention in a household interview when Thuliswa said the oldest of the two high-mast lights servicing PJS belonged to P-Section, and therefore PJS did not have public lighting when she first arrived in 1992. The high-mast light in question is technically situated in P-Section, ten metres away from the PJS boundary. Considering the light is forty metres tall, ten metres is nothing.

This rationalisation came up often in our PJS survey. Residents, specifically from the darker D-Section, said they did not have public lighting. A few added that they used the light from P-Section, the formal neighbourhood next to PJS.

> Female, DB-Section: No public lighting— We use the high-mast which is for P-Section not for us in PJS, we don't have light

> Male, DB-Section: No public lighting— We are helped by a high-mast light which is not inside our section, it's in P-Section

> Female, DB-Section: No public lighting— There is only a high-mast light at P-Section

> Female, DC-Section: No public lighting— No light in PJS, but we are helped by streetlights from another section

> Male, DC-Section: No public lighting— No lights here, only at P-Section

> Female, DC-Section: No public lighting— High-mast light from P-Section

This clue led to further investigations into the answers people gave when asked whether their neighbourhood had public lighting or not.

In my public lighting preference study, we asked residents within Khayelitsha what public lighting they had in their self-built community. In response, 64.44% (n = 90) said their neighbourhood did not have public lighting (Table 1). Contrary

What public lighting does your self-built community have? (n = 90)	% average
No lighting	64.44%
High-mast lighting	20.00%
Street lighting	13.33%
Electricity pole lighting	2.22%

Table 1 Table indicating the perceived public lighting in self-built communities in Khayelitsha

to their perception, many settlements fall within a high-mast light or street lighting service radius. **Graph 1** shows that most participants came from RR-Section and Greenpoint Informal Settlement. I reviewed these two settlements to see whether access to public lighting (according to the public lighting data) reflected a participant's response. Greenpoint covers 20.3 hectares and has lighting coverage of 56% with a combination of street lighting and high-mast lighting. However, in the survey, 72% of participants answered that they did not have public lighting in there. In RR-Section, which covers 26.2 hectares, lighting coverage is similar, with 58% coverage. There, 77% of respondents said they did

not have public lighting, reflecting the poor coverage in Greenpoint.

PJS is much smaller than Greenpoint, at 3.9 hectares. As shown in **Map 1**, the area receives 98% lighting coverage, but 24% of respondents still felt PJS did not have public lighting. According to the CoCT regulation on a high-mast light coverage area, the P-Section light covers 754 PJS households, yet 22% of those households said that PJS did not have public lighting. The high-mast light next to Dora Educare serves 511 households according to regulation. Here, 21.5% of households felt that PJS did not have public lighting. Of these households,

What public lighting does your self-built community have?

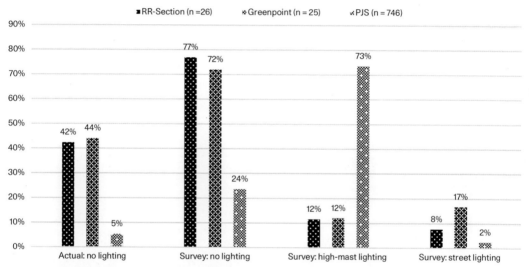

Graph 1   Public lighting coverage versus whether participants felt that they had public lighting or not

What public lighting does PJS have? (answers by lighting coverage area)

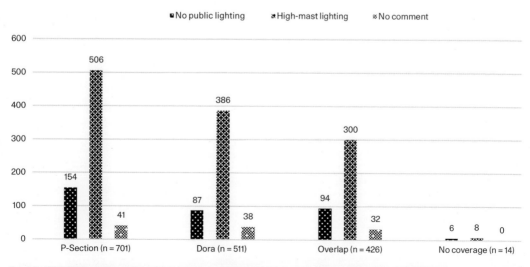

Graph 2   What lighting residents think PJS has, divided according to the coverage areas of high-mast lighting in **Map 1**

Opinion: PJS Informal Settlement does not have public lighting

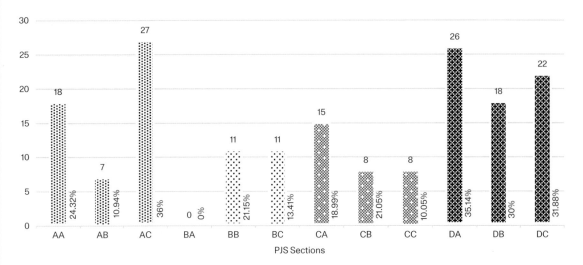

Graph 3   Residents' opinions on whether or not PJS Informal Settlement has public lighting provision

Map 1   High-mast light coverage in PJS Informal Settlement

426 reside within the service radius of both lights. Their lighting situation should therefore be improved with more uniform light and fewer shadows. Yet, 22% of households in this overlap area said that PJS did not have public lighting (Graph 2).

The PJS data by section revealed that the distance from lights correlates with the respondent's answer. Residents in A- and D-Section are further away from the lighting. More people in these sections said PJS did not have public lighting. In B- and C- Section, more people said PJS had high-mast lighting, although some still answered that PJS did not have public lighting. All these areas in PJS, except for fourteen houses in DC-Section, fall within a high-mast light coverage area (Graph 3).

In Greenpoint, many residents in RR-Section and PJS feel that public lighting in their neighbourhood is inadequate. A significantly higher percentage of people say they do not have public lighting than the actual lack of public lighting according to public lighting coverage, pointing to high-mast lighting's insufficiency.

There are several reasons for people saying they do not have public lighting. The most significant complaint about high-mast lighting, and a possible reason people felt they did not have public lighting, was that the light was too far away from their house or neighbourhood. This was a theme mentioned many times in my workshops and in participatory photo interviews in PJS and in other self-built communities. Mrs Filifili from PJS and another anonymous workshop participant from RR-Section explain:

Mrs Filifili: We are walking in these dark pathways all the time. These pathways are dark because the nearest public light is very far from these pathways that I travel. (female, elderly, participatory photo interview, PJS)

Anon: There are high mast lights that are very far away from seven sections. (Workshop participant, RR-Section)

Evidence of this distance also came up in a sketch-mapping workshop. Some participants drew high-mast lighting "far-away" from their neighbourhood, represented on the drawing's border (Figures 1 - 5). These drawings were not just the imagination of residents in self-built communities—high-mast lights are mostly peripheral lighting, as explained in Chapter 2.

As a result of this distance, a sense of ownership of the lighting was missing. In general, people did not report faulty or broken high-mast lights. Some knew how to report it, while others did not. The lack of reporting ties in with the theme of ownership over infrastructure, where people were less likely to report a fault than with decentralised infrastructure. The consensus was also that leaders and the ward councillor should report broken lights. Problems in the community were generally reported through a decentralised channel, by reporting to the local leaders.

People often associated darkness in their neighbourhood with the high-mast light being too far away, even though their house was fairly close to the light. High-mast lights are designed to illuminate open areas such as football stadiums and parking lots. They do not provide even lighting in densely built-up areas with narrow pathways, but instead cast dark shadows. At 95%, PJS is well serviced with light coverage, but the high density of 204 single-storey dwellings per hectare results in very narrow passages where the high-mast lighting casts dark shadows. Most of the light falls on roofs. Average density for self-built communities in Cape Town is 183 dwellings per hectare. However, when a pathway is at the correct angle to the high-mast light, it is very brightly lit. Pedestrians move continuously from overpowering light to absolute darkness while walking through the pathways at night. This poor uniformity negatively impacts eyesight when adapting to the fluctuating lighting levels. Nombulelo, a photo interview participant in PJS, noticed the inefficiency of high-mast lighting when I asked her what she had learnt through the process of taking photos:

Stephanie: *Did you learn anything about PJS?*

Nombulelo: Yes, the pathways at night are dark, but there is a light, but the light does not travel and get to the other pathways. I live close to one of these pathways, but it's not too small; at least two people can walk at a time through the path at my area, but we depend on the high-mast light to light our pathways.

I was also struck by the juxtaposition between bright and very dark pathways during my night visits to PJS. I stayed in Kholeka's house. The front door was very dark, but when we went for a night walk, the pathway to the toilets was very bright, so bright that I thought we might have chosen the wrong settlement for a public lighting research project. This confirmed that high-mast lighting needed to be considered in many situations. At the beginning of my sleepovers, I spent most of my time filming in the wider, very well-lit pathways and little time in the narrower, darker parts of PJS. When I did lighting measurements in June 2019, I experienced very dark

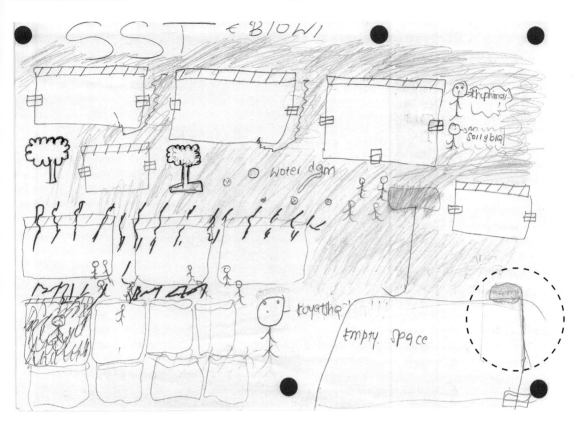

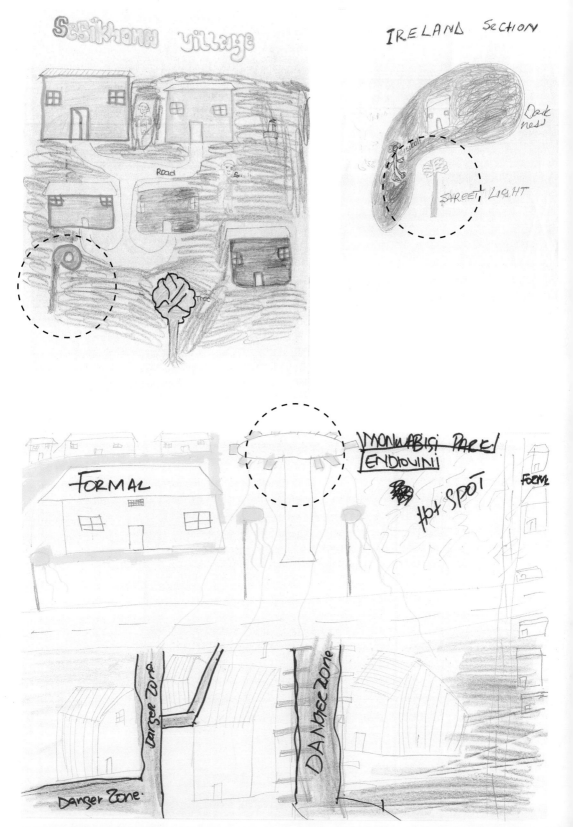

Figures 1 – 5 Sketch mapping in the nighttime workshop, indicating high-mast lighting often drawn on the periphery of neighbourhoods

Map 2   Lux measurements taken at each household's front door, where less than one lux (blue) is below the City of Cape Town's accepted standards

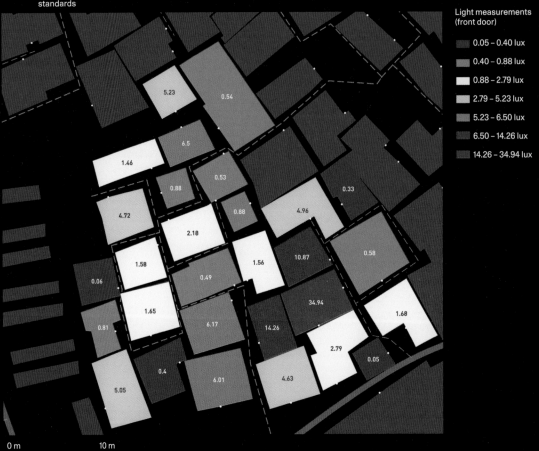

Light measurements
(front door)

0.05 – 0.40 lux

0.40 – 0.88 lux

0.88 – 2.79 lux

2.79 – 5.23 lux

5.23 – 6.50 lux

6.50 – 14.26 lux

14.26 – 34.94 lux

0 m   10 m

pathways. I stopped to take a light measurement[11] at every house and realised that each one had a different lighting experience depending on proximity to the two high-mast lights.

After my lighting measurements, my research partner and I collaborated with two community leaders to do more detailed lighting measurements using a lux metre at twenty-nine front doors. Several areas within the 175-metre servicing radius of the high-mast light had readings below the required one lux lighting level, shown in **Map 2**. For example, one reading at 70 metres and 199 metres away from the two high-mast lights servicing PJS measured 0.06 lux—slightly higher than the light of a quarter moon, and far below the minimum requirement. Just over twenty-three metres away from this reading, a second reading (79 metres and 178 metres from the high-mast lights) showed 34.94 lux. In comparison, twilight measures 10.72 lux.

Due to the constantly changing lighting situation, people had different experiences of high-mast lighting in their neighbourhoods. They struggled to characterise it exclusively as good or bad. Instead, interviewees often presented contradictory statements about the lighting, saying either that it was very dark in their neighbourhood or that they could see the high-mast light was helping their community. These statements often related to scale, for example, "the lighting in front of my house is bad, but the lighting is good for the community".

Many residents feel their neighbourhood does not have public lighting for various reasons, even if their settlement is well-serviced with high-mast lighting. The planning boundaries and zoning regulations set in policy materialise on the ground, with lights on the border outside self-built communities. This reduces a sense of infrastructure ownership and reinforces a perception that communities do not have public lighting. This acute awareness of legislative boundaries and planning in the minds of residents who live in self-built communities was surprising. (Figure 6)

Individual experiences of lighting in PJS

My first fieldwork conducted in PJS involved household interviews primarily focused on public lighting experiences. The five interviewees assisted in reaching some broader conclusions on the individual's perception and experience of high-mast

lighting. Understanding the lived experience of high-mast lighting allows a more nuanced explanation of the impact of the infrastructure on daily life. This section focuses on individual perspectives and the daily experiences of high-mast lighting in their neighbourhood, also referred to as "apollo lights", "streetlights" or just "that light".

Thembeka

Thembeka, an adult female who has lived in the same house in PJS since 1991, indicated on **Map 3**, did not know what I was referring to when I spoke about public lighting. She had mistaken it for the electricity in her house. Once I clarified, she said that the high-mast lights were already in PJS when she moved there in 1991.

Stephanie:	*Was there lighting [in 1991]?*
Thembeka:	They put the electricity in 2009. No, the tall lights were there. The big ones, they were there. I didn't understand; I thought you were talking about these ones [points to light in her house]. When I arrive here, they were there already.

Thembeka's memory of the lights from so long ago indicated their strong presence in PJS, no matter whether that presence was good or bad. When I asked her if she remembered the lights in association with apartheid, she had nothing to say except that she liked the lights.

Stephanie:	*Do you remember these lights from then [1991]?*
Thembeka:	[Shrugs]
Stephanie:	*What is your experience when you walk home in terms of the public lighting?*
Thembeka:	No, the public lighting is fine for me, sister. I like it.

The interview later turned to more pressing issues that Thembeka wanted to discuss, which were nighttime issues related to living next to a *shebeen*. For this section, however, I will only look at what she spoke about in technical relation to lighting.

The nearest high-mast light to Thembeka's house was 153 metres away, shown in the map to the right. Her house therefore was just inside the service radius of 175 metres. Because she lived in a wide pathway, the dim light fell directly onto her house, lighting up her front door. It was therefore understandable that she would say "the light is fine" because she had sufficient light at her front door.

---

1   The SI unit of illuminance, equal to one lumen per square metre. The City of Cape Town standard is a minimum of one lux in public space.

Fig 6   Neighbourhood-scale view of high-mast lighting in SST Informal Settlement

Thembeka often worked night shifts, so she had to walk to and from the taxi in the very early morning and at night, after dark. Although she felt the lighting was good, she felt fear and a lack of trust while walking. She spoke about not recognising people walking past her at night.

Thembeka: ... so I'm just getting scared, but I can't stop them because I don't know who they are... No, you will never trust anyone at night.

After I interviewed Thembeka in her home, we walked her route to and from the taxi at night, shown on **Map 3**. The brown dots on the map indicate all the pathways perpendicular to the route, where she said she feared the *skollies* (youngsters causing trouble) might hide. The danger points were all on narrow pathways and pathways receiving minimal light from the high-mast lights, compared with the pathway where she lived. However, Thembeka did not refer to darkness when showing me these hiding places. The position of the high-mast light relative to her walking route cast several dark patches, shown on the map. Her recollection of her fears of walking and dark hiding places only surfaced when walking us along the route and describing the nature of the walk at night.

Thembeka did have one strange thing to say about the high-mast lighting during the interview. She said the actual light bulbs turn around, and when they turned away from her house, the light was not good. Thabisa, my research assistant, immediately told her this was not possible, and I agreed. But after two years of working in PJS, I learned that some of the six light bulbs on the high-mast lights fused occasionally. Broken bulbs combined with strong winds caused the bulbs to move from time to time, which resulted in inconsistent lighting. (Map 3)

Mvelisi

Mvelisi is a young male living with his wife in PJS and occasionally works night shifts. Mvelisi also did not have much to say about high-mast lighting. His statements were both positive and negative. Mvelisi said he liked the high-mast lights but that it was very dark in front of his house, as shown in blue on **Map 4**. This made him feel insecure when he got home at night.

Stephanie: *Public lighting—how is the lighting working for you at the moment?*
Mvelisi: Light, which light?
Stephanie: *The tall ones outside.*

Mvelisi: Yes, the public lighting is lighting, but it's too far for us on this side. Because it's there next to the police station that light but its lighting for all of us, but it's too far for us. When I'm coming to my house, there's a darkness here in front of my house, yes, it's too far for us.

We walked outside, and he showed me where the darkness was, which was in direct relation to the dark shadow the high-mast light cast. He referred to the Dora high-mast light, at the police station, 234 metres away from his house. This said, Mvelisi's house was eighty-four metres away from the P-Section high-mast light, relatively close when considering the high-mast lighting service radius. The contrast between light and dark increased with closer proximity to the light, resulting in darkness in front of his house. This darkness was also more apparent because Mvelisi lived next to the wide, brightly lit main road in PJS, indicated in grey on **Map 4**. Additionally, his route walking to the taxi drop-off point, shown in brown on the map, was much darker than the main road. These contrasts in lighting made it challenging to have a clear opinion on whether Mvelisi approved of high-mast lighting or not.

I asked Mvelisi whether the high-mast lights ever switched off. He responded that the *skollies* sometimes switch them off, but the next day, they are on again. He thought the *skollies* were switching the lights off because every time the light was switched off, he heard stories of robbings the next day. (Map 4)

Fundiswa

Fundiswa is a young woman living with her mom. Working in the catering industry, she leaves for work early and returns home late, depending on her shift. Fundiswa made similar remarks as Mvelisi about shadows in front of her house. Her mom installed a wall-mounted light on their house in 2010 because the high-mast lighting "did not reach their house". They installed the light after PJS received its second high-mast light (the Dora high-mast light) in 2009, which was only ninety metres from their house.

Stephanie: *When did you put up the light?*
Fundiswa: In 2010.
Stephanie: *Why?*
Fundiswa: Before we put up this light, there was no light outside, no streetlight, it was dark, so we decided to out up this light.
Stephanie: *So the light from the high mast doesn't get here?*
Fundiswa: No, it doesn't get here when it's dark.

Map 3 Thembeka's nighttime experience related to public lighting

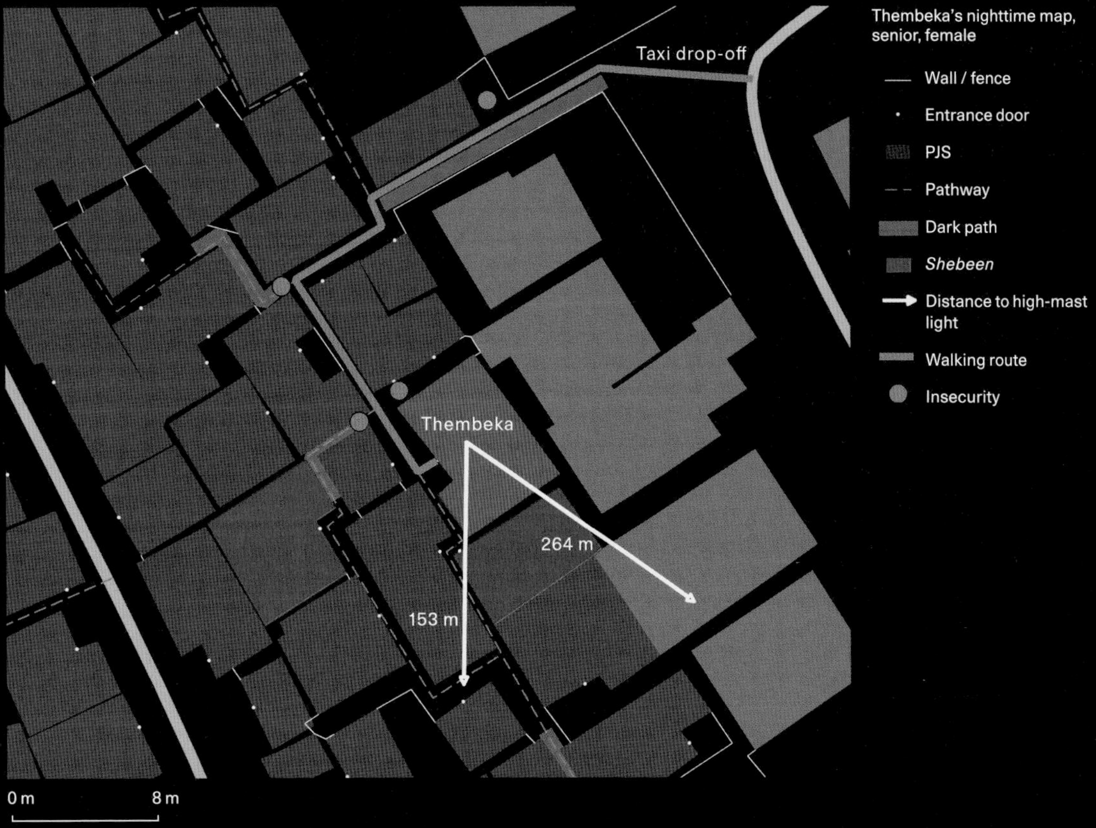
Taxi drop-off
Thembeka
264 m
153 m
0 m
8 m
Thembeka's nighttime map, senior, female
Wall / fence
Entrance door
PJS
Pathway
Dark path
Shebeen
Distance to high-mast light
Walking route
Insecurity

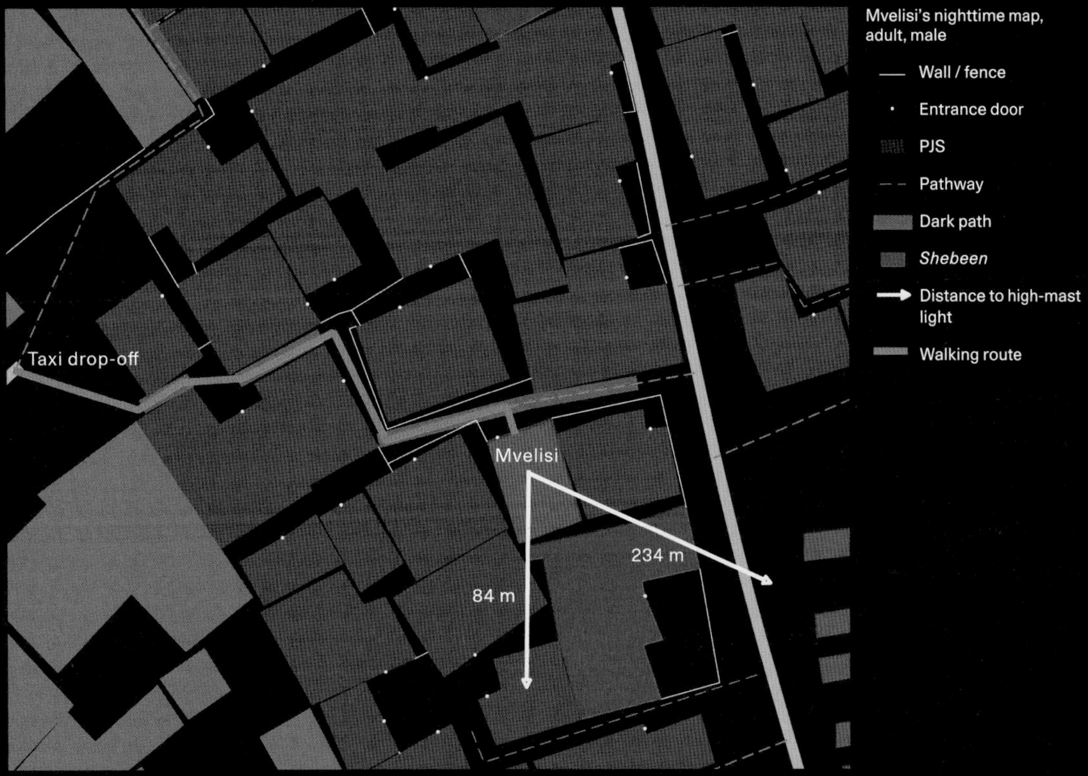
Taxi drop-off
Mvelisi
234 m
84 m
Mvelisi's nighttime map, adult, male
Wall / fence
Entrance door
PJS
Pathway
Dark path
Shebeen
Distance to high-mast light
Walking route

Map 4 Mvelisi's nighttime experience related to public lighting

I visited Fundiswa's house at night, in the middle of winter, and I noticed that living only seventy-five metres from the closest high-mast light did not improve the lighting conditions. **Figure 7**, taken at position *1* on **Map 5**, shows that the pathway beyond her front door was very dark. **Figure 8** in position *2* on the map is around the corner from Fundiswa's house. The path was brightly lit with one high-mast light directly in front (118 metres away) and the other high-mast directly behind the camera, eighty metres away. The pathways were very close to one another yet had very different lighting conditions, showing the lack of uniformity of high-mast lighting.

We discussed the benefits of having a wall-mounted light. Fundiswa enjoyed the light because she could sit outside at night in December, during summertime in South Africa. Her friends wanted to visit at night because her outdoor space was big and well-lit, but her mother did not allow that. She said her neighbours also had a light, and because of their light, they spent time outside at night. As with most people who had an outdoor light, Fundiswa's family switched their light on for about three hours per night from 18:00–21:00.

I ended the interview by asking Fundiswa what she thought about PJS when walking around at night. Her answer contradicted the previous complaints about the inadequacy of high-mast lights. The conclusion was that she approved of the lights at a neighbourhood level but not at a household level.

Stephanie:	*When you move through PJS at night, what is your experience?*
Fundiswa:	I can see the streetlights are helping us.
Stephanie:	*Those two tall ones are helping you?*
Fundiswa:	Yes.
Stephanie:	*They just aren't helpful for here?*
Fundiswa:	Yes.

Sibongile

Sibongile is a senior male who has lived in BB-Section, PJS, since 1991. He confirmed that the P-Section high-mast light, as he and many others called it, was in PJS when he arrived. The Dora light, fifty-seven metres from his house, was installed when PJS received electricity in 2009. Before the Dora light was set up, he had an outdoor light above his front door but felt that he did not need it anymore after the CoCT installed the second high-mast light in PJS. He complained a lot about this "new" high-mast light continuously being out of order.

Stephanie:	*And how is it lighting for you?*
Sibongile:	No, it's not right that light, sometimes the globes is another one is not light; maybe it's working maybe two globes. This new one.
Stephanie:	*And when everything is working? When it is working, do you like it?*
Sibongile:	I like it because this one here inside is all right [referring to his indoor lights], but that one outside [high-mast light] is not right. That one is not right. But it's taking a long time to change the fused globes. The municipality is doing it.
Stephanie:	*When it is shining, is it shining nicely?*
Sibongile:	Everything is good when it is working right.

Sibongile's house borders BA-Section, where every person acknowledges the high-mast light as PJS's public lighting, according to the household survey. Sibongile's front door directly faces the high-mast light, as shown on **Map 6** and in **Figure 9**. Because of the high levels of light at his house, he always noticed when the light broke. **Figure 10**, labelled *2* on the map, shows what the lighting is like at Sibongile's house. The house in the background, where a woman is walking past, is Sibongile's house.

When one high-mast light malfunctions, the entire community is left in the dark. I asked Sibongile why he said the high-mast light is "not right". He told me that when it broke, he was left in darkness. It seemed to break often and it took a long time to get fixed. I noticed the light was broken in March 2020 when we implemented the first phase of the lighting intervention. People in B-Section mentioned how happy they were to receive a solar light because the high-mast light was out of order. At the same time, a team was taking lighting measurements in PJS as part of the project. They had to redo the measurements because the light in B-Section frequently malfunctioned. They reported the broken light several times, and the City did fix it, but it broke more than once. Some City officials and technicians say that power surges due to loadshedding[2], South Africa's planned power outages, cause the lights to fuse and that is why it was defective so often.[3] With loadshedding predicted for the foreseeable future, many damages to electrical infrastructure are to be expected.

---

2   Loadshedding is a series of planned nationwide power outages to compensate for an energy backlog experienced by the country's energy utility, Eskom.
3   This was also the case with people's electricity metres, which would break due to power surges.

Map 5   Fundiswa's nighttime experience related to public lighting

Fundiswa's nighttime map,
young adult, female

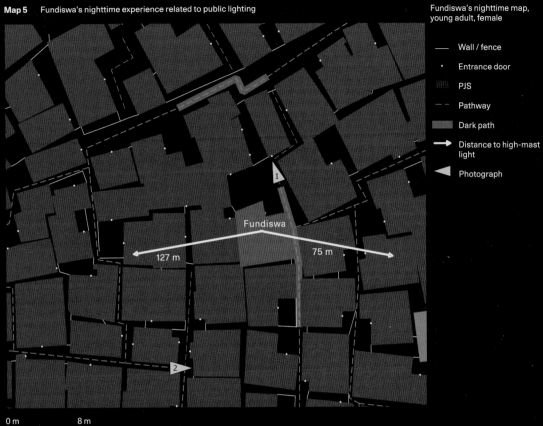

—   Wall / fence

•   Entrance door

▦   PJS

– –   Pathway

▨   Dark path

→   Distance to high-mast light

◄   Photograph

0 m   8 m

Fig 8   Fundiswa's light, lighting up the path in front of her house.
Photo position 1 on the accompanying map

Fig 7   A pathway close to Fundiswa's house, brightly lit by the two high-mast lights in PJS. Position 2 on the accompanying map

Map 6 Sibongile's nighttime experiences related to public lighting

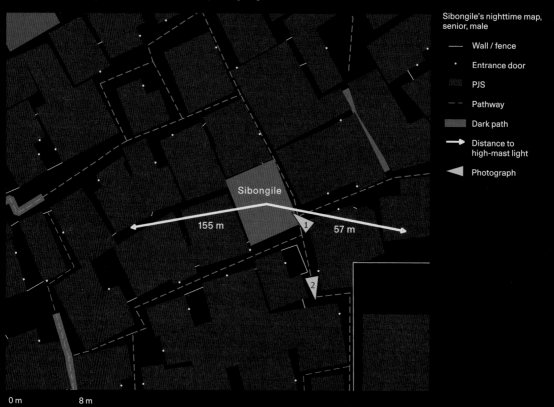

Sibongile's nighttime map,
senior, male

—— Wall / fence

· Entrance door

▦ PJS

--- Pathway

▬ Dark path

→ Distance to
high-mast light

◀ Photograph

Sibongile

155 m   1   57 m

2

0 m   8 m

Fig 9 Taken from Sibongile's front door, the high-mast light is clearly
visible, showing that Sibongile's house receives direct and bright
high-mast lighting at night. Position 1 on the accompanying map

Fig 10 Position 2 on the accompanying map shows the bright
lighting conditions in B-Section, where Sibongile lives. His house
is in the background, where the woman is walking past

Sibongile's interview highlighted the high-mast lighting maintenance and repair issues aggravated by loadshedding. (Figures 9 and 10) (Map 6)

Thuliswa

During my first sleepover in PJS in November 2018, I noticed a wall-mounted light indicated on **Map 7**, which was on at 21:47. I captured an image (Figure 11) of this light to show the improved colour rendering of the light compared with the orange colour rendering of the background's high-mast lighting. I asked for an interview to find out more about the light.

Thuliswa is an elderly woman who moved to PJS in 2001 and started selling snacks and cigarettes from her house to earn a living. She said there was no lighting in PJS in 2001 and that they only got electricity in 2009. I then asked about the high-mast light more specifically:

Stephanie:	*When you moved here, was there any public lighting?*
Thuliswa:	No, there was no electricity at that time.
Stephanie:	*No high-mast lighting?*
Thuliswa:	There was the high-mast in P-section.

Like many others, Thuliswa attributed the high-mast light as belonging to P-Section. I asked her if she liked the high-mast lighting, and her response was:

Thuliswa:	Yes, I like the light, but we need lights in PJS. It doesn't cover us all. I do like the high-mast, but it's not enough for everyone in my area; it doesn't cover us all.

Thuliswa installed her light to see the customers' faces when she served them. It attracted customers to her shop by offering a brightly lit area at night, even though she failed to mention that the high-mast lighting was not illuminating her front door enough. Her light also signalled that she was open for business, and she was always open for business. People knocked on her window at any hour, waking her up to serve them. We discussed vandalism. Thuliswa said: "*skollies* like taking the bulb", so she installed a cover on the light (Figure 12). Evidently, vandalism was an issue. I kept track of this light, and in February 2019, two months after our interview, I noticed that the light cover and bulb were missing. She told me the *skollies* stole the bulb to use it for drugs. She had not replaced the bulb for fear that they would steal it again, but that the light would still work if she bought a new bulb. I asked how her business was affected by not having a light, and she responded that it had not been affected.

Stephanie:	*And now? You used to use the light because it would help you with your shop at night; what now?*
Thuliswa:	No, it does not affect my business so much. If someone wants to buy something, we use the window to sell to them.

I gathered that selling through the window must have affected her and her customer's experience because when I returned to PJS five months later, she had upgraded her light to a spotlight with a cage around it, as shown in **Figure 13**. It was clear to me how important the light was for her business. She went through much trouble to protect it, opting also for an LED light so that *skollies* would not steal her bulb anymore.

In March 2020, when we wanted to install Thuliswa's solar light, she said that she already had a light above her door and that we could install the light on the corner of her house, as shown on **Map 7**. A few days later, we received a demand from *skollies* via word of mouth to remove it because the corner of Thuliswa's house is their business turf, and the light would negatively affect their business. On the community leaders' recommendation, we did not remove the light. In September 2020, when we repaired the faulty lights, we repaired Thuliswa's light on the corner, but when I returned in March 2021, the light was missing. (Figures 11 – 13) (Map 7)

This is not specifically related to Thuliswa but is important to note with reference to economic activity at night. When I attended a night march organised by the Social Justice Coalition in SST, a self-built community, I noticed the importance of lighting and economic activity. I documented several *spaza* shops with wall-mounted lights outside their shops, forming a little hub of activity in the darkness, as seen in **Figures 14 and 15**. The difference was not about whether the *spaza* shop had sufficient light from the high-mast light or not; it was about the atmospheric quality that the small, human-scale lights created, which supported the nighttime economic activity. The photographs below show how lighting changes the atmosphere, and how people gather around the *spaza* shops at night. (Figures 14 and 15)

These are all small and specific instances showing that high-mast lighting is not adequately serving individuals. It is precisely in these everyday lived experiences where we can make broader conclusions about the inefficiency of this form of lighting.

Map 7 Thuliswa's nighttime experiences related to public lighting

Thuliswa's nighttime map,
elderly, female

— Wall / fence

· Entrance door

— PJS

▨ Food stall

▨ *Spaza* shop

--- Pathway

▨ Dark path

→ Distance to high-
mast light

◀ Photograph

Thuliswa

98 m   159 m

0 m   8 m

Fig 11 Thuliswa's light, shining brightly into the pathway.
Position 1 on the accompanying **Map 7**

Fig 12 Thuliswa's light with a covering to protect the bulb
from theft

Fig 13 Thuliswa's new LED light, its vandal-resistant
cage protecting it from theft.

Fig 14   *Spaza* shop lighting in SST Informal Settlement

Fig 15   *Spaza* shop lighting in SST Informal Settlement

Public lighting preferences

My research methods included the use of images, virtual reality and especially household interviews, but we were still unclear what people's lighting preferences were, and furthermore, which decisions influenced their preferences. In response, my colleague Michael Walczak[4] and I conducted a study with ninety self-built community members in Khayelitsha to better understand public lighting preference. We also conducted the study with eight people in the CoCT Energy Directorate and Public Lighting Development. For details on the method itself and a critical reflection on the method, refer to Chapter 3.

Before we revealed the different public lighting solutions, we asked participants to rate eleven factors contributing to their decisions around lighting. I identified these factors from two interviews with a senior officer at the CoCT Public Lighting Development and my fieldwork in self-built communities to date. Participants had to rank the factors in order of importance, from one to five, five being very important and one not important. Although the results were not very dramatic, it was clear that people found certain factors to be more important than others when they thought about their lighting preferences. **Table 2** shows the results, ordered from the highest-scoring factor to the lowest.

According to participants, the most important factor related to the ability to see more, with 'very bright light' rating the highest. Brightness was also often mentioned during my interviews and informal

---

4   At the time, Dr. Michael Walkzak was a PhD student based in the Urban Research Incubator at the Institute of Science, Technology and Policy, ETH Zurich.

conversations throughout my fieldwork, especially in the SST pilot, where we tested the solar lights. Aphiwe, a young adult, helped install the pilot lights in SST and was happy to discuss them via WhatsApp. He remarked that lights should be very bright in the pathways of SST.

Stephanie:	*Hi Aphiwe! How did the lights work last night?*
Aphiwe:	They are working, very! The whole passage is extremely brighter now.
Stephanie:	*Do you like it? Is it too bright now?*
Aphiwe:	Yes, I like it and the passage is too bright now.
Stephanie:	*Too bright? Like there should be less light?*
Aphiwe:	[They are bright] like they should be.

Junior, a young male also living in the SST pathway where we installed pilot lights, reiterated what Aphiwe said, saying that no light is too bright in the narrow pathways of self-built communities.

Stephanie:	*We installed two of them [wall-mounted lights] on Saturday.*
Junior:	Yes. It's more bright than the one installed on my house.
Stephanie:	*Yes, definitely much brighter. Maybe too bright?*
Junior:	In these passages, there's nothing too bright. A light is a sign of relief to tell you the truth.

I asked Junior's mother which light she preferred, between streetlights and high-mast lights, and her answer indicated that she did not have a preference as long as the light was bright.

Stephanie:	*Which light do you prefer- high-mast or streetlight?*
Junior Mom:	I prefer the brightest light.

	Which factors are important to you when deciding what lighting you prefer?	Total (n=90)	Male (n=32)	Female (n=58)
1	The light makes it easier to see more clearly outside after it gets dark.	4.81	4.66	4.81
2	The light makes walking outside easier after it gets dark.	4.66	4.38	4.72
3	The light is very bright.	4.66	4.41	4.70
4	The light reduces my fear of crime.	4.59	4.34	4.64
5	The light allows me to do activities outside after dark, like socialising or selling things.	4.51	4.44	4.53
6	The light makes the outdoor space look inviting after it gets dark.	4.47	4.19	4.53
7	The light is a short distance from my house.	4.23	3.72	4.43
8	The light is difficult for a person to break.	4.22	3.91	4.31
9	The light is difficult for a person to reach.	3.56	3.22	3.66
10	The light is quick and easy to install.	3.48	2.81	3.76
11	The light takes up little space in the pathway.	2.83	2.34	3.09
	Total average	4.18	3.86	4.29

Table 2   Factors that influence people's decisions around lighting preferences, listed from most important to least important

It was clear that brightness was the most important factor residents considered when thinking about public lighting preferences. Walking at night ranked as the second most important factor that public lighting enabled, confirming that people needed to walk outside after dark and that lighting would make this easier. Whether light increased the ability to walk because it reduced fear of crime or whether it was a practical or safety aspect is not clear, but due to the high levels of fear of crime in self-built communities, I would argue that walking more easily at night is strongly linked with a reduction in fear of crime.

Malume: When this light is on, it's better.
Stephanie: *Why?*
Malume: You walk freely when it's on.

Reducing fear of crime ranked fourth. I thought it would rank first, but this result shows that people are concerned about other factors *interlinked* with fear of crime. The ability to carry out activities at night ranked fifth, which again shows a desire to be outside after dark, and lighting to reduce crime should not be the central focus of public lighting design.

Even though it did not rank very high, people felt it was important for the outdoor space to look inviting at night. This category ranked sixth, with a rating of 4.47. This ranking shows a concern with spending time outside at night. In an interview with a woman who received a pilot light in SST, she compared her pathway to that of the Southern Suburbs, a predominantly white middle-class area in Cape Town. The atmospheric quality introduced by the six pilot lights reminded her of an aspirational place like the Southern Suburbs, and she seemed to enjoy this, explaining that she was more confident outside at night now.

Surprisingly, according to the survey, the distance of the light from the person's house did not matter that much, even though this comment came up many times during my interviews, when people felt that the high-mast lighting was too far away.

Protecting the light from vandalism also ranked low. It did not matter so much to people whether the light was easy to reach (3.48) and difficult to break (4.22). The low ranking of vandalism was surprising because vandalism was raised as a significant concern during my interviews, especially in the pilot project in SST.

Stephanie: *What about the streetlights with poles?*
Anon18:   I am scared of street poles because people will vandalise them.

For residents, the lowest ranked were technical factors, in other words, how easy the light was to install and whether it took up a lot of space in the pathway. A notable point about this finding was that what the CoCT saw as the most important factors (installation and maintenance) were the least important for residents in self-built communities (Graph 4). It makes sense that CoCT officials are concerned about how to roll out and maintain public lighting effectively, but it also shows that the City is more concerned with the technocratic approaches to infrastructure than the concerns of the residents centred around daily life in self-built communities. For residents, factors related to improving daily life and the quality of the lighting were most important. (Graph 4)

An additional observation was that, on average, women rated all factors influencing lighting preference higher than men, with an average ranking of 4.29, compared with 3.86 as the average factor ranking for men. One could speculate that this indicates women feel more strongly about having public lighting than men because women feel more vulnerable outside at night. The response could also be attributed to the average age of women, at 33.88 years, against the men who were younger on average, at 24.22. Generally, older women are more apprehensive and active in voicing their concerns than young men.

Moving beyond the influencing factors mentioned above, we looked purely at which lighting people prefer from a visual perspective, as shown in **Figure 17**. Next I discuss the results of the image survey and the virtual reality survey and conclude by looking at the results as a whole. The difference between the two survey styles was that participants moved through the pathway in the virtual reality survey and could look around. The image survey showed still renders, as seen in the images to the right. (Figure 17)

Graph 5 shows that street lighting received more choices in the image survey than the VR survey (Img.=807, VR=519). High-mast lighting received more choices in the VR compared with the image survey (Img.=264, VR=445) but got the fewest choices overall out of the three lighting types, as illustrated in the two charts below. Wall-mounted lighting scored very consistently in the two surveys (Img.=622, VR=620). (Graphs 5 and 6)

The study revealed wall-mounted lighting to be the most stable choice in both VR and image surveys. The choices for streetlights and high-mast lights varied significantly between the VR survey and the image survey. In the image survey, the streetlight

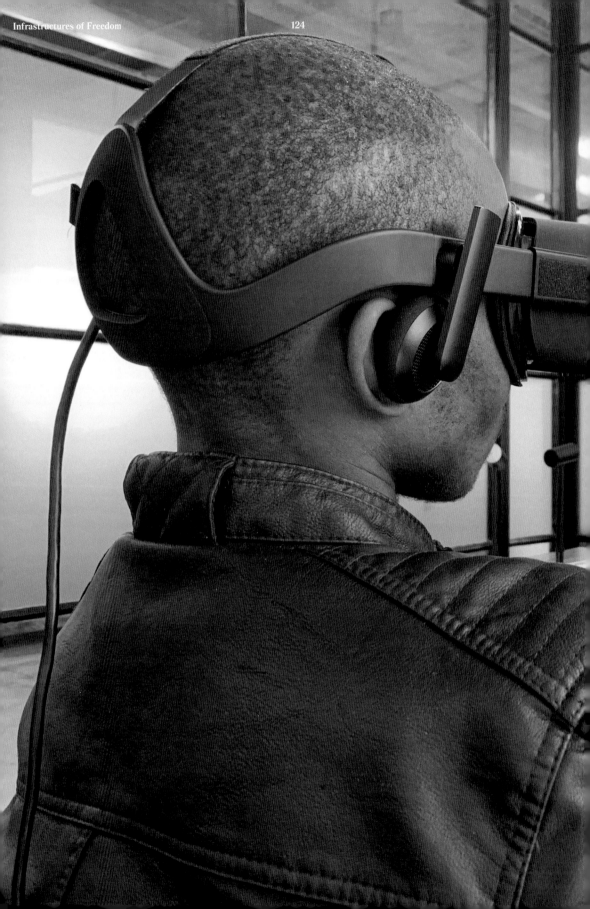

Fig 16   Participant doing the virtual reality preference study.

Which factors are important to you when deciding what lighting you prefer?

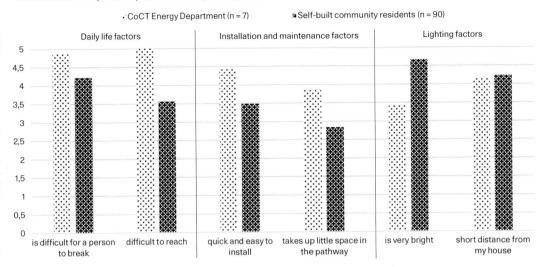

Graph 4 Ranking of factors considered when thinking about public lighting, CoCT versus residents of self-built communities

was a focal point in the image, and one could clearly see the light falling onto the pathway **(Figure 18)**. Appearing framed in the image could be why street lighting scored very high in the image survey but much lower in the virtual reality survey.

Another hypothesis for the large difference between virtual reality and image scoring for street-lights and high-mast lighting was the static viewpoint in the image survey that did not accurately portray the lighting uniformity. The uniform illumination of wall-mounted lighting resulted in more consistent choices between the virtual reality and image surveys, because no matter what the participant's viewpoint was, the lighting was shown to be evenly distributed. For streetlights and high-mast lights, the lighting uniformity was low. Participants may have seen a very bright or very dark area, depending on where their attention was in the VR and which viewpoint the image survey framed. This poor uniformity of lighting could have been the reason for more varied choices.

The colour temperature was much more subtle in the surveys, and both image and virtual reality surveys revealed no preference **(Graph 6)**. Across both VR and image surveys, the choice of colour temperatures was spread equally. Although the colour temperature is more noticeable in reality, in the survey, participants may have focused on which

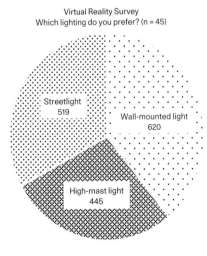

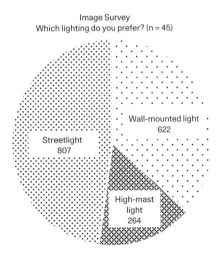

Graph 5 Number of times the different lighting solutions were chosen in the virtual reality survey

Graph 6 Number of times the different lighting solutions were chosen in the image survey

Fig 17   Lighting solutions shown in the image survey and virtual reality survey.

Wall-mounted light

Streetlight

High-mast light

Fig 18   Render of street lighting shown in the image survey

lighting they preferred (wall-mounted, street lighting or high-mast lighting), and this was the basis of their decision. When the same lighting type was presented with two different colour temperatures (Figures 19 and 20), I could tell from my observation that participants were slightly confused and suspected that the choice was a random selection.

Interestingly, while testing lighting in SST, I also tested different colour temperatures, as shown in **Figure 19**. The feedback I received was that some lights were brighter than others. While this was true, the most significant difference in the lights was the colour temperatures. The cool white lights have much better colour rendering. In other words, you can see distinctions between different colours better than with warm white light, which causes everything to look slightly yellow. A light with 600 lumens and a colour temperature of 6000 Kelvin will appear brighter than a 600-lumen light with a colour temperature of 2000 Kelvin because of the increased colour rendering. **(Figure 20) (Graph 7)**

The final step of the survey was rating the three lighting types before and after the survey to understand whether opinions changed after seeing the images compared with virtual reality. The average preference rating of streetlights was 3.47/5 before the survey and 4.22/5 after the image survey. This perception change was the most significant for all the lighting types in both the image and the VR survey. The increase in preference for street lighting after the image survey illustrated the impact an image can have on the viewer and why it can be misleading to show people images rather than virtual reality. We could say the same for high-mast lighting, which was rarely chosen in the image survey.

Although this result supported our study, it demonstrated how the image exaggerates lighting conditions. In virtual reality, participants could see that some areas were well-lit with high-mast lighting, which would account for the increase in high-mast lighting choices during the VR survey, compared to the image survey.

In the above preference study, residents in self-built communities had to choose between three public lighting solutions. From a purely visual perspective, wall-mounted lighting was the most stable choice in the preference study. This can be attributed to the uniform lighting conditions achieved with wall-mounted lighting. People also liked street lighting, while high-mast lighting scored the lowest. Nonetheless, public lighting preferences are not straightforward, and people find certain factors more important than others when thinking about lighting. Residents in self-built communities felt that a very bright light, resulting in increased ability to see, was the most important lighting factor. The CoCT, on the other hand, were more concerned about implementation and maintenance factors.

Takeaways

This empirical chapter explored the lived reality of high-mast lighting in self-built communities at two scales—beginning with a neighbourhood level and ending with individual perspectives and experiences of public lighting, including understanding more about public lighting preferences. When combining these levels, a holistic view of public lighting in self-built communities is understood. Some conclusive themes are given below.

Uniformity and dark pathways

Many interviewees related darkness to narrow pathways and did not consider high-mast lighting's uniformity. When I asked people how lighting could be improved, a considered solution was that the paths should be widened or more high-mast lights should be added like Mrs Filifili mentions below:

> The lighting situation could be better if we were to get proper roads in these pathways. If you look at other houses [that] have proper roads on the side, we are just in need of proper roads. Even the children would be safe.

Widening roads would work to an extent because high-mast lighting casts dark shadows, and wider

Colour temperature choice across both surveys (n = 90)

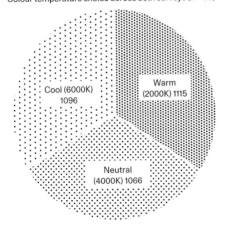

Cool (6000K) 1096

Warm (2000K) 1115

Neutral (4000K) 1066

Graph 7   Number of times the different colour temperatures were chosen in the virtual reality and image survey

Fig 19 Image survey showing wall-mounted lighting with different colour temperatures

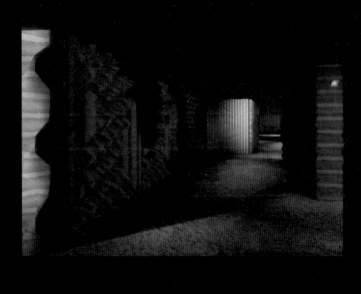

Fig 20 Different colour temperatures used in the preference study

roads would mean fewer shadows. The narrower the pathway, the more shadow is cast on the pathway. That said, widening the pathways of more than 600 self-built communities is an implausible solution. It only treats the symptom of a bad lighting solution rather than finding a more suitable one.

Periphery, distance and ownership

High-mast lights are often located on the periphery of self-built communities due to zoning restrictions and density. This light position results in poor lighting conditions and inefficient use of the light, compared with centrally located lighting. Peripheral lighting locations leave many residents in self-built communities feeling that the lighting is too far away from their house. This is a frequently repeated comment. This distance and the fact that lights are located on land other than that of the community causes a missing sense of ownership of the light, adds to feelings of neglect and to notions that the government is not providing for their community specifically.

Different scales of lighting

People had different opinions on high-mast lighting, depending on their situations or the different scales they were considering. People tended to consider public lighting at neighbourhood and the household level. They expressed both happiness and dissatisfaction with high-mast lighting. They might use a well-lit pathway, which made them happy, but on the other hand, they may have total darkness at their front door.

Resilience and centralised infrastructure

When I first started my research on public lighting, people were not overly opinionated about the topic. However, a wave of loadshedding hit South Africa while research was underway, and suddenly everyone was concerned about light. When asked how loadshedding affected people, interviewees complained that it was unpredictable when the lights would go off—they may be out, going to the shops or toilets when loadshedding started and would be left in total darkness, where they felt that "anything could happen". Loadshedding exacerbated grid-dependent and centralised infrastructure issues—if one light broke, an entire community would be left in the dark. Centralised infrastructure also caused maintenance issues for the City. Due to the infrastructure's size, the City needed to locate it in easily accessible areas, which was often not the most efficient position in terms of illuminating the self-built community.

Supporting nighttime activities

Thuliswa taught me that lighting her shop at night was important beyond providing light to see her customers. Light invited customers, signalling a trading space, which was open and ready to serve. This was evident throughout my visits to self-built communities at night, where I noticed that all shops had small lights or even large, sophisticated lights outside their shops. While high-mast lighting provides general lighting for a neighbourhood, human-scaled lighting supports nighttime activities, such as night shops, *shebeens* or socialising outside a house.

Public lighting policy needs to address these conclusive themes at a technical and a social level, specifically for self-built communities, to produce resilient public lighting infrastructure that addresses the needs of people and specific spatial conditions found in those communities. By investigating everyday experiences of high-mast lighting, we can conclude that this lighting does not meet the nighttime needs of self-built communities.

The lived insufficiency of high-mast lights

Understanding how public lighting policy materialises on the ground and in people's minds is an important component of infrastructure, often overlooked by governments. Public lighting policies have a material and perceptive representation that affects people in a variety of ways. The great distance from a high-mast light, in a sense, is manifested in the minds and everyday interaction of residents in self-built communities. Why would you value and take care of something that is 170 metres away from your house and not located in the neighbourhood where you reside? A sense of ownership is important to the maintenance and acceptance of infrastructure, especially in self-built communities. People often do not feel a sense of ownership over centralised infrastructure, and fewer people watch over and report problems with the infrastructure. The technical difficulties relating to high-mast lighting, such as poor lighting uniformity, also reflect on the ground and in people's opinions, where many people both like and dislike high-mast lighting.

How individuals think about, feel and experience public lighting is nuanced, and so are their public lighting preferences. Through my fieldwork, I realised that people did not think much about high-mast lighting. High-mast lighting was forty metres above their houses and similarly distant in their minds. When asked about other infrastructure, like taps and toilets, people had more opinions, because of their daily, tangible interaction with these necessities, compared with lighting. After comparing interviews and observations, I noticed some recurring themes emerging around high-mast lighting. Although people did not speak directly about high-mast lighting's insufficiency, they experienced it in their everynight lives as the *lived insufficiency* of high-mast lighting. The next chapter investigates darkness as the materialisation of high-mast lighting's insufficiency and looks at how darkness impacts everynight life in self-built communities.

Trapped by Darkness

Chapter 5

Darkness is part of the reality of everynight life in self-built communities in Khayelitsha, whether as the lived insufficiency of high-mast lighting or experienced as being forgotten by the state. What does it mean to confront darkness and the associated practices, relations and perceptions in everynight life? When I asked people about their life at night, other issues would take centre stage, and I never got the clear answers that I was hoping for. Participants were overwhelmed with daily struggles of access to sanitation, commuting to work, social conflicts such as drug abuse and violence, to name a few.

> I have never heard of a place as extreme as Marikana, and it made me realise how insignificant the questions of light were to the interviewees because they were so caught up in everyday stories of trauma that thinking about lighting almost seemed arbitrary. (fieldnotes, November 2018)

Yet, when further investigating the scope of these topics, I realised that most daily struggles participants raised were temporal and that these struggles were often amplified at nighttime. I wanted to understand how daily struggles and perceptions related to nighttime, darkness and public life. For example, interviewees often raised concerns over undignified living conditions due to inadequate access to sanitation, as well as long daily commutes. When probed further, in both of these issues, darkness emerged as a contributor to feelings of fear and lack of dignity. When I considered daily struggles as interrelated and temporal, a holistic picture of everynight life where darkness plays a key role in self-built communities began to emerge.

Chapter summary: This chapter on daily life at night—what I specifically refer to as everynight life—suggests that darkness complicates the task of providing inclusive, safe, resilient and sustainable access to urban life at night. In Khayelitsha's self-built communities, everynight life is often associated with fear and insecurity, and yet there is remarkably little research on life at night and the impact of darkness in those communities. The chapter moves between scales and self-built communities within Khayelitsha. While doing fieldwork between 2018 and 2021, I engaged with numerous residents at various depths using a mixed methods approach. Most of my empirical research is based on my primary case study—PJS Informal Settlement. I also engaged significantly with residents from Marikana and SST. In this chapter specifically, the mixture of visual data plays an essential role in allowing the reader, and me as a researcher, to gain a better understanding of the lived realities and consequences of darkness in self-built communities. For this reason, this chapter features rich visual and often emotive content produced by residents of self-built communities and by me during my immersion in PJS Informal Settlement.

Social dynamics at night

Darkness changes the way people relate to others. It creates strangers and uncertainty—people are either trusted or feared. Many different social dynamics develop at night, often related to darkness. How you greet someone, which areas you avoid to evade certain groups, and who you find outside at night are all influenced by darkness. This section discusses nighttime, everynight life and how darkness influences life socially. It looks at who ventures out at night, the nature and importance of social relations, and the type of social conflicts that happen at night. The section concludes by looking at the spatial and temporal elements associated with the fear of crime and violence in self-built communities.

Characters of the night

Various groups venture out at night in self-built communities, including groups of children, young adults, men, so-called "irresponsible" people and *skollies* (petty criminals). During my immersive fieldwork in PJS, I would assess the safety of a place based on which characters were there. I gauged my safety based on how many children were around at night. The presence of children always made PJS feel safe, even after dark. Adults did not spend much time outside at night, and if they did, it was hardly to socialise but to run a necessary errand. After sunset, children continue to play outside and gather in public spaces. There were children at the *spaza* shops throughout the day until the shops closed at 22:00, and they would also meet at the public open space close to the toilets. Children generally did not spend time in the narrow pathways, especially not at night, perhaps because they were much darker, not as safe, and too small to play in.

The youth in PJS wanted to, or did, spend time outside at night more than older generations. When I asked older interviewees whether they spent time outside at night, they mostly said "never" or referred the question to younger people in the room. Younger people spoke of being the "new generation" (the post-apartheid generation), and with this, they had a stronger sense of freedom and need for socialising at night. However, they felt that their freedom was being restricted by "gangsters" outside at night as described by a young male participant:

Anonymous: You need to walk free at night. We are the new generation, we love to walk at night, enjoy ourselves, go to parties at night with our friends or a family party but now we can't go because out there are gangsters. (male, teen, youth workshop, PJS)

From this and other similar comments in my interviews, one can speculate that cultural and historical contexts influence whether people spend time outside at night. Older people, with embedded memories of night curfews, police brutality and raids, as expressed below by anti-apartheid musician Rodger Lucey, do not want to spend time outside at night. Older people have never spent time outside at night, and more deeply ingrained habits are more challenging to change.

Rodger Lucey: There are cops on every corner
And they know what they don't like
And if you're it then you know
That the streets no place for you at
night. (Lyrics from Lungile Thabalza—
Rodger Lucey, protest singer-songwriter, 1979)

Men spent much more time outside at night, whether to access basic services or socialise, especially around *shebeens*. The Sakikamva Youth Group raised women's safety as a major concern in the context of nighttime experiences. They felt women were discriminated against at night because nighttime was a masculine space, where women were vulnerable and unwelcome. Some interviewees also felt that women should not be outdoors at night. During a spontaneous discussion with a young male living in C-Section, Khayelitsha, he said that any woman who hangs about outside at night is promiscuous. He felt that respectable women belonged inside at night. Women also believed the same, as mentioned by a young female in Sakikamva Youth Group, who felt that women get raped at night because they are outside and drunk.

Anonymous: At night the most people get hurt or raped because they got drunk.
(female, teen, youth workshop, PJS)

Many people stereotyped those outside "late" at night (after 21:00). With the exception of people walking to and from work, community members considered people outside at night irresponsible or suspected of taking part in some illegal activity. Participants spoke about drunks being out at night and perceived them as targets for crime. Generally, people feared two groups, *skollies* (also "*amapara-para*") and gangsters. When I asked Sbu, a young male living in PJS, what the distinction was, he responded:

Sbu: Criminals (gangsters) mainly do robberies only, and *amapara-paras* smoke

any kind of drug they can get. (male, young adult, participatory photo interview, PJS)

When a woman from Marikana described the young *skollies* and the respect they demanded, she seemed almost surprised by her own words.

Monica: Yoh! They are very small, we are talking about 14-year-olds who want you to call them Bhuti (brother), they want you to be afraid of them. (female, adult, participatory photo interview, Marikana)

Skollies are mostly young—between twelve and eighteen years old. They are especially active at night and not scared of anyone. They are generally drug addicts who harass and often mug people in dark pathways at night. They are also known for stealing any easily accessible items, such as laundry left outside. According to interviewees, *skollies* demand respect, despite their youth. People often described *skollies* as pathetic, and though they can be very dangerous, people do not respect them in any way as elderly Mrs Tsitsi from Marikana describes below:

Mrs Tsitsi: And if you suspect anything and go and check outside, they will call you out and say, "why you being nosy" or "come here". If you approach one of them, they will ask you why are you looking at them, you must not look them in the eye, or they will find that disrespectful, and these *skollies*, they are very young about twelve, thirteen, fourteen years. (female, elderly, participatory photo interview, Marikana)

Gangsters are positioned on a higher rung and usually carry guns. They are often drug dealers and known to earn their income from organised crime, which involves more serious crimes such as stealing cars and murdering people. Gangsters often live in formal areas and view the self-built community as their hiding place or "forest" for their crimes. While people are afraid of gangsters, they know that if they do not interfere in their business, they would be safer than around *skollies*, who are thought to be more dangerous because of their drug addiction.

Nighttime relations and fear of the dark

When people spoke about nighttime, they mostly told fear-filled stories of their friends or other people who had experienced crime and violence at night. With violence and substance abuse emerging as overpowering themes, I questioned whether darkness contributed to these perceptions. In other words, whether people referred to darkness when they spoke about nighttime and whether darkness actually exacerbated social issues rather than nighttime. In changing perspective from nighttime to darkness, a major fear of darkness often emerged. When interviewees mentioned darkness, this was often in the context of a story about crime, violence and substance abuse. As part of his participatory photo interview, Khayelethu, an adult male living in Marikana, captured an image to show that Marikana had no formal access to electricity, and candlelight posed a considerable risk of shack fires. His image of a dark, candle-lit house was, to my surprise, the one that got the most attention during a keywording exercise with workshop participants. This photograph received many comments and endorsements, mainly around danger and fear of darkness. A specific comment on criminals robbing and raping in darkness was endorsed nine times (Table 1).

These anecdotes often reinforced people's fear of nighttime. To understand whether fear increased at night, we asked respondents how safe they felt in

PJS at night compared with during the day. Although many participants answered that they never felt safe in PJS, there was a definite increase in fear at nighttime compared with daytime, as shown in **Graph 1**.

The fear of social conflict at night works at two levels—the fear of these conflicts occurring, as discussed above, and actual incidents. We reviewed actual incidents of violent crime—robbery, vandalism and physical attack—in PJS by asking respondents whether they or anyone in their household had experienced violent crime in the last twelve months. Violent crime is a legitimate fear in PJS (Graph 2)— one-quarter of respondents reported a robbery in the last twelve months. These actual incidents of violent crime drastically perpetuate fear of social conflict, especially in a community where people have strong social relations. News of an incident of social conflict is often widely discussed, inciting more fear.

To understand the types of social conflict people feared would affect them most, whether personally or a household member, we asked respondents to rate the following social conflict risks: drug addiction, alcohol addiction, street mugging and

	Comment	Endorsements
1	In darkness, criminals take advantage of people, like robbing and raping them. (9)	········· (9)
2	It's not safe the *skollies* mug people. (1)	• (1)
3	Unsafe. (3)	··· (3)
4	Darkness, no lights, unsafe. (1)	• (1)
5	Darkness. (4)	···· (4)
6	Danger.	
7	It is terrible when it gets dark. (3)	··· (3)
8	The *skollies* mug us because it is dark. (5)	····· (5)
9	Unsafe. (4)	···· (4)

Table 1 Nighttime workshop comments and endorsements of a photo from the participatory photo interview (male, adult, Marikana)

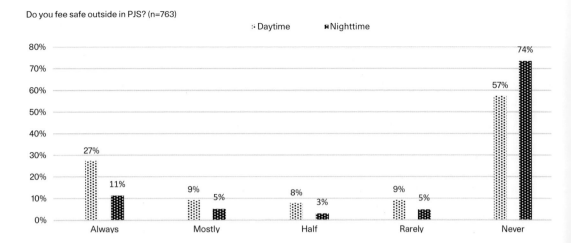

Graph 1 Household survey question asking whether respondents felt safe outside at night versus at daytime in PJS

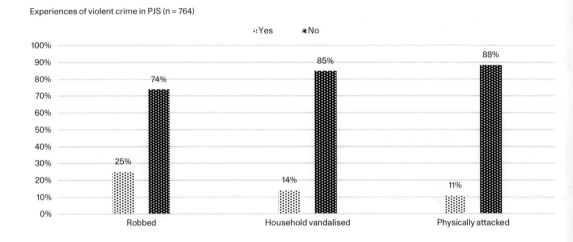

Graph 2 Survey question asking respondents what type of violent crime they had experienced in PJS in the last twelve months

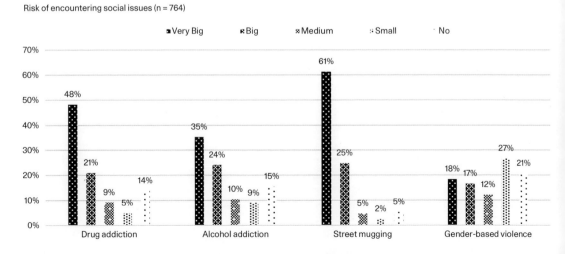

Graph 3 Survey question asking respondents what social issues they are most at risk of encountering in PJS

gender-based violence. The data showed that respondents were very fearful of drug and alcohol addiction as well as street muggings (Graph 3). The risk of gender-based violence is imprecise due to low reporting globally, and within the South African context, gender-based violence is also not widely reported (Lange and Young, 2019). Contrary to this, violence and especially gender-based violence was persistently raised during my qualitative work.

Street mugging was mentioned most frequently in workshops and interviews and being mugged was almost normalised when spoken about. In our survey, most respondents stated that street mugging was a very high risk (sixty-one per cent) or a high risk (twenty-five per cent) in PJS. A quite significant and important point was that they did not get physically attacked in the process.

Darkness played a role in many of these feared social conflicts, and when we spoke about nighttime, interviewees often focused conversations around matters such as substance abuse, crime and violence, especially gender-based violence. When Mveliso, a youth leader in PJS, spoke about nighttime experiences in PJS, he concluded that nighttime in self-built communities was all about violence.

Mveliso: It's all about the violence. Night is about violence. (male, young adult, youth workshop, PJS)

Violence tended to occur at night for two main reasons. Firstly, people drank alcohol at night, which often resulted in violent behaviour; and secondly, violence — specifically gender-based violence, such as rape — happened in the veil of darkness.

Comment: Darkness is very dangerous, for children are being raped in places which are dark. (photograph comment, nighttime workshop)

People often spoke about the abuse of women and children in dark pathways and toilets. A workshop participant explicitly said, "stop women abuse in the dark". Participants continuously related darkness to rape, as if rapists used darkness to stay anonymous and not get caught. Thabisa, a PJS leader, mentioned that a man tried to rape her when breaking into her house at night, but she did not recognise his face because it was too dark. Months later, she recognised his voice and confronted him, with the help of her cousins. Other accounts of gender-based violence occurred in the dark pathways and most often inside or around shared darkened sanitation, which I discuss later in this chapter.

A male youth participant expressed his concern about darkness as a space where gender-based violence happens. He expressed it in a way that suggested darkness was used to hide the act and identity of the perpetrator:

Anonymous: Our parents, even females, youngsters, get raped by our closest friends and even strangers in darkness. (male, young adult, youth workshop, PJS)

Alcohol abuse, which has become a major public health issue in South Africa, is another major social issue related to nighttime and darkness. Among those who consume alcohol, 70.8% of men and 33.7% of women, engage in heavy episodic drinking (World Health Organization, 2018). Alcohol consumption happens mainly at night after work, and interviewees and workshop participants often referenced intoxicated people when considering nighttime. Those who drank too much were seen as irresponsible and "walked freely" in dark pathways, becoming victims of crime. An elderly woman, Mrs Filifili, expressed fear of her neighbours, associating their drinking and suspected criminal activities to darkness:

Mrs Filifili: These are my neighbours, and they like to drink until 10 or 11 at night. This house is not safe ... there are criminal activities that like to happen by that house, and it's very dark behind that house at night. (female, elderly, participatory photo interview, PJS)

Mihali, a young adult in PJS, also expressed his views on his peers drinking alcohol, saying their consumption was against his values and resulted in problematic behaviour at night.

Mihali: Many peoples' values are to have some fun in the middle of the night and get drunk and cause trouble. Some of them don't have time for their school, all their time they give to booze. (male, young adult, youth workshop, PJS)

Over and above nighttime being related to drinking, darkness specifically reminded many of drug addicts or drug dealers using darkness to conceal their habits or drug dealing. Owam, a boy living in Marikana, showed me his photo of an open field that filled up with drug addicts after dark.

Stephanie: *How is this place when it is dark?*
Owam: It becomes full of drug addicts because there is a man who has a house that

sells drugs near there. There is a pathway that leads to his house. **(male, child, participatory photo interview, Marikana)**

During her participatory photo interview, Lona, another child participant, took me to all the pathways frequented by drug addicts and drug dealers in PJS. She is only twelve, but Lona was very preoccupied with and fearful of drug-related activities, and most of her photos were about drug dealers and drug addicts. In her photos and explanations, the "drug spaces" related strongly to darkness and not to nighttime.

Lona: This place needs light because there are drug dealers that operate there because it is dark. **(female, child, participatory photo interview, PJS)**

Monica also spoke about drug addicts in her photo interview based in Marikana, and she related drug use to theft, extreme violence and murder:

Stephanie: *Did they* (skollies) *steal those cables?*
Monica: Yes, and then they take them to the scrapyard, get money from there, go and buy drugs, come back and kill us. **(female, adult, participatory photo interview, Marikana)**

Darkness supports anonymity, a vital component of social conflict, which contributes to fear and exacerbates social conflict at night. Building strong social relationships and trust plays an important role in coping with nighttime fear in self-built communities.

Relationships are built and practised in different ways, sometimes to avoid certain people and other times to seek out people who make you feel safe. I regularly experienced neighbourliness and familiarity during my fieldwork in PJS, where it felt almost mandatory to greet passers-by and neighbours. This feeling of familiarity offered a powerful sense of security. People even greeted others through the walls of the house as they passed by. Mrs Filifili, an elderly female, mentioned that she wasn't afraid to take photos for the photo interview because the people were familiar:

Stephanie: *Were you scared of taking these photos [at night]?*
Mrs Filifili: No, I was not scared because I know this area very well. It is only when you are not so familiar with a place, then it gets challenging because you don't feel safe. Here I am safe cause I know my neighbours. **(female, elderly, participatory photo interview, PJS)**

Mr Fukazi, an elderly man in RR-Section, attributed his survival to knowing people there.

Mr Fukazi: I have survived because the people know me. It is a really dangerous place. **(male, elderly, participatory photo interview, RR)**

Many mentioned that they checked on friends or family members to ensure that they arrived safely at their destination when they ventured out at night. Social relations also determine which pathways are

You see this passage here; this is where my friend was murdered; she died here in May (2018). She was walking here, and then the *skollies* told her to move out of the way, and then they shot her in her head, they said to her "get out of our way you are disturbing us", and then they shot her.

Table 2 In this photo, Monica describes the fear of making eye contact with the wrong people in Marikana (female, adult, Marikana)

used and avoided when going out at night, as described later in this chapter. Interviewees also mentioned strategies to determine whether they knew someone or could trust them, such as observing subtleties in someone's stride, whether they make eye contact or greet you. I also used these indicators when walking through PJS. At times I would greet a group, and the subtleties within their response made it clear they were not from PJS and that I should approach with caution. Making eye contact with people is a way of acknowledging that they pose no threat and are not *skollies*. However, if you make eye contact with the wrong people, it could be dangerous. Monica's interview brought home this point. Her photo in **Table 2** tells the story of losing a friend because the friend made eye contact with the wrong people. Mrs Tsitsi also spoke about how the *skollies* stared into your eyes as an intimidation tactic, which she tried to avoid.

Stephanie: *How do you know if someone is a* skollie?
Mrs Tsisti: If you are suspecting someone, just walk looking down because they look directly into your eyes to scare you. (female, elderly, participatory photo interview, Marikana)

Skollies rely on anonymity when robbing people. Making eye contact means you could recognise them. *Skollies* generally move to other areas to rob people rather than robbing their community. This seems to be a motif for anti-social behaviour. Being anonymous helps perpetrators of crime and violence avoid being caught or reported to the police or shamed by the community. Recognising whether someone is from your community or not offers security to residents, as Mr Fata explains. For him, knowing people offered more security than light did.

Mr Fata: I usually see other *skollies* from other sections that come this side to rob us. They usually swop around. The *skollies* from PJS would usually go to K-Section to rob and K-Section would usually come this side to rob us. I feel safer at that darker place on the other side compared to this place where there's light because there they know me. (male, elderly, participatory photo interview, PJS)

In PJS, the local *skollies* loitered around by day and made themselves quite visible on prominent corners and at *spaza* shops. People try to get to know the *skollies*, because making yourself known to them contributes to a sense of safety, even if only perceived. I also made an effort to win them over when I strategically asked them to help me change my car tyre. *Skollies*, in a sense, are also the protectors of their communities because their dangerous activities in other communities are well-known, and their "dangerous" reputation protects those who are close to them. Mrs Tsitsi used this technique during her photo interview, where she got to know the *skollies*, and they even agreed not to harm her if she did not get in their way.

Stephanie: *What I would like to know is how this task helped you?*
Mrs Tsitsi: As much as it was challenging taking these images because I was always trying to find a time where the *skollies* were not around, I learnt different ways of getting myself out of potential trouble, even though I was trying to do my task. Sometimes the *skollies* would ask me why I am walking around, while I am trying to do my task. I would just say I am "stretching my legs" or "I am going to check on my friends." Now that I have built that courage to talk to them every now and then, we have some sort of relationship; they assured me that I am free to walk around and that I am safe when I want to go out. There was a space that they usually go to and hang out at, but I could not risk it. (female, elderly, participatory photo interview, Marikana)

Social relations are an important component, providing a sense of safety at night. Many people expressed the insecurity they felt when they could not recognise people in the dark—recognising people related to knowing whether you can trust the person or not; even though some, like teen Silisizwe, said that they do not trust anyone at night.

Silisizwe: It's nighttime, we aren't safe anymore, there are few people on the street, and I don't trust any of them, even when I know them. (female, teen, youth workshop, PJS)

However, darkness makes it virtually impossible to judge subtle social cues and understand whether someone is trustworthy or not. As Mr Fata explained before, recognising whether you know and trust someone is almost impossible in the veil of darkness.

Map 1 Map of feelings of insecurity and fear in PJS

Map of insecurity and fear in PJS

- Unsafe (according to interviews)
- Corners where *skollies* hang out
- Narrow pathway
- Toilets
- *Spaza* shop
- *Shebeen*

0 m   100 m

Mr Fata: Yes, it's dark, you can't even tell if it's the *skollies* from PJS or from the other section. It's hard to recognise them.
(male, elderly, participatory photo interview, PJS)

Fearful spaces, fearful times

Darkness and fear of social conflict reflect both spatially and temporally. Some spaces are darker at night and attract *skollies*, while temporal aspects and the period of darkness also influence people's behaviour. People associated their fear of crime with specific spaces in self-built communities. The photo interviews helped in understanding fear spatially. Places mentioned were *spaza* shops and *shebeens*, narrow pathways, open spaces, corners, dense places (relating to narrow pathways) and public toilets.

Map 1 visualises those spaces, along with excerpts from interviews with people talking about places associated with crime and violence.

People commented on fearing *shebeens* and their immediate vicinity because intoxication tends to fuel fights and gender-based violence. *Skollies* hang around *shebeens* and target less vigilant intoxicated people who likely have money on them to buy alcohol. Thembeka, a senior female, expressed her feelings about the stress of living next to a *shebeen* in PJS:

Thembeka: I'm not getting happy because sometimes I used to get the people with the drugs; I don't even know if they are coming from the *smokkel huis* (*shebeen*), or they are just coming or rob them, you see? I don't understand, but it's not nice to stay close to the *shebeen*. (female, adult, household interview, PJS)

Although only a child, Owam spoke about the level of violence outside a local *shebeen*, which eventually led to its closure (Table 3).

Skollies also prefer to loiter around *spaza* shops, sometimes asking for money or as a strategy to identify people carrying valuable items. Interviewees talked about these stores related to *skollies*, although less fear was expressed in terms of *spaza* shops, likely because of numerous passers-by on the streets around the shops.

MamQ: The Somalian shops [*spaza* shops] are next to the *shebeens* and are the main targets for the *skollies*.
(female, adult, nighttime workshop, RR-Section)

Sbu: Normally you would find *amapara-para* [*skollies*] standing or loitering around the shops, but when the shops are closed, they also leave. (male, young adult, participatory photo interview, PJS)

During the first round of participatory interviews, it became clear that people feared large, peripheral open spaces in self-built communities. Several participants captured images of open fields and described these spaces as dangerous. This is evident

This site next to this house, there was a *shebeen* where people got stabbed and killed. The owner of the place even closed the place because a lot of people there used to fight, get stabbed and killed.

Table 3 In this photo, Owam describes the violence taking place around *shebeens* in his neighbourhood, Marikana (male, child, Marikana)

Table 4 In this photo, Owam describes his fear of open, peripheral spaces in Marikana. Many workshop participants related to this fear (male, child, Marikana)

Owam: This is also a place where dirty things get dumped. On this grass there are holes that are dug. They use these holes to throw away rubbish and bury dead dogs. People also complain about this place because there are houses nearby and it really smells.

Stephanie: How is this place when it is dark?

Owam: It becomes full of drug addicts because there is a man who has a house that sells drugs near there. There is a pathway that leads to his house.

	Keywording comment	Endorsements
1	It's these kinds of public spaces that give an opportunity to criminals to kill people and dump them there.	•• (2)
2	This area is very dangerous.	•• (2)
3	This place is close to the road, meaning people who are using public transport are unsafe when passing through, whether it's during the day or night.	••• (3)
4	Dark	•• (2)

We walk on this grass and go sit by the crèche and have our meetings, and yet in this very same place, a lot of people have lost their lives. This area is where people should be passing freely through to get to their public transport when they go to work, but this place is so unsafe that people don't walk there or are afraid of crossing cause it's so unsafe because people get killed at any time of the day. This route is from Lower into Marikana.

Table 5 Monica's photo of an open space she fears in Marikana (female, adult, Marikana)

Table 6   In this photo, Monica describes her fear of narrow pathways in Marikana, and many workshop participants confirmed this fear (female, adult, Marikana)

If you look at this image, here is the passage, my house is behind this one, it's that orange one, and here we have the road we can't walk here at night, it's very unsafe. (Monica, female, adult, participatory photo interview, Marikana)

	Keywording comment	Endorsements
1	This shows how unsafe we are at night, anything can happen, and it would be difficult to run from criminals because of the passage you have to pass through when running	•••• (4)
2	Our kids are being finished by these *skollies*	•• (2)
3	We live a terrible life because of these *skollies*. We get mugged in the dark by these *skollies*	••••••••••• (12)
4	It's challenging living here. When you leave the house, there is a possibility of meeting a *skollies* on one of the pathways	•••••••• (8)
5	Fear of darkness on pathway	••(2)

in Owam's explanation of his photograph in **Table 4** and Monica's in **Table 5**. Workshop participants who reviewed Owam's image also associated it with danger and social conflict, as shown in the table.

The exact opposite also scared people, where dense environments and narrow pathways were associated with a risk of being trapped and not visible to the public if in danger.

Anoxolo: If you take a look at this area, Marikana is a squeezed [dense] community that if one were to get mugged, they would not be able to run. **(female, child, participatory photo interview, Marikana)**

Interviewees believed that *skollies* targeted narrow pathways as strategic spaces to rob people. Narrow pathways were tricky to navigate, and many people complained about not knowing who would be around the next corner. Monica's image in Marikana, in **Table 6** shows how intimidating it can be to walk down the narrow pathways in self-built communities.

PJS has extremely narrow pathways. Sibongile, a senior male, describes PJS as a "forest" where people hide and where the police cannot enter.

Sibongile: When the guys rob you there in the [formal] road, they are just coming here [PJS] like in a forest; you can't see anything here, you go up and down, up and down, because the houses, the other one is here, the other one is here, you can't see anything. **(male, senior, household interview, PJS)**

Nombulelo describes below how density and narrow pathways also relate to a darker environment, where high-mast lighting casts shadows in the pathways. These shadows fuel fears among pedestrians that someone may be lurking in the darkness.

Nombulelo: These are the houses that stand very close to the pathways; it's very cramped, and it gets very dark here at night. **(female, adult, participatory photo interview, PJS)**

The most dangerous space in self-built communities were almost always the shared public toilets, especially at night. When interviewees viewed

Fig 1   Sketch map of PJS showing *skollies* on the corner, annotated with "The Rhanavithi Gang where you won't find peace (they are killers)" (male, teen, youth workshop, PJS)

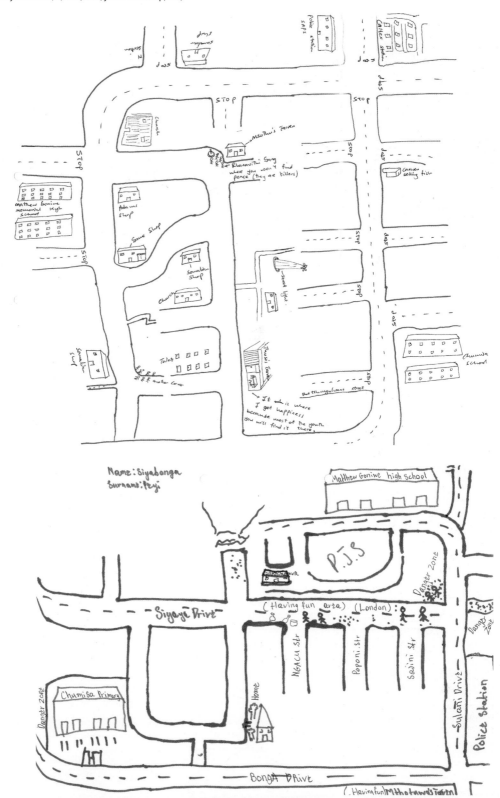

Fig 2   Sketch map of PJS showing *skollies* on the corner (male, young adult, youth workshop, PJS)

photographs of toilets or were asked whether they use shared toilets at night, they often told stories of violence, involving rape and murder.

MamQ: And at night it is dark. They either get robbed, raped or killed at these toilets. (female, adult, nighttime workshop, RR-Section)

Mr Fata: I took an image of these toilets here. This area is dangerous; it is also close to the shops, and people like killing each other here. (male, elderly, household interview, PJS)

Many also mentioned that skollies gathered around toilets, often smoking drugs there.

Sibongile: You find them (skollies) in specific places, near the toilets, not the whole of PJS. (male, senior, household interview, PJS)

Local skollies tend to loiter on neighbourhood corners. However, people do not fear these corners as skollies tend to move to other self-built communities to rob people. Instead, people are very aware of other locations where local skollies hang around and approach these with caution. Yandisa explained that the men who frequent the corner in PJS actually protect the community.

Yandisa: Those who sit around the corner actually look out for those who live around here. (male, child, participatory photo interview, PJS)

During the theatre workshop, participants indicated via their sketch maps that dangerous skollies hung about on corners in PJS—as shown in Figures 1 and 2. For them, the danger was more about being bullied and less about getting robbed.

Beyond the spatial elements of fear, people referred to safety as temporal. This temporality varied between seasons, months, weeks and times of the day, mostly related to when it was darker and when people were likely to have more money and become targets. When we tested lights in SST Informal Settlement, Junior, one of the household members who helped install and monitor lights, told me that we would see the lights' real impact when crime worsens in the winter months.

Junior: But I honestly think we shall judge the [wall-mounted] light during winter when the sun goes down early and rise late, and basically that's when crime in these pathways escalates. (male, young adult, WhatsApp chat, SST)

PJS community leaders Thabisa and Nontando spoke fondly of the summer months. They were confident that crime data at the police station would reflect their hypothesis, which was that crime was higher in winter.

Thabisa: If we could go to the police station and ask when is the crime starting, I think there's more crime during the wintertime in Khayelitsha because of the weather. On rainy days people hide in dark places so that they can rob people, and mug them, and murder them. (female, adult, interview, PJS)

Although increased discontent in self-built communities coincides with the winter season in Cape Town (Lancaster, 2018), violent crime statistics actually decrease in winter (Breetzke and Cohn, 2012). This decrease in incidents could be because people spend less time outside, and perpetrators have fewer opportunities than in summer, even though there are more eyes on the street then (Jacobs, 1992). It is much darker during peak pedestrian traffic in winter. This darkness could increase the fear of crime and could be the reason for Thabisa's hypothesis.

Based on my own experiences in PJS, I considered whether fear of crime increased over winter. During one sleepover in summer, I woke up at 05:00, hoping it would still be dark outside for my observations, but it was already light. The streets were quiet, but people were slowly waking up. I observed them meeting to walk to work together, while others were emptying their night pails. Dogs were also up earlier than in the winter and came to greet me. These dogs often accompanied me throughout my observations, offering a sense of security. By 06:00, activities increased rapidly, with commuters almost always travelling in groups. By 07:00 it felt like midday, with the whole of PJS buzzing with activity. During long summer evenings, front doors are open, children play outside until after sunset (around 20:30), and people gather outside, talking to one another, even after it gets dark.

My sleepover in the winter was very different. I woke up at what I thought was the middle of the night, but it was 07:00 in the morning, and Sindi, my host, was leaving for work. When I asked how she would get to the bus stop in the dark, she said she usually walks with people, but because it is Saturday and others are not working, she would "run through the passages" all by herself. Outside, at 07:50, it was only five degrees Celsius, and the sun was just rising. There was very little movement, and the few commuters were walking fast through the foggy pathways. During winter evenings, people go outside only when necessary because it is cold, wet and dark.

There is little research proving that fear of crime increases in winter, and the only study I found dealing with this issue is a work in progress (Semmens, 2002). However, based on Thabisa and Nontando's hypothesis and my own experiences in PJS, I believe that fear of crime increases in winter because it gets dark earlier and light later, and there are fewer eyes on the street in the cold weather.

Commuting was also temporal. Morning rush hour felt less safe than in the evening. More people were walking in groups during early morning compared with the evenings, even if it was equally dark. As a reaction to the temporal nature of crime and fear of crime, PJS residents observe an informal curfew, like residents in other communities. People retreat indoors at 21:00 because it becomes "late", and the outside is declared as a "no-go zone". From 21:00 onwards, it becomes quiet outside. *Spaza* shops close their gates, and people can only buy products through the gate. Front doors are closed, and outdoor lights are switched off. Minutes before 21:00, there would still be activity outside, but at 21:00 everything quietens down. Our survey data also showed that by 21:00, most people are at home and go to bed between 21:00 and 22:00. This "curfew" was consistent, regardless of the season.

Stephanie: *For you to walk around between 6 and 8, is it dangerous?*

Fundiswa: It's not dangerous at night, but around 9 pm till 10 pm, it's dangerous to walk outside. (female, young adult, household interview, PJS)

Stephanie: *Is it busy here at night?*

Lona: Yes.

Stephanie: *But not with the right people? And do they sit outside or inside?*

Lona: No, not the right people. At night around 9 pm, they usually roam around. (female, child, participatory photo interview, PJS)

Another temporal aspect of crime occurs at weekends and at the end of the month. Interviewees estimated there were more robberies at the end of month because people received social grants or

salaries. At these times, alcohol also increased significantly, providing more opportunities for less vigilant, intoxicated people to be robbed. Weekends are also considered to be more dangerous because of increased alcohol and drug use.

Angel: Most crime happens at the end of month and weekends. (male, senior, household interview, SST)

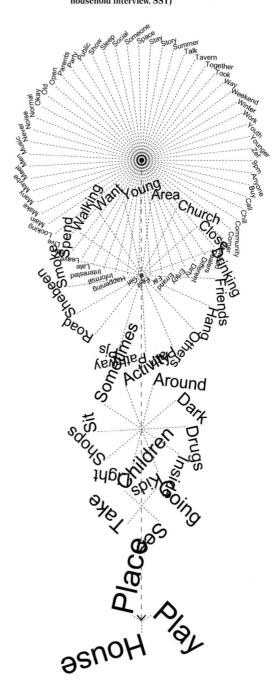

Fig 3　Word cloud on activities in self-built communities based on data collected during my research

December was also considered a dangerous month. Crime, especially theft, increased, usually to make money to go home for the festive season and to buy gifts for loved ones. It is a known fact that many receive Christmas bonuses and have more money or valuables available to be stolen.

Darkness exacerbates social conflict

Nighttime, and specifically darkness, has a profound social effect on residents of self-built communities. At night, strong social relations are an important mechanism to cope with the fear of social conflict. Much social conflict is associated with nighttime and darkness, and many living in self-built communities associate violence, contact crime and substance abuse with darkness and nighttime. Darkness and social conflicts reflect spatially and temporally, and certain spaces such as *shebeens*, narrow pathways and toilets are feared more than other places. The time of year, month and day of the week also play a role in the levels of fear felt by individuals. Many speak of the winter more fearfully than the summer.

Everynight practices

Nighttime is associated with fear of social conflict in the dark. Living with fear of the night results in certain nighttime practices that differ substantially from daytime practices in self-built communities. While there are activities outdoors at night, these are often governed by fear, shaping everynight practices that entail coping mechanisms to deal with a fear of social conflict and darkness. Walking practices and accessing services at night are linked to these fears. This section elaborates on nighttime practices in self-built communities or everynight

practice. Everynight practices were investigated through observation, full immersion, photo interviews and workshops. It is important to note that these practices differ significantly between communities. The following section is based mainly on PJS and Marikana and is a snapshot of various nighttime practices in self-built communities.

Activities at night

Interviewees were asked whether a particular space was busy at night, with social and pedestrian activity in mind. Their answers, however, mostly related to drug dealing and criminal activity. After 21:00, "busy" was construed as negative. I would consider a busy pathway as safer, but participants almost unanimously thought of "busy" as dangerous. People often spoke about a pathway being busy without me asking, and when asked whether that made them feel safe or unsafe, they mostly replied "unsafe".

People did not seem go out at night—49.09% of survey respondents said they never left their homes at night. Despite this, through my interviews and experience in PJS, I discovered that there were some nighttime activities inside and outside PJS. Most youths wanted to leave PJS at night, saying that there was nothing to do there. Sbu, a young male, said his friends refused to visit him in PJS because they were too scared, so he had to go out and visit them in the formal area, P-Section. In **Figure 3** and **Graph 4** are some other activities people mentioned in the qualitative work and the household survey.

Many people said they left PJS at night for social activities, visiting people in the surrounding formal neighbourhood, going to bigger taverns, attending church

If you went outside at night in the last 7 days, where did you go? (n = 764)

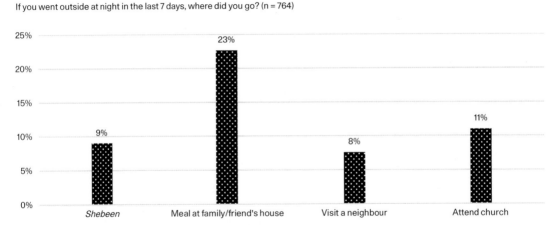

Graph 4   Asking respondents where they went out to in the last seven nights

Fig 4   Our walk to drop Xolelwa's daughter off at her uncle's house

Fig 5   Arriving at church by taxi with Xolelwa and Thabisa, along with three other taxis

Fig 6   Documenting the Khayelitsha nightscape on my outing to church

Map 2   Social attractions and activities in PJS

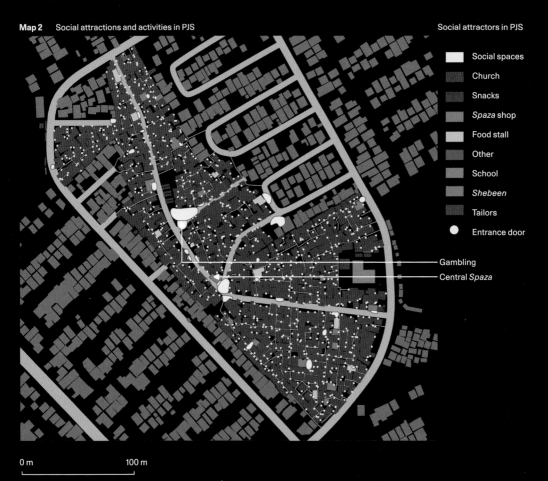

Social attractors in PJS

Social spaces
Church
Snacks
Spaza shop
Food stall
Other
School
Shebeen
Tailors
⬤ Entrance door

Gambling
Central *Spaza*

0 m   100 m

Fig 7   Typical *spaza* shop activity in SST

or group practices such as choir. Attending activities outside PJS required some planning. People arranged transport pick them up, or if they were going to visit a nearby area close by, they would ask someone to accompany them. During one of my sleepovers, Xolelwa's daughter wanted to visit her uncle in the surrounding formal section, and we (Xolelwa, Thabisa, Kolekha, Nonthando, another woman and I) accompanied her to the street where he lived (Figure 4). It is also common to call and check if someone made it home safely. The Sakikamva Youth Group explained that they went out as a group, never leaving anyone behind. One participant only went out with his friend who owned a taxi; that way they would be driven home and would always be safe.

Mzimasi: When we are going to party we take the taxi so that we don't have to rely on anyone when we want to go home. All of us would go; we don't leave anyone behind because we grew up together. It is very much safer when you go out with your friends. **(male, teen, youth group workshop, PJS)**

As Mihlali, a Sakikamva Youth Group member explained, the youth also arrange social events earlier, so they do not get back at a dangerous hour.

Mihlali: At night, maybe my friends want to go out and have some fun. [It is] Ideal to do those things at an early time so that terrible things cannot affect me. Or we will have fun in the afternoon. **(male, teen, youth group workshop, PJS)**

Going to church with Xolelwa and Thabisa one evening was quite an organisational feat. Xolelwa organised a taxi, for which everyone paid her R25 ($1.50). The taxi collected us at a certain point and then drove to other points to collect more people. When we arrived at the church, which was inside someone's house in a formal area of Khayelitsha, many taxis dropped off other groups as well (Figure 5). The church service lasted until 21:00, and after church, the taxi dropped everyone off at their houses and dropped us off as close to Kolekha's house as possible. During my taxi ride, I captured some snaps shots of Khayelitsha by dark to show the empty streets and high-mast lights dominating the nightscape (Figure 6).

Inside PJS, people were apprehensive about going out and also complained that there were no fun nighttime activities. When people were asked what they did, most immediately mentioned the *shebeens* and taverns and then said they stayed inside and watched TV—there was not much else to do. The survey revealed that quite a few people visited friends or family members at night. Though most people stated during interviews that they did not go out, there was activity at night, mainly before 21:00. Nighttime activities were revealed through my observations, the photo interviews and the household survey. On the following page is a map showing the social spaces in PJS. Some were not open at night and others were.

Spaza shops, snack shops and *shebeens* are generally open at night. *Spaza* shops close at 22:00, and *shebeens* and snack shops close according to client demand and agreements between neighbours.

Ten *shebeens* were mapped in PJS, catering to different crowds, older, younger, men and mixed demographics. *Shebeens* often functioned throughout

How often do you go to the *spaza* shop in the centre of PJS?

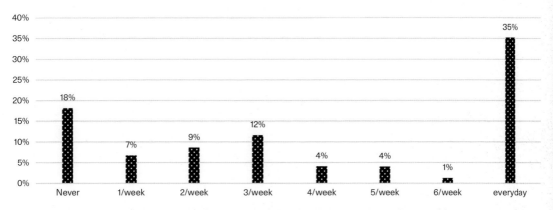

Graph 5 Asking respondents how often they visit the *spaza* shop in the centre of PJS

Fig 9 – 11   Temporary and repurposed objects for social spaces. A tyre planted in the ground, buckets and crates for sitting

Map 3   Outdoor space in PJS differed in degrees of publicness and privateness, the degree of privacy also changed at night

Outdoor space in PJS

- Private yard
- Shared yard
- Common yard
- Common space
- Vehicular route
- Pathway
- ● Entrance door

0 m   20 m

Fig 12 – 15 The same common space in PJS hosting activities ranging from gambling (bottom right), hand-washing (top left and bottom left), choir practice (top right) and children playing (bottom left)

the day well into the night. They attracted many people and are probably the most common social spaces where people linger for longer at night in PJS. However, *spaza* shops were the most active places in PJS at night. Adults lingered for long periods, as did children and some teens, especially to access free public WiFi. The central *spaza* shop shown in **Map 2** was particularly active, with eighty-two per cent of respondents visiting it once a week (**Graph 5**) and forty-three per cent of respondents saying that they visited the *spaza* shop in the centre of PJS after sunset. **Figure 17** shows very typical night-time activity outside a *spaza* shop in SST.

Mrs Filifili spoke about how much she enjoyed walking to her favourite shop, even at night. She spoke about going there several times a day, but as much as she enjoyed walking there, she was anxious in the darkness due to loadshedding.

Mrs Filifili: Let me show you the route I take when I go to my favourite shop. I like taking this route when I go to my favourite shop; I take this route even at night. ... This is my favourite shop. I can't even count how many times I come here in a day.
It gets very dark and causes anxiety when it's dark, and I don't want to go to the shop because the pathways are dark.
(female, elderly, participatory photo interview, PJS)

Using observations and interviews, I documented several social spaces through fieldwork in PJS— represented as "social spaces" in **Map 2**. These spaces were temporary and challenging to document. Some days, children would gather around a fire (**Figure 8**), other days, women would gather around a temporary barbeque stand. These events happened spontaneously and often in different places. However, some were more regular social spaces, such as the gambling space and the corner where the same group of young men gathered daily. Even with regular spaces, if no one was there, there were no obvious material traces hinting that this was a social space. I looked for signs of sociability and found only crates, upside-down buckets, car tyres, reappropriated dustbins and large concrete pieces or rocks used as outdoor furniture. All these objects were worthless or multi-functional, and if they had value, they were often easy to move (**Figures 9–11**).

Along with the ephemerality of outdoor social spaces, there is often a temporal blurring of public and private space, with different spaces assuming different degrees of publicness depending on the time of day, as shown in **Map 3**. A public

thoroughfare by day may become a private courtyard by night, and activities in a common space may vary from washing clothing to hosting a public meeting (**Figures 12–15**).

By day, people sit outside, washing areas attract people, and open spaces in front of houses attract smaller social groups. By night, socialising is done on the move (**Figure 16**), while walking to shops or toilets, or preparing to retreat at 21:00. People generally linger around spaces of economic activity, such as at the woman selling meat from her house or the *spaza* shop. Parents or guardians often send children to *spaza* shops to run errands at night (**Figure 17**). None of the children talked about being robbed but mentioned older children or *skollies* taking their money and teasing them—the difference between robbing someone and taking their money is unclear. Some interviewees suggested that children playing outside at night signalled neglect by parents drinking at *shebeens*. I did sense that even when children were properly cared for, they stayed out quite late, protected to a degree from social conflict because they are very young and are less likely targets.

People often mentioned hearing things at night. They could not see because they were inside and too afraid to go out. They heard violence outside and heard stories the next day. Like Malume from SST, people often talked about hearing noises and not knowing what people were doing, but knowing they were up to something bad.

Stephanie: *What happens at night, late?*
Malume: At 9pm you can hear things, they are up to something. It is dark because the streetlight has been off for one month.
(male, adult, household interview, SST)

Junior's mom, who also lives in SST next to the streetlight Malume mentions above, thought there was less noise at night when the light was working.

Junior's mom: I can hear whispering at night. The streetlight is off since September/October.
Stephanie: *How have things changed since the light went off?*
Junior's mom: When the light is on, there are less people late at night talking.
(female, senior, household interview, SST)

A theatre workshop method, vocal imaging, raised the discussion about many nighttime sounds. Participants found it difficult to express themselves but were much more expressive when asked to make a nighttime sound. These were only sounds of

Fig 16 Peak hour at 19:00 during the winter in PJS. Streets are busy with people socialising while moving

Fig 17 A child on a nighttime errand to buy milk, and other children gathering around the *spaza* shop around 19:00

distress—dogs barking, gunshots, women screaming, a baby crying, stone-throwing, loud and persistent music.

Walking at night

People often commented on daily realities related to mobility, "when I pass by here, this is what I see", or "on my way to work, I walk past this area", or "people pass through here to get to x or y". Walking is a way of life in self-built communities, and many people are concerned they cannot walk freely. People were most concerned about their safety when walking, and walking at night is particularly filled with fear. Angel from SST described how he was kept awake at night by the sounds of people running through the pathway where he lives out of fear.

Angel: People run in the passage to get out as soon as possible which keeps me awake all night (male, senior, household interview, SST)

Residents of self-built communities must walk outside at night to use shared basic services, such as taps and toilets. A workshop participant explained how he lived very close to the shop, but it was scary to walk there in the dark. In this sense, darkness and fear also increase the perceived distance to services and amenities.

Phelo: The distance between the tuckshop and my house is not that long, just that it is so dark and the streetlight is far from there, so it becomes scary at night. (male, teen, Sakikamva Youth Group workshop, PJS)

People often have no choice but to walk at night. Many self-built communities in Cape Town are located on the urban periphery. Residents walk to access public transport in the dark morning and nighttime hours and face long daily commutes to access opportunities. While PJS is centrally located, interviewees often referred to daily commuting struggles. Survey data revealed that one-fifth of people enjoyed living in PJS because of its access to transport and other facilities, even if they still struggled daily to access public transport in the dark early morning hours and at nighttime.

In PJS, 48.89% of respondents are employed full-time or part-time, with commute times between thirty minutes to one hour (forty-two per cent of employed respondents) and one to three hours (39.39% of employed respondents) as shown in **Graph 6**. Observations and interviews revealed that many people wake up between 05:30 and 06:00 to get ready for work, get children ready for school, do some household chores and then hasten to public transport at approximately 06:00. Residents consider 06:00 to 07:00 peak pedestrian traffic hour in PJS, when most people are travelling to work. Survey data suggests a three-hour peak from 06:00–09:00. Commuter traffic drops significantly after 09:00. Traffic peaks with kids travelling to school between 06:00–08:00. People felt safer during peak commuting times because there were many people around, and in summer as it was light outside.

When people leave for work in PJS (n = 763)

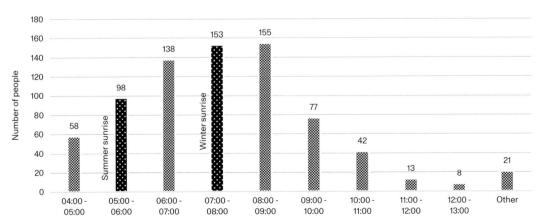

Graph 6 Time respondents leave to go to work in the mornings, also indicating winter and summer sunrise and sunset

Some residents leave for work much earlier—and some as early as 04:30.

Sibongile: In the morning, it's busy from 04:30, because someone is taking a taxi, someone is going to the train, someone is going to the bus, like that. (male, senior, household interview, PJS)

Residents travelling at such early hours are often alone and feel very vulnerable without the reassurance of fellow commuters, but they have no choice but to pass through the dark pathways in PJS as quickly as possible. Thembeka, a female PJS resident who works night shifts, shared her stress about off-peak commuting.

Thembeka: No, sister, I'm just taking every step because I can't do otherwise. I am not safe, there's a lot of things happening here at night, I don't want to lie, but I can't do otherwise because I am working for my children.

To work at night is not safe. Especially when you are living in these types of houses, it's not safe to be here. (female, senior, household interview, PJS)

Peak hours differ quite significantly from summer to winter, as shown in **Figures 18 and 19**. The mid-winter sun only rises at 07:51 and commuters are forced to walk to public transport in the dark. In summer, this is a different story—the sun, and most of PJS, rises at 05:30. I slept over for the first time in November 2018 at Kolekha's "summerhouse" in PJS. She explained that she called it her summerhouse because she only lived there during the summer months, when it was light enough to walk to the bus stop in the morning. During the darker winter months, she moved to her mother's house in the adjacent formal neighbourhood, P-Section. The bus stop was closer, and it was lighter in P-Section, presumably due to the high-mast lights illuminating the wider formal roads more effectively. When commuters travel during off-peak hours, taxis often pick them up or drop them off as close to their house as possible, as Thembeka explains. PJS, like most other self-built communities, is mostly inaccessible by car, and people have no choice but to walk a significant distance from the taxi drop off point to their home.

Stephanie: *You arrive with the taxi at night?*
Thembeka: Yes, and walk here. The taxi stays there in the street. (female, senior, household interview, PJS)

Mvelisi, who sometimes works overtime, suggested this was not always possible. If the taxi was too full, the drop off point was further away from his house .

Mvelisi: Sometimes I'm working overtime, I finish my overtime at 8pm, so the taxi maybe drops me off there in the street, on the main road, they drop me there, 9pm or 9:30pm, it depends how many people are in the taxi.

Stephanie: *And then you have to walk?*
Mvelisi: Yes, I have to walk to the main road to come here. (male, adult, household interview, PJS)

In the early mornings, I observed people walking to bus stops together. Groups would gather at a meeting point, or men would fetch their female family or friends from their homes and accompany them. When unable to walk in groups, people ran through pathways to avoid spending any more time than was absolutely necessary in the narrow and dark pathways. Mzimasi, participant in one of the youth group workshops in PJS, walks his mom to the taxi rank every morning before school. Sibongile also spoke about not being scared of the *skollies* at the train station anymore because he walked in a group with other men. It appears that there is, without a doubt, safety in numbers in self-built communities.

Sibongile: They [commuters] must have a plan to move there. Maybe you call the guys,

Reasons for taking a different route to the *spaza* shop at night (n = 97)

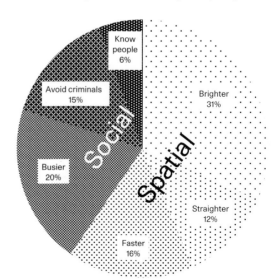

Graph 7   Spatial and social reasons for taking a different path to the *spaza* shop at night

you say "Hey guys, I'm going to the station", yes I need the guys who are going to the station. You are going together. They can't rob us; there are too many. **(male, senior, household interview, PJS)**

Some interviewees said they did not carry their cell phones at night for fear of being mugged. Others hid them on their bodies. Some younger girls, like Akhona, complained that people would even steal their wigs in the darkness. She talked about how this affected her sense of freedom.

Akhona: We live in a generation where we have this thing called *weave* [wig]; when you have it you can't walk out with your weave because you will get robbed and get killed for your things; we don't walk freely at night. **(female, teen, Sakikamva Youth Group workshop, PJS)**

Some participants like Thembeka, an older woman living in PJS, shared their experience of hiding valuables on their bodies. She spoke about how young *skollies* touched her all over her body to search for hidden valuables.

Thembeka: I put it [cell phone] like this [points to her crotch]. Because they feel here [refers to her breasts], they go straight to the private parts. They touch everywhere. They are not scared because they are children, because they are young, but they can catch you here [referring to body] and look for the phone. Maybe it is not even my children's size, it is like my grandson's size, but they can catch you here [Laughs]. Seriously! **(female, senior, household interview, PJS)**

There are different reasons why some change pathways at night to feel safer, as shown in **Graph 7**. Some change routes to avoid or encounter certain people — knowing people living along a route offered a sense of safety. Interviewees also described how they avoided specific pathways because they were aware of crime or gang-related activities and, at times, were intimidated into changing routes. Other reasons for changing routes at night were more spatial than social, choosing alternative routes that were faster, straighter or brighter. Certain pathways are brighter than others, depending on the angle to the high-mast lights. Spatial reasons for taking a different path at night were mentioned less in my interviews but much more often during the survey. Most of the ninety-seven respondents who said

they took a different route to the central *spaza* shop at night specified reasons related to space (brighter, faster and straighter routes). Social reasons (busier, avoids criminals and familiarity of people) were also mentioned fairly often, but not as much.

My own walking practices in PJS

I also adopted various personal walking strategies at night, and my walking style depended primarily on my intuition. I experienced some intimidation when I walked around in PJS, especially when passing unfamiliar faces. I would behave nonchalantly, while the group would walk past me, teasingly asking whether I was scared of them. As a reaction, I felt that walking slower would show a group of gangsters that I was confident. I also greeted people to prove that I had protection and was familiar with the residents of PJS. At other times, I walked very fast, as if I had a mission and knew where I was going and as if I belonged in PJS. My strategies depended on the situation and my intuition. I refrained from looking lost or confused. If this happened or if I needed to read a message, I would knock on an open door and ask to sit down for a moment, or enter a house with an enclosed yard until I figured out where I was, before continuing.

I also walked in groups, sometimes with adults, other times with children, and often with a dog. I always suggested that a team member walked with me, or when that wasn't possible, I would ask children nearby to follow me because they tended to walk fast. I would say "Iza" ("come") to the children, and they would excitedly follow me, making me feel secure. I did the same with Miguel, a community leader's dog. Miguel was my bodyguard. Knowing and walking with her made me feel secure and accepted by the community. To me, it felt as if residents accepted me when they saw the dog following me around, which made me feel protected. When a dog barks at or does not like you, it is a sure sign of not belonging in an area, so gaining the dogs' approval was important. Miguel also followed her owner everywhere, and she was always around during our nighttime monitoring, adding to our sense of security.

I dressed very discreetly at night, dark jeans, a dark jacket with a hood and many pockets so I didn't need to carry a bag. The team I worked with called me *Amapara-para* (the *skollie*) because of how I dressed at night — I wanted to blend into the dark and not stand out as a target. I also adopted a strategy at night and when I was afraid of making confident eye contact with people and greeting them in Xhosa (the

Fig 20   Open field in Marikana with infrastructure in the far distance. Photo taken during a participatory photo interview (male, child, Marikana)

Fig 21   Toilets in Marikana Informal Settlement. Photo taken during the participatory photo interview (female, adult, Marikana)

predominant language spoken in Khayelitsha and PJS). Furthermore, I befriended those considered to be *skollies* in PJS. Familiarising myself with the *skollies* and getting to know as many people in PJS as possible made me feel much more secure while walking around at night. A final strategy was to always walk on the main road that cuts through PJS. It was wide, well lit, and the most active space, with many eyes on the street.

Walking is a widespread practice in self-built communities—many areas are not accessible by car or bicycle. And yet, as seen in interviews and observations, much fear and insecurity are attached to walking, specifically when needing to access distant job opportunities and having to commute during the dark and quiet hours; or having to access basic services after dark. People have adopted several walking strategies that help them feel safer.

Darkness and accessing basic services

This photo (Figure 20) struck me. It was taken by Owam, a twelve-year-old boy living in Marikana. The open field between the infrastructure in the distance and Owam taking the photo was almost ironic—all the electricity distribution cables and streetlights are visible, but Marikana has no formal access to electricity. During his photo interview, Mr Fukazi, an elderly male living in RR-Section, expressed the same irony when looking at Owam's photo.

Mr Fukazi: We don't have [formal] electricity yet, and other people have. We are right beneath the poles under the connection lines. (male, elderly, participatory photo interview, RR-Section)

This section investigates nighttime practices in accessing basic services in self-built communities, especially sanitation, and also discusses residents'

perceptions of being left in the dark (metaphorically and literally), without access to basic services. The section also shows that darkness exacerbates the lack of access to basic services, resulting in onerous coping mechanisms and negative perceptions of the state.

In **Figure 21**, Monica, a female resident in Marikana, captured her everynight life struggles to access sanitation. When she presented this photograph, it was clear that shared sanitation was mostly inaccessible by night, and that using shared sanitation after dark was a major safety risk. A recent study on sanitation practices in various self-built communities in the Western Cape region showed that people do not use shared sanitation facilities at night despite adequate availability, mainly due to safety concerns (Muanda et al., 2020). During my fieldwork, many people expressed fears around using dark toilets at night, for example, MamQ, who voiced the dangers she and her community faced while accessing the toilets in RR-Section:

MamQ: And at night it is dark. They either get robbed, raped or killed at these toilets (female, adult, nighttime workshop, RR-Section)

Even elderly residents, like Mrs Filifili in PJS, feared being raped in the toilets. During our walking interview, she expressed concern about the sudden darkness around toilets when there is a planned power outage for loadshedding:

Mrs Filifili: Anything can happen to me if I am on my way to the toilets or if I am already there. I could get robbed or raped at these toilets by these *skollies* when there is loadshedding. (female, elderly, PJS)

StatsSA's General Household Survey asks a question about residents' main concerns regarding shared sanitation (by day and night). For five out of

	Poor lighting			Physical safety threatened		
Year	%		ranking	%		ranking
2013*	25.1		2	22		3
2014	25.9		1	19.5		3
2015	24.7		1	18.2		3
2016	23.3		1	17.8		3
2017	23.7		1	16.3		6
2018	23.2		1	11.9		7
Ave.	24.31		1.17	17.62		4.17
*2013 was the first time this question appeared in the StatsSA GHS						
(General Household Survey, 2014, 2015, 2016, 2018, 2019)						

Table 7   StatsSA's General Household Survey asks a question about residents' main concern (by day and night) regarding shared sanitation. Light was mentioned repeatedly (General Household Survey, 2014, 2015, 2016, 2017, 2018, 2019)

the six years since this question was included, poor lighting was the largest concern out of the twelve concerns listed, including safety. **Table 7** shows that a lack of lighting is a persistent concern for residents accessing shared sanitation in self-built communities.

Interestingly, the threat to physical safety is not nearly as great a concern as the lack of lighting. Safety concerns seem to be decreasing slightly each year, but lighting concerns are dropping at a much lower rate. From all my interviews and reviewing secondary data, it was clear that people were petrified of using shared sanitation facilities at night. From the StatsSA results and the prevailing fear, it can be deduced that residents feel safety concerns would be solved with better public lighting. Could it be that they, therefore, chose poor lighting as the most critical concern the government needed to address?

Xolelwa, a community leader in PJS, linked the lack of safety when accessing the public tap and toilets to the lack of lighting and distance of the infrastructure.

Xolelwa: At night you can't walk such a distance to get water, it's not safe, and there is no light over there. For instance, the toilets, [if] the toilets moved closer; then one can have their own tap and toilet close to their home. Because at night you can't walk such a distance to get water, it's not safe, and there is no light over there. **(female, adult, nighttime workshop, PJS)**

Alternative sanitation practices are used in response to the clear concern about darkness and safety at night when accessing shared sanitation. Muanda et al. (2020) found that ninety per cent of participants (n=345) in various self-built communities in Cape Town used plastic buckets in their homes at night, and sixty-five per cent used porta-potties (when provided). Other practices included open defecation and using plastic bags. In our household survey in PJS, we found the same practice of using buckets, but numbers were not as high, at 25.72% (n=196). Some practices we found were not mentioned by Muanda et al. (2020). These were to ask for someone to accompany them to the toilet at night (17.45% (n=133)); and 25.72% (n=196) of respondents in PJS simply do not relieve themselves after sunset. In PJS, a surprising 26.12% (n=199) of residents walked to the toilets alone at night, with 60.3% being male. Out of the 763 participants, 73.88% had different sanitation practices after sunset compared with during the day.

Using a night pail is a common sanitation practice in South Africa, where shared sanitation facilities are the norm in self-built communities. Before dark, water is collected in a large plastic bucket, used as a toilet inside the house and emptied in shared sanitation facilities or the sewerage system in the morning. Colloquially known as a pota-pota, this practice has been considered very undignified for decades in South Africa. No matter the government's efforts to provide dignified shared sanitation for all, nighttime access is a big problem, leading to the use of a pota-pota. Monica, who lives in Marikana, described the undignified use of night pails in her photo interview:

Monica: We can't go out at night, even if you have a tummy bug, you have no choice but to use it (baby's potty) at night, close to the door. **(female, adult, participatory photo interview, Marikana)**

In Muanda et al.'s useful study, using night pails resulted in dirtier toilets because of the messy process of emptying the pails out in the morning. They also found that residents who did not use the toilets much and instead used night pails, as shown in **Figure 22**, were less likely to clean the toilets or be mindful of not dirtying them (Muanda et al., 2020).

In PJS, open defecation is not a common nighttime sanitation practice, mainly due to density—there is little space for open defecation. Workshops and interviews in other less dense self-built communities or those that had access to open fields revealed that open defecation was a more common practice. Open defecation is perceived as undignified. In a workshop where we reviewed photographs, a man said he was quite affected by the photo of the open field. The photo reminded him of the lack of dignity within self-built communities where people do not have toilets and have to relieve themselves in the open. He mentioned a bush would be better, but there are only open fields and no bushes, so you have to go further away to be less visible. He spoke shamefully about open defecation at nighttime, saying he had no choice but to do this. Others in the workshop also described open defecation as a shameful act that was done at night so that no one could see you. In my interviews, it generally happened in areas with inaccessible sanitation by night, especially in Marikana. Muanda et al. (2020) also found open defecation to be a nighttime sanitation practice in self-built communities, where people generally went in between houses because of safety concerns related to shared sanitation. In my workshop with self-built community residents in Khayelitsha, I showed participants an image of a

Table 8 Monica's photograph of an open field reminded workshop participants of open defecation and the associated lack of dignity (female, adult, Marikana)

"Do you see how open this area is, we live close to this container, even today we are going to have a meeting at this place. We don't have facilities such as community halls, so we hold our meetings at the field. On Tuesday, we were with our community leader at this place." (Monica, female, adult, participatory photo interview, Marikana)

	Comment	Endorsements
1	When we want to go to the toilet, we go to a dark area. It makes us scared to go out at night time.	••• (3)
2	It's quite dangerous to go to the bushes because you will find yourself sometimes pressed and needing to go release yourself at night time in the bushes.	••• (3)
3	In my area, we don't even have a toilet, we use the field as our toilet.	(0)
4	It's dirty, we want change, we have children who play in this place	• (1)
5	Dirty	•• (2)
6	Dirty. The kids drink this water which causes skin allergies and breakouts.	• (1)
7	The kids play around with dirty items which causes them to fall sick.	(0)
8	This place is dangerous for kids for they could get murdered.	• (1)
9	It's not a safe area just to walk around, it's better in this afternoon.	• (1)
10	It's not a safe area to walk around at night, it's better in the daytime.	•• (2)
11	We will die of diseases because its very dirty.	•• (2)
12	This place is stinky, it causes diseases.	(0)

field that Monica captured in Marikana. The primary response to the photo was that the open space reminded them of a scary area where people were forced to defecate, raising intense feelings of lack of dignity, as shown in **Table 8**.

Den: I will rather use the pota pota. Sometimes the pota pota is right for your life and safety, but it's also not right for my dignity. (male, elderly, focus group, PJS)

As Den, an elderly male in PJS, says, the effect of the inability to access shared sanitation in the dark is a lack of dignity associated with nighttime sanitation practices. Again, I refer to the study by Muanda et al. (2020) and data gathered around dignity and sanitation practices. In their study, 82.8%

of respondents experienced feelings of "shame, being neglected, lack of dignity, discomfort, and desperation" (Muanda, Goldin and Haldenwang, 2020, p. 243). These feelings also appeared in a keywording exercise with Monica's photo of toilets at night (Table 9).

In the sketch and explanation in **Table 10**, Patrick, a male workshop participant from Sesikhona Village, explains his sketch map of his neighbourhood at night, beautifully phrasing what he felt about not having basic services. He related it to darkness, symbolically being left in the dark and literally living in darkness. His response only highlighted how so many people also felt about infrastructure during this research. Feelings of being forgotten, undignified living conditions and not having any hope

Table 9 Keywording exercise of Monica's photo of the toilets in Marikana at night, with round stickers indicating endorsement (female, adult, Marikana)

Then here on the side are the toilets. Here we are challenged because especially at night, for our children, as you can see, these houses are close to the toilets. When they change the buckets all of that sewage stench comes into my house and I have a sickly premature baby.

	Comment	Endorsement
1	Dignity	••••• (5)
2	Dignity	•• (2)
3	Dignity	• (1)
4	It is unsafe for women. Unhealthy and you can get raped while going to the toilet. It has happened once in one of the areas in Khayelitsha SST Section, where a young girl got raped and killed while in the toilet. (5)	••••• (5)
3	People fight over here	•• (2)
4	Fear, unsafe (1)	• (1)

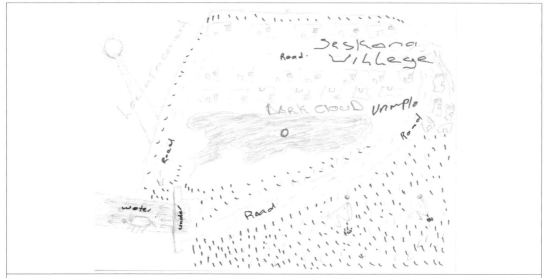

As you can see here, I have written law enforcement. Inside the law enforcement station, there is a light that lights for the whole township. So over here there is a cloud, a dark cloud. You see when there is a darkness, and they say there is a dark cloud over me. So there is that dark cloud due to the lack of services... Here I have drawn the moon that is covered by that cloud, you see. The moon at times also acts as light, so you can see from a distance when someone is approaching you or could possibly attack you. This moon you can't be seen, because of this cloud that is covering us, that is dark, such as lack of sanitation, waste removal services, electricity, water and unemployment. Yes [we are] unemployed at that place since that place is surrounded by unemployment, I am unemployed. If I was employed, I would not be here but being here means that I am unemployed, so its situation like that.

Table 10 Sketch map and explanation by nighttime workshop participant showing a literal and metaphorical dark cloud over his neighbourhood (male, adult, Marikana)

Fig 22   A typical night pail in PJS ready to be emptied in the morning

Fig 23 A collection of sketch maps indicating the theme of self-built communities situated within a dark shaded area in participants' sketches

Table 11 Keywording comments of two photos from the participatory photo interview related to not having services and the act of "borrowing" services

(Photo: Mr Fukazi, male, elderly, RR-Section)	(Photo: Khayalethu, male, adult, Marikana)
Keywording comments	
Lack of water. There is no water; we are using street taps to survive.	Illegal connection is happening because of no basic services.

for change were consistent themes that arose when people discussed access to basic services and darkness. MamQ, who works for SJC and lives in RR-Section, illustrated her area at night and explained that RR-Section had all the needed services, but they were living in darkness.

MamQ: *Our community has everything that is necessary, but it is dark.* **(female, adult, nighttime workshop, RR-Section)**

In the workshop, many participants drew the same dark shaded area, as seen in Patrick's drawing. The shaded area was often in the centre, with services drawn outside the shaded area to show a "forgotten" or "excluded space". The drawings often contained people, presumably residents of self-built communities, inside the dark shaded, forgotten or under-serviced area as shown in **Figure 23**. These dark areas also indicated danger zones with *skollies* drawn or labels such as "danger". When participants talked about their drawings, they described basic services as inaccessible and also described their undignified coping mechanisms, such as illegal dumping and open defecation, often in the veil of darkness.

Stephanie: *Who dumps at this place? Is it the people who live there and do you stop them?*
Khayalethu: This activity happens late so we can't catch them at times and yes, it is the people that live around that area who dump at that place because people regard it as a dumping site. We wake up with the place filled with trash because they dump at this place at night. **(male, adult, participatory photo interview, Marikana)**

Along with not having basic services, interviewees frequently mentioned borrowing or "stealing" public services and infrastructure. Participants frequently mentioned stealing electricity from a light or another house or borrowing water from a tap in another community. In **Table 11** are two comments from workshop participants when looking at images captured in the participatory photo interview. The first image in **Table 11** is of a man carrying a bucket of water. The workshop participant noticed this, emotively describing water access as related to survival. The second image was also taken by a participant in the photo interviews in Marikana, where you can see households informally connected to electricity with many wires running above houses.

The lack of basic services, including public lighting, evoked in participants emotions of being forgotten and not being cared for by the state. Darkness at night emphasised those feelings of exclusion, where participants often felt little sense of ownership over the infrastructure they were using. Their interaction with infrastructure was often described in illegal and even criminal terms, as a workshop participant from OR Tambo expressed when explaining her sketch map:

Anonymous: You see these arrows? That is electricity we "steal" from those with houses, we pay R350 ($20) per month. **(female, adult, nighttime workshop, OR Tambo)**

Access to electricity was a major concern for residents in self-built communities, and people referred to electricity with lighting in mind. When people indicated they wanted electricity, they also pointed out the need for public lights, and when asked about

Table 12 The keywording exercise revealed that participants referred to light as electricity (male, child, Marikana)

Keywording comment*	Endorsement
"Darkness is very dangerous to children who are being raped in places which are dark, having no electricity" (anonymous workshop participant)	•••••• (6)
*not all comments are shown	

Keywording comment*	Endorsement
Darkness, we need electricity (anonymous workshop participant)	(0)
*not all comments are shown	

the public lighting in their neighbourhood, people often answered the question with household electrification in mind. Thuliswa, an older woman living in PJS, and Khayalethu and Monica from Marikana had similar responses in the photo interview when I asked them about public lighting.

Stephanie:	*When you moved here, was there any public lighting?*
Thuliswa:	No, there was no electricity at that time. **(female, adult, household interview, PJS)**

Stephanie:	*Is the [public] light in Marikana close to you?*
Khayalethu:	There is no electricity yet installed in Marikana. We steal electricity. **(male, adult, participatory photo interview, Marikana)**

Stephanie:	*And there is no lighting on this road at all?*
Monica:	We don't have electricity. I ask the police to accompany me there. **(female, adult, participatory photo interview, Marikana)**

Thuliswa, Khayalethu and Monica related public lighting to electricity access, although household electricity and public lighting are not installed simultaneously in practice (Chapter 2). I began to realise that interviewees' notion of access to electricity included public lighting as part of their expectations, as seen in comments made by participants during a workshop (Table 12).

Darkness exacerbates daily struggles

This section looked at everynight practices in self-built communities and the often-detrimental effects fear of social conflicts in dark environments can have on nighttime practices. Social activities are greatly affected by these fears—many do not leave their homes at night, especially after 21:00,

and the only way of experiencing the outdoors at night is through hearing sounds. Those who do venture out often make elaborate arrangements to ensure their safety. Walking at night affects all residents in self-built communities, since most people do not own cars. Houses are only accessible by foot, and navigating dark pathways at night sparks feelings of fear and lack of freedom. Some strategies alleviate the fear of walking at night, but the dangers of walking remain the main topic of discussion when talking about nighttime in self-built communities.

When I asked participants about their nighttime experiences and practices, the conversation quickly turned to basic service access and quality of services. Reading between the lines in their responses, darkness exacerbated the poor access to and people's dissatisfaction with basic services, emphasising general feelings of being forgotten by the state. People do not feel safe to use shared sanitation after dark. Instead, they use onerous coping mechanisms at night, such as night pails and open defecation. These practices have detrimental effects on their sense of dignity. Regardless of the availability of adequate shared sanitation by day, nighttime sanitation access needs to improve in self-built communities. To solve prevailing access issues, adding more shared taps, toilets and janitorial services will not necessarily improve nighttime access nor resolve residents' feelings of being forgotten by the state.

Nighttime perceptions

Fears of encountering social conflict and onerous nighttime practices result in very negative perceptions of the night, as Masi, a teen living in PJS, expressed.

dangerous	killing one another	people don't walk at night because they are too scared
drinking too much	always fight when they are drunk	walking in the streets at night you don't feel safe because in your mind you think maybe they will rob you, rape you, hurt you
house break-in	use drugs	when you are going out at night alone, you have that fear that someone will do something bad to you
robberies	rob each other while I'm on my way home	there's a lack of trust; you have to run into your house with the dog
rape	too violent	others get stabbed
won't see gangsterism at night, can't identify the people doing it at night		

Table 13   Nighttime perceptions of youth living in self-built communities, explored through a theatre workshop

Masi: In day time is where people walk freely, they are not afraid of anything, but at night, it turns out to be a nightmare to them because they are afraid, they are not comfortable to go outside at night. And people do [bad] things at night, they don't do it in the daytime. (male, teen, participatory photo interview, PJS)

As soon as nighttime and everynight life was mentioned, interviewees and workshop participants immediately related nighttime to fear, referring to people fighting, stabbing each other, drinking and raping women. It may sound brash but that was how people related to the night, as demonstrated by a young workshop participant living in PJS, who expressed the cause of her fear of night:

Anonymous: My fear at night is that we get robbed, killed, and raped. (female, teen, Sakikamva Youth Group workshop, PJS)

A theatre workshop helped to explore the kinds of thoughts and emotions triggered when people thought of the night. When the workshop collaborator, Mandisi, asked the group of youngsters about the first thing that came to mind when they thought about nighttime, their perceptions, listed in **Table 13**, were incredibly negative.

At this point, I had tried many different techniques to initiate a discussion on things people valued about nighttime, but nothing seemed to work. After the group expressed their thoughts, Mandisi, knowing my desire to dig into positive nighttime aspects, asked the group to think of one positive aspect of nighttime. Out of fifteen participants, only his wife responded, saying that she enjoyed listening to her neighbour's music through her shack walls. The rest were silent. Even her response was ironic; she experienced nighttime through sound heard within the confines of her home.

Fear made people feel various other emotions, and many described their nights with strong emotions, using words such as loneliness, no peace, sadness, anger; and referring to hardship caused by fear and the inability to go out at night. One member of Sakikamva Youth Group described his loneliness and negative emotions because of nighttime fears:

Phelo: Because I'm scared of going out at night, I stay at home. It becomes lonely and boring. I start thinking about negative things like nobody cares for me; my friends don't come to check on me. (male, teen, youth group workshop, PJS)

At the beginning of my fieldwork, I was struck by the nightmarish stories people told me about nighttime and darkness. Social issues related to darkness, but in turn, darkness and nighttime related strongly to trauma. I heard many traumatic stories through my interviewees, either personal or experiences involving loved ones. Some were told vividly and in detail, while others were relayed in a normalised fashion, as if to say, "This is life, we have no choice but to accept it and live on".

Extreme levels of violence were ever-present, to the point where I questioned the truth behind some stories. In a participatory photo interview, Monica presented a photo of an open field. She told a horrific story of how young boys killed a pregnant woman at night, wanting to see inside her belly and using broken bottles to cut it open. She ended the story by saying, "that is Marikana" as if to say, "that is life", and to normalise the horrific event.

Monica: The reason why I took these images is because there was a pregnant lady two years back. She was attacked by three boys; they tore her tummy and placed a glass bottle in her tummy. That is Marikana.
Translator: *Where these men ever found?*
Monica: Others ran away; others died; others got beaten up by the community. Otherwise, the baby died when they tore the mother's tummy. They said they wanted to see how a child sits inside a mother's womb because they have never seen such. (female, adult, participatory photo interview, Marikana)

This story shocked both my translator and me, and Monica broke down and cried. Almost every photograph she presented was associated with a horrifying story of extreme violence and a sense of absolute helplessness. Owam, a young boy living in Marikana, told another nightmarish story. Young boys who had dropped out of school had raped an older woman at the toilets at 05:00. Owam was a twelve-year-old boy who had experienced too much for his young age. Everything seemed like a nightmare. A playground became a burial site, a toilet became an invitation to be raped and a pathway became a death sentence at night.

Owam: They even make shallow graves and hide people who were murdered. There is a little hill there; another man was hidden there. He was stabbed and was found in the morning. His foot was visible, and that is how he got discovered.

Table 14 Sketch map of Siliziwe's walk home from Sakikamva Youth Group and her imagined experience of walking home

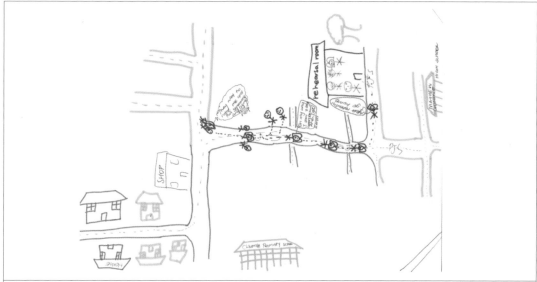

I go home from rehearsals... On my way, I saw two boys approaching me; I got scared... They want to rape me, and I'm screaming and crying for help.

Stephanie: *Why are people walking this way?*

Owam: People don't usually go there. It is usually us who play here. When people want to hide, or they want to dump dead people, they come here. **(male, child, participatory photo interview, Marikana)**

A male participant in a workshop told us of another horrific incident that he was reminded of when looking at the nighttime photos. He told a heart-breaking story about a rat eating a baby's face while the baby slept, and no one noticed this because it was so dark.

In SST, Angel, a senior resident, told stories of the *skollies* who "come to life" at night, as if they were zombies.

Angel: You hear them at night; they run on the roofs; I do not know what they are doing out there. **(male, senior, household interview, SST)**

I heard many more stories about the *skollies* at night, almost making them seem like night terrorists who made life a living hell for anyone who dared to go out at night. These *skollies* were nameless, faceless, identity-less. They committed crimes under the veil of darkness.

Anonymous: Those are gangsters over there, they can see in the dark **(female, senior, nighttime workshop, Ireland)**

People told imaginative stories about nighttime, and when I asked participants whether they had ever experienced any of the events they described, they replied that they had not. These stories were anecdotes they had heard about, which transformed into somewhat fact-based fictional stories about nighttime in self-built communities. Mostly youth and children told these imagined incidents. Siliziwe, a member of Sakikamva Youth Group, drew her walk from Youth Group practice to her house **(Table 14)**, depicting two boys trying to rape her in the street. I asked her if this actually happened to her, and she replied that it had not, but that she imagined it could.

Whether the stories were real or imagined events, these nightmares were true in the interviewees' minds, as a manifestation of the extreme fear felt every night by many people in self-built communities. These horror stories all seemed to have one thing in common—they happened in the dark. I often noticed the temporal nature of space in most stories—what seems to be a vibrant and reasonably safe space by day transforms into a nightmare come darkness. After some time, I was beginning to think that people did not like nighttime, no matter how much light and how little crime there was. In a series of three workshops, I began to explore what people enjoyed about nighttime. The first sign of positivity I saw was a young teen's comment, relayed below:

Anonymous: When I grew up, I used to hear stories about things that happen in the nighttime, and they were all bad. But when I went outside at night, I didn't experience all bad things. At night is when peace comes, and people mind their own business. (female, teen, Sakikamva Youth Group workshop, PJS)

I began to explore these very subtle positive aspects of the night by asking people what their favourite parts of nighttime were or what they wished for at night. Mveliso framed it quite positively in his comment below.

Mveliso: At night we do dream. We dream at night; we don't dream during the day. And when you dream at night, you wake up and implement your dream. In order for you to be successful, you need to dream and have goals that you plan during the night. (male, young adult, Sakikamva Youth Group workshop, PJS)

While people are overwhelmed by negative nighttime perceptions, positive aspects emerge when explicitly asked about their hopes and dreams for nighttime. In these workshops, several main keywords emerged: peaceful, gathering, friends, share, quiet, family, comfortable, freedom, party and dream.

Anonymous: You cannot live in fear, and it must be clear that we are in a free country, not in a fear country. (male, young adult, Sakikamva Youth Group workshop, PJS)

I could not have summarised this section in better words than by this quote by a youth group member during a theatre workshop, which created an "ah-ha" moment for me. After all this time, I wanted to find out about positive nighttime experiences and how people were enjoying everynight life. However, fear of social conflict exacerbated by darkness governed people's daily lives, causing people to feel imprisoned by their fear; they were not free. Many people spoke about the need to walk freely at night (something that people cannot do because of fear) and described the fear of venturing out at night as not having freedom. In a few interviews with youngsters, they spoke of being the new generation, and they needed freedom to walk at night.

Anonyous: You need to walk free at night. We are the new generation, we love to walk at night, enjoy ourselves, go to parties at night with our friends or to a family party, but now we can't go because out there are gangsters. (female, teen, Sakikamva Youth Group workshop, PJS)

The "born free" generation (born post-1994) needed to be free in all regards, while older generations, born before 1994, have a comparatively different relationship with being outside at night. Several interviewees also mentioned the need to be confident and comfortable when walking outside at night.

Darkness trapping everynight life

Everynight life in self-built communities is both under studied in academia and an undervalued component in governments' attempt to improve living conditions in those communities. This chapter elaborates on everynight life through three focal areas — psychosocial, practices and perceptions of everynight life.

Social dynamics are greatly affected by poor spatial conditions at night and generally exacerbate social conflict in self-built communities resulting in fear of the night. Fear prevents many people from venturing outdoors at night, and mostly only children, young adults, men and those who are considered "irresponsible" spend time outside at night, alongside *skollies* who own the night. Strong social relations link to coping with nighttime fear, where forming close and trusting relationships in the community provides a sense of security. Knowing who to avoid or to befriend is an important strategy in dealing with nighttime fear of social conflict. Such social conflict, often underpinned by violence and substance abuse, tends to happen in the dark, often to hide the perpetrator's identity. Social conflict is also spatial and temporal; it increases around and in specific outdoor spaces in self-built communities, at specific times of the week, month or year. Therefore, these spaces and times are associated with more fear.

Despite the immense fear people experience outdoors at night, outdoor nighttime practices exist out of necessity (getting to work or accessing services) and for social reasons (playing outside at night or visiting friends). Social activities at night are affected by these fears — many arrangements have to be made to ensure safety when venturing out at night. Although there are outdoor social activities in PJS, most outdoor social spaces are ephemeral and disappear after 21:00, leaving behind little trace of their existence. After 21:00, PJS moves indoors, and people experience the night through sound.

Nighttime walking practices are largely shaped by fear. To cope with this fear, people adapt walking practices at night spatially, such as taking brighter walking routes, or socially, such as walking on pathways where people are familiar, or avoiding the wrong people and walking in groups. During off-peak hours, commuters make additional arrangements to spend as little time as possible in dark pathways.

Nighttime access to basic services is a practice that challenges a safe and dignified standard of living. Darkness in self-built communities exacerbates poor access to basic services and raises more symbolic associations of being left in the dark by the government. Onerous nighttime sanitation practices, such as using a night pail inside the house, directly relate to the fear of venturing out at night to access dark shared sanitation facilities. Living with dignity is very important to residents in self-built communities, as much as it is for any other citizen.

These nighttime struggles, largely related to darkness, raise negative nighttime perceptions. Layers of negative emotions accompany fear, and nighttime has become a real and imagined nightmare for residents of self-built communities. Nevertheless, it is often the only time that people have to run daily errands and socialise with family and friends, and there is an expressed need to go out at night, especially among youth. Framed as the need to be free instead of being trapped by darkness, these dreams of a better night are expressed through a range of emotions as well as practical needs like needing nighttime access to the toilet. This chapter highlights an everynight life dominated by a fear of darkness. The next chapter looks at what role public lighting could play in alleviating that fear and moving towards the dream of a better night.

Freeing the Night, Co-producing Light

Chapter 6

As we learned in the last two empirical chapters, everynight life in self-built communities means being trapped by darkness, and darkness exacerbates the daily struggles in these communities. In addressing darkness every night, residents experience the insufficiency of high-mast lighting—mainly due to the distance of the lights from residents. Besides the technical insufficiency, lighting from a distance above and beyond the community reduces a sense of ownership over the light and contributes to the feeling of being forgotten by the state.

Chapter summary: What would happen if we were to light from within self-built communities rather than from above? Furthermore, what would happen if the lighting process itself also came from within self-built communities, with residents co-producing and maintaining public lighting? This chapter considers these questions, evaluating an action research public lighting project in PJS Informal Settlement using a highly visual and ethnographic mixed methods approach.

In March 2020, we co-produced and installed 283 solar-powered wall-mounted lights in PJS to understand the impact of public lighting in everynight life. This was only the first phase of the lighting project, in which approximately 780 households received wall-mounted solar lights. Chapter 3 describes the intervention design, process and stakeholders. **Map 1** illustrates the positioning of the phase 1 lights. Lights were placed close to the household's front door to create a sense of ownership and prioritise the entrance of houses.

Many unexpected events impacted the project after the installation, such as the global COVID-19 pandemic, the introduction of public WiFi in PJS and increased loadshedding. Due to the multitude of changes, the co-production of light in PJS allowed people to venture out at night more willingly, to access toilets, visit friends or sit outside their houses under lights during loadshedding. With a new agency over the night, people felt more free and less afraid of crime and were emboldened by the sense of security that being able to see, and being seen, provided them.

Co-producing light

Co-production was integral to the success of the lighting project. Even if we wanted to "fake it" and show a participatory process on paper, PJS residents did not allow us to make any move during the project without them by our sides—and we needed the community on board. We relied on each house to allow us to install a public light, to be surveyed and to report any problems with the lights. We also depended on local teams to survey the households (Figure 1), install the lights (Figures 2 and 4) and maintain

the. PJS leaders were aware of the project status and expected us to deliver monthly reports via the local maintenance team. In a sense, the co-production of these lights can be attributed to the PJS community's insistence on being fully involved at all times. Co-producing also taught us valuable lessons about management of infrastructure in self-built communities and helped to understand the solution's feasibility and scalability. This section elaborates on the importance of using a participatory approach to infrastructure management and discusses how we managed project conflicts.

I asked the maintenance team what would have happened if we were the CoCT and installed 250 solar lights without a participatory process. Their response clearly reflected the importance of involving the community to ensure the success of the project.

Yamkela: By the time you are finished installing the lights, the lights are all going to be gone. Because the City of Cape Town installed the lights and they have money and will replace the lights.

Sibongile: And they [the community] never got information about the lights.

Yamkela: They didn't get the information about the lights, what's going on. They [the City of Cape Town] just put the lights, then go.

Sibongile: They do their own thing without informing the community, without consulting us.

(maintenance focus group, PJS)

Co-producing the lighting project resulted in a process that worked within the community dynamics and facilitated a sense of care and ownership over the solar lights. There were hints of increased collective pride in PJS and anecdotes about individual pride in having a light. Residents displayed a sense of ownership over the lights—referring to their light—but also spoke collectively about the lights and how they were helping PJS as a community. When I asked interviewees, such as Thembeka, an elderly woman from the focus group, if they thought lights on their houses belonged to them, they usually laughed and said yes, the lights belonged to them.

Stephanie: *And do you see this as your light? Does it belong to you?*

Thembeka: I thought so, this belongs to me [laughing]. (female, senior, household interview, PJS)

Stephanie: *Do you see that light as your light?*

Nonicikelelo and Nomzamo: Yes [laughing]! (elderly, focus group, PJS)

Fig 1   The baseline survey team and community leaders

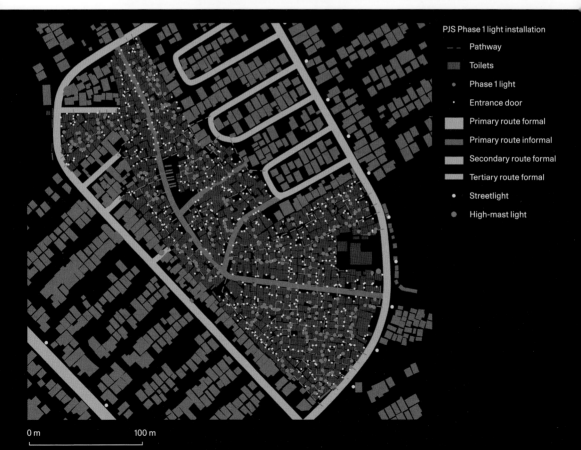

PJS Phase 1 light installation

– –   Pathway

    Toilets

•   Phase 1 light

·   Entrance door

    Primary route formal

    Primary route informal

    Secondary route formal

    Tertiary route formal

•   Streetlight

•   High-mast light

0 m   100 m

Map 1   Phase 1 lighting installation, with a light above or close to the front door of 283 households

Fig 2   The phase 1 local lighting installation team

Some interviewees, like Xolelwa, a PJS leader, mentioned that people from other neighbourhoods asked when they would receive similar lights.

Xolelwa: There is a lady from Harare here for church service; when she came to the service, she saw the light, and she said, "Where do they get electricity because there is loadshedding?" We say no, it's not the lights; it's the lights we are installing in PJS. She said, "Yoh, PJS is nice! You've got these lights!", and we said yes, but not all of us; the second phase is coming. She said, "Yoh, PJS, wow!" (female, adult, leadership focus group, PJS)

Bandla expressed how he appreciated that the light was marked with "property of PJS" because no matter where he found the light, he would know it belonged to PJS.

Bandla: Whenever I see this light, I know that it belongs to PJS. It belongs to PJS! No matter if I see this light in another township, I know this light belongs to PJS; why is it there? (male, senior, household interview, PJS)

Mveliso, a prominent community member, decided to make a documentary about our lighting project to emphasise the need for more effective public lighting in self-built communities. He followed us for two days, filming our installation process and interviewing different community members about the project and the need for better public lighting (Figures 5 and 6). This gesture showed the real commitment of the PJS community regarding the project, choosing to create their own awareness around the need for more effective public lighting in self-built communities.

Through the co-production process, we fostered a sense of pride in and ownership of the project, including agreeing where the light would be positioned on each house and employing locally. The PJS community felt responsible for their lights and were proud they had co-produced them in PJS. It was important to create a sense of ownership of the lighting infrastructure to ensure it would be maintained, but also to foster "infrastructural citizenship" (Lemanski, 2020), as discussed in Chapter 1.

Using a local team made it easier to report broken or stolen lights. Alongside reporting to the maintenance team, we tried a centralised reporting system with a WhatsApp hotline, but this did not work well. Generally, people tended to report other infrastructure issues in a decentralised manner, either to a leader or neighbour who would report to the ward councillor, who would in turn report to the central maintenance hotline. When asking interviewees who they would report light-related issues to, most replied they would report to either the leaders or the maintenance team.

Siya: It's great that you give them skills because there are fewer opportunities here, so we run it from our community; we are thankful for that.

Stephanie: *So there is no jealousy?*

Siya and
Lenox: No!

Stephanie: *Would you go and speak to them or the leadership?*

Siya: I go to the maintenance team because they are the ones who installed the lights; we will go and report it there. (male, young adults, household interview, PJS)

Mveliso summarised the importance of reporting to a local maintenance team, saying it eased reporting and encouraged community members to report more actively.

Mveliso: I think, for us, we know each other from PJS, so for us, it's easier to approach someone from PJS. Even if they didn't notice that there is a light that is off, you could say, "Hey Lucky or Yamkela, I was passing by BC-Section, and I saw that there is a light that is not on. Because I used to use that path there and then it was on, and now I see there is no light." So it's easy for them to interact with them with light issues. (male, young adult, youth focus group, PJS)

The maintenance team did not mind the extra responsibility of receiving reports randomly, but this meant the job became a full-time responsibility. This additional effort was no problem for them because they were "helping their community", as Anele explained.

Stephanie: *Does it bother you to be the face of the project and that it puts you in a position where you are always on standby? Does it not disturb you?*

Yamkela: No.

Sibongile: No.

Anele: Because we know our people. We are helping them. (maintenance team focus group, PJS)

Many people said they would report light problems to the leadership committee. For the project to be successful, respecting and actively involving the leaders was essential. As Zianda expressed, reporting problems to the CoCT is difficult because they are 'unavailable'.

Stephanie:	*If you had a problem with the light, do you know who to report it to?*
Zianda:	I think I'll go to the committee. Like if I have got a problem, I am going to report to them, then they will be fast to come and fix these lights.
Stephanie:	*So for you, it's about fixing the lights fast, and the City of Cape Town?*
Zianda:	It's too far for us. **(female, adult, household interview, PJS)**

Stephanie:	*If you have a problem with the light, who would you speak to?*
Mrs Filifili:	The committee to maintain the light. **(female, elderly, household interview, PJS)**

The leadership manages almost all social processes, including social conflict in PJS, so it was very important to work with them from early on in the project to gain community acceptance. The importance of their role is also why having an active leadership committee was a non-negotiable criterion when choosing where to work. Yamkela, a young male in PJS confirmed this when we discussed the thefts during our SST pilot lighting project.

Yamkela:	I think the reason that that happened in SST is because they don't have good leadership. When you have good leadership, they can know who is stealing here. They know the criminals, and whenever there are lights missing, they are going to go and ask them, where is that light from? So I think one of the advantages that we have here is good leadership. Our leadership is active. **(male, young adult, youth focus group, PJS)**

The PJS leaders insisted on being involved from the beginning, and they learned how to be involved in such projects. Xolelwa expressed how much she, as a leader, learned from our process of always involving the leaders, even when we employed fieldworkers.

Xolelwa:	The lesson that I have learnt from you guys is that when you come with employment, you communicate with the leadership and work together in terms of employment because it's the

leadership who know the people in the community who are not working. So that's a lesson that I learned from you. **(female, adult, leadership focus group, PJS)**

Indeed, ensuring fair employment was one of the most important leadership tasks—it even resulted in a new leadership committee being elected when the youth were not happy with their process. Some youth felt that leaders were choosing their friends to work on the project. After the community elected a new leadership committee, we developed an application process, including interviews and a policy to not hire the same people for each phase.

Working so closely with the PJS community required inclusivity and transparency. We communicated all processes at public meetings. However, as much as we tried to inform everyone about the process, many were frustrated with employment issues, or that they did not receive a light, as the maintenance team describes:

Thabile:	Some people got very angry that they didn't get a light, even before you guys left. Because the whole pathway doesn't have light and there is a lot of traffic on that pathway and most people use that pathway and there is a lot of crime. And then there's no light.
Sibongile:	And then also there's one path that has four or five lights, that makes people angry as well. How come all these people got lights, and we don't have.
Thabile:	I think it was more about communication. People weren't informed about what was happening. Yes, there were flyers about what was happening, but some people didn't read them. **(maintenance team focus group, PJS)**

I asked the group how we could improve communication. Everyone agreed with Anele's idea to have more routine checks, which was when they informed people about the project and received many reports on the lights.

Anele:	We must do more checking. Some people don't have time to read. Maybe once or twice a week so that we can explain to them. Some aren't at home. One woman was in the Eastern Cape region, and then when she came back, she found the light not working. We didn't have time to go around and check with her, so if we do check-ups it's better. **(male, young adult, maintenance team focus group)**

Fig 3   Installation team sharing information on the wall-mounted solar lights before getting a household's consent to install

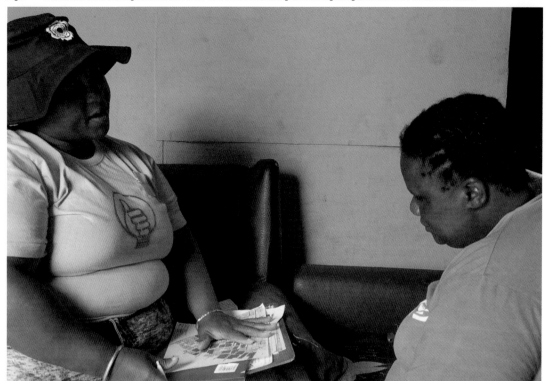

Fig 4   Installation team installing a wall-mounted solar light

Fig 5   Mveliso interviewing community members about public lighting for his documentary film

Fig 6   Mveliso filming our lighting installation team at work for his documentary film

The leaders also felt communication was the most important part of successfully implementing and maintaining the public lighting. This required community members to take care of the lights and report problems to the leaders, who would then communicate those issues to the maintenance team.

Tera: There is only one thing—communication between the leadership and the installers and you guys. That is very important. The three of you are the workers of the project. (male, senior, leadership focus group, PJS)

Thabisa: And understanding of the project, it must be clear. (female, adult, research assistant, PJS)

Tera: Everybody must be on the same level of the project. (male, senior, leadership focus group, PJS)

Communication and co-managing the project further ensured that conflict, which inevitably arises in any project, was managed effectively. We experienced some complaints and conflict over the lights, but issues such as theft and vandalism were not as severe as first predicted. Between March 2020 and May 2021, thirteen of the 283 lights were stolen, and seven were vandalised. Two houses moved the light for use indoors. We expected vandalism and theft to be the biggest problem in the project, especially after most pedestrian mobility sensors in the quantitative study were stolen.

Interestingly, the sensors were targeted while the lights were not. Mveliso felt that the lights were useful to everyone, including the *skollies*, and that is why they were not stolen or vandalised as much. He further mentioned that destroying a light was also destroying a community project, and people were aware of that.

Mveliso: So by destroying those lights, we are not destroying the lights only, we are destroying the community. And even for the criminals, even though they won't say that, it's benefitting them. They even have their enemies; they can see when the enemies are attacking them. (male, young adult, youth focus group, PJS)

Mveliso added that the lights' positioning was an important factor in why they were not stolen and why the sensors were:

Mveliso: The lights are installed on top of the house door, so it won't be easy to take it off. Someone inside won't think that you

are taking off the light; they will think that you are attacking him in his house. Those sensors were installed on the sides of the house. When you are in the kitchen, you won't hear anything. So when it's above the door, we are waiting for everything at that door. Some doors aren't open, so you don't know who is inside. Maybe by the time you are uninstalling the light, someone comes. Some lights are installed on the pathways that are being used most, so it won't be easy to take them off. (male, young adult, youth focus group, PJS)

Perhaps the sensors were stolen because the community did not feel ownership over them, nor did they understand the benefits of the sensors. On the other hand, it was easy to see how the lights were benefitting PJS, especially considering the co-production process, and the sense of ownership people developed over their lights. Bandla explained how worried people became when the lights malfunctioned at the beginning of the installation in March 2020, again highlighting the importance of the lights for the community:

Bandla: People talk about the lights, they love them, and then the lights went off because of the solar things; people were worried why the lights went off because people love the lights; they are so bright. (male, senior, household interview, PJS)

In fact, the only complaint interviewees voiced about the lights was that not everyone received a light at the same time. The maintenance team had to deal with this challenge during their routine checks and maintenance work. Community members would ask when they would receive their light, often growing impatient.

Anele: But I also want to ask that everyone gets a light so that everyone is happy because most of the time when we are working, the neighbour comes to us and asks where is the light. I also hope that in the second phase we can do all the houses so that everyone can be happy. Because now sometimes we have load-shedding and then it gets very dark. (male, young adult, maintenance team focus group, PJS)

Another dissatisfactory aspect of the phased intervention was that there were still many dark pathways. Even if a house or pathway had a light or lights installed, residents were still afraid of *skollies* hiding in the surrounding dark pathways, as Mveliso said in the youth focus group:

Mveliso: Yes, yes, because not every [path has a light]. Maybe someone can hide in those dark pathways and then when you arrive, they can catch you. If every path has a solar light, then maybe it's going to be better. (male, young adult, youth focus group, PJS)

Lenox: That's the other thing that they were complaining about. When the lights were installed, maybe two lights, here and two lights there, and it's bright. And the other pathways that are supposed to have light don't have light. (male, young adult, household interview, PJS)

Sibongile, a maintenance team member, believed that there would be less vandalism if lights could be installed for everyone simultaneously. Anele agreed with her.

Sibongile: I think it (vandalism) would have been less if everyone had a light.
Stephanie: *Why?*
Sibongile: Other people who are angry about not having the lights.
Stephanie: *Is it something you heard?*
Sibongile: Something I think personally.
Anele: I agree. Some of the people see we work, and they will do anything to get a light. (maintenance team focus group, PJS)

Thankfully, there were relatively few cases of vandalism, even with the discontent described above. To our surprise, renovations were a bigger issue than theft and vandalism, especially as members of some households tried to remove lights and panels themselves, sometimes breaking one or the other. Between March 2020 and May 2021, when I conducted my endline fieldwork, our maintenance team received twenty-one service requests related to renovations. The maintenance team worked hard to inform households not to remove systems by themselves. If households wanted to renovate, they would generally ask the maintenance team for help. Renovations are likely to be one of the biggest challenges with decentralised solar lighting infrastructure.

Working in such a participatory manner requires significant energy and sensitivity, but the results are well worthwhile. Co-producing lighting was important on many levels, and everyone believed that the project would not have been such a success without this process. Through co-production, people understand the project, accept it as theirs and feel responsible for its care and effectiveness. By co-producing the lighting project from within PJS, the project's resilience and longevity was assured. The next section elaborates on how the co-produced lighting improved everynight life in PJS, from going to the toilet at night to sitting outside during loadshedding.

Lighting everynight life

Rather than directly correlating the shift in everynight life with the intervention, the shift needed to be considered within a complex network of change (and anticipation of change). This section therefore speaks in dynamic terms, using words like adjusting, processing, shifting and evolving to describe the change in everynight life after the co-produced public lighting intervention. After three weeks of endline fieldwork, my impression was that of dynamic change. One cannot and should not conclude that the lighting project directly correlated with a change in everynight life but rather consider the addition of public lighting as part of a dynamic system in constant flux. The most significant result was the sense of freedom that light gave people, to be outside at night because they could see people and be seen. Seeing instilled confidence in people as well as a sense of control over their environment, which they lacked in the dark shadows of area lighting. This section elaborates on how this new sense of freedom changed everynight life in PJS. **Figures 7, 8 and 9** give an impression of the degree to which lighting conditions improved.

From strangers in the dark to familiarity in the light

Not being able to see or recognise people when walking in the dark raises considerable fear. Darkness creates strangers, and suddenly everyone becomes an untrustworthy, feared stranger. This fear negatively affects social relations. Fear of crime raises many other emotions, such as loneliness, anger, hopelessness, as well as lack of freedom and trust. The addition of light in PJS addressed this inability to see and brought more people outside — strangers became familiar faces in the light. This section discusses how seeing and being seen positively affected social relations in PJS.

Social relations changed for most interviewees. Many related stories of suddenly talking to people

Fig 7   Before installation, shadows cast by high-mast lighting

Fig 8   Brightly lit courtyard after installing new solar public lights in PJS

Fig 9   Brightly lit pathway after installing new solar public lights in PJS

Map 2   Mrs Filifili's nighttime map after she received a light above her front door

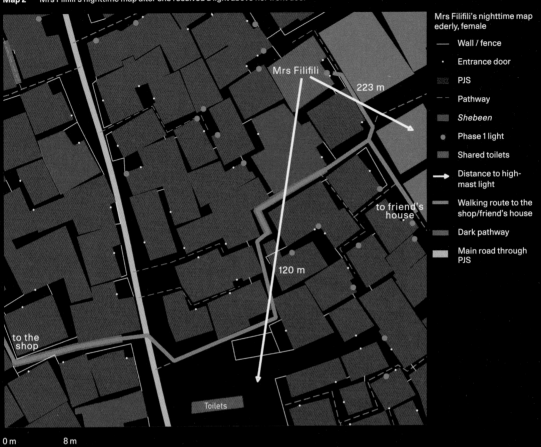

Mrs Filifili's nighttime map
ederly, female

— Wall / fence

· Entrance door

▨ PJS

-- Pathway

▨ *Shebeen*

● Phase 1 light

▨ Shared toilets

→ Distance to high-
mast light

▨ Walking route to the
shop/friend's house

▨ Dark pathway

▨ Main road through
PJS

0 m   8 m

they had not spoken to before the lights were installed or of changing social habits since the lights arrived. In her first interview in 2018, Thembeka talked about always being afraid of strangers walking up and down the pathways. However, since the lights were installed, her fear has lessened, and she even greets them from time to time. She now finds strangers less threatening because she can see them and describe them if they try to rob her.

Stephanie: *When we spoke the last time, you also said there were those people going up and down [the pathways], but you didn't like them?*

Thembeka: ... But at that time, I couldn't see anything.

Stephanie: *So it's the same people, you're just not ...*

Thembeka: Not scared of them.

Thembeka: There were people, a lot of people coming this side [before the lights]. Sometimes they are standing here, and I don't understand their language. But now, seriously, I am free. One day I met someone on that corner, he was going to R-Section, and I was coming to my corner. He didn't say anything to me; I didn't say anything to him. Sometimes they say, "Hello, Ma." [I say] "Hi Baba.", and I get inside. That's it. There's no one even saying, "do you have R10 for me?"
(female, senior, household interview, PJS)

Mrs Filifili also mentioned recognising people. Even though she had not noticed more people outside than before the lights were installed, she was able to recognise more familiar faces on her regular walking route to her favourite shop at night, shown in her nighttime map (Map 2).

Mrs Filifili: When I am going through the pathway, I pass many people that I know. Sometimes they are going to the shop; sometimes they are coming from the shop.
(female, elderly, household interview, PJS)

From my interviews, it seemed that the lights encouraged more street-level interaction between neighbours. While there has always been a strong relationship between neighbours in PJS, they now seemed to interact more at night, spending time together outside. I elaborate more on this in the section titled "Being outside at night". Being able to identify people was by far the most prominent theme raised in the interviews. Interviewees often contradicted themselves by saying the lights did not impact crime but would later comment on how they felt safer in PJS because they could see and identify people, as Lenox, a young male, describes:

Lenox: It's much easier now that we have lights because if you get robbed, you can easily see the person who robbed you because of the brightness. But before, you could not see who is robbing who. So now we can identify the person.
(male, young adult, household interview, PJS)

Thabisa, my research assistant, told a story of someone who could retrieve his belongings the day after he was robbed because the lights made it possible to identify the robber.

Thabisa: I just remembered an incident. Xolelwa's husband got robbed when he was reaching his house, and then he identified the person, and he was drunk at that time, but in the morning, he knew who took the phone and went to take the phone back. Because there was a light, even though he was drunk, he could recognise the person.
(female, adult, research assistant, PJS)

Some elderly and senior interviewees described how they enjoyed the lights because they could observe the outside from inside their homes at night. They still perceived outside to be unsafe but believed they benefitted from the lights purely from an observational point of view. It made them feel more secure at night and they could address any incidents when they felt safe to go out in the morning.

Stephanie: *So you are all saying that there is still crime, day and night, and the lights don't help. So what difference do the lights make for you?*

Nomzamo: There is a difference because even if there is a person who is dead, who is left there, you can identify that person, or who stabbed that person. Before, it was dark, and you did not know who did this, but now we can identify people.

Nonicikelelo: I agree. (elderly focus group, PJS)

Stephanie: *So even now that there is light, it doesn't make a difference?*

Nomzamo: They make a difference. Even if I'm inside, I can see very clearly outside. I can watch my neighbour because he drinks a lot. When I hear a noise, I can go to the curtain and watch. I can switch my light off and see that it's just my neighbour getting home. You can even see the person who's trying to break into houses through my curtains that that person is tall/short and identify them.

Stephanie:	*How does it make you feel to be able to see/look outside?*
Nomzamo:	I feel right because I can identify if my neighbour is there or at work, and I can hear the door banging, and I can know that person is breaking in there.
Nonicikelelo:	I also feel right because I can identify people.
Den:	Yes, I agree with them because dark is not the same as light. You can see who is there.
	(elderly focus group, PJS)

Thembeka, a senior female in PJS, also described how, with the light, she could watch over their pathway through her kitchen window at night, as shown in **Map 3** and the accompanying photo, **(Figure 10)**, observing who is fighting, allowing her to address the incident in the morning.

Thembeka:	Because sometimes I hear people fighting or I hear some rumours outside. I go to my kitchen, and I just stand there; I don't put my light on, I just stand there, and then I can see, "Oh."...When they are fighting for their stuff, they are drunk, but just because they are passing here or sometimes I just want to see, "oh, it was who and who", and then tomorrow morning I will go to them, that's it.
	(female, senior, household interview, PJS)

Identifying familiar faces was also important to reduce fear in the pathways. Once people recognised someone they knew and trusted, they felt safe.

Yamkela:	It's to recognise. No matter if you don't recognise the face, to see my body, you can see, OK, that's Yamkela. Because most people are putting those polo neck masks so ... **(female, adult, maintenance team focus group, PJS)**

It seemed as if social conflict was still present. People were still afraid of getting robbed and were vigilant when outdoors at night. However, some shifts in social conflicts had occurred, such as the habits of perpetrators and consequently the nature of their crimes. Some interviewees also felt that the nature of crime had changed because of the risk of being identified. For example, now that there was light, Thembeka was no longer as afraid of being violated as she was before, when young boys attempted to touch her inappropriately. They would no longer do so because of the risk of being recognised.

Stephanie:	*So they are not going to touch you anymore?*
Thembeka:	You see that other house had a light, when I am coming to that passage, the light is like that, so no one ...
Stephanie:	*No one is going to touch you.*
Thembeka:	No, no. They were taking chances because they saw it's dark. **(female, senior, household interview, PJS)**

The maintenance team all gave their opinions on how crime had changed in PJS. Yamkela mentioned *skollies* being more active during the day, stealing groceries and alcohol, as opposed to handbags and cell phones being stolen in the dark morning hours.

Yamkela:	I think most of the time they [*skollies*] are doing it during the daylight because they are robbing alcohol and some groceries.
Stephanie:	*So they steal food and alcohol more than cell phones?*
Yamkela:	Yes.
Stephanie:	*One or two years back, was there a difference in the* skollies*. Like were they robbing at night, were they more, were they more aggressive?*
Yamkela:	Early in the morning, around four/five, when people were going to work and even when they were coming back [from work]. So then they were busy with phones and that stuff.
Stephanie:	*They were, and are they still now?*
Yamkela:	Not quite. **(female, adult, maintenance team focus group, PJS)**

Anele indicated an increase in gang-related crime but a decrease in petty theft by *skollies* in the pathways.

Stephanie:	*Is this gang-related crime, or is it* skollies*?*
Anele:	You can call it gang. I can't talk about *amapara-para* [*skollies*] running around, but this is gangsterism.
Stephanie:	*Would you say the smaller* skollie *crime has decreased?*
Anele:	I can say it, yes. **(male, young adult, maintenance team focus group, PJS)**

Initially, Sibongile said the crime rate remained unchanged. However, when asked if the nature of crime had changed, she agreed with Anele's statement. The decrease in *skollies* operating in the pathways meant that PJS residents felt safer because they were the targets of *skollies* more than of dangerous gangsters.

Map 3   Thembeka's nighttime map after she received a light above her front door. Compare this map to her previous map in Chapter 4

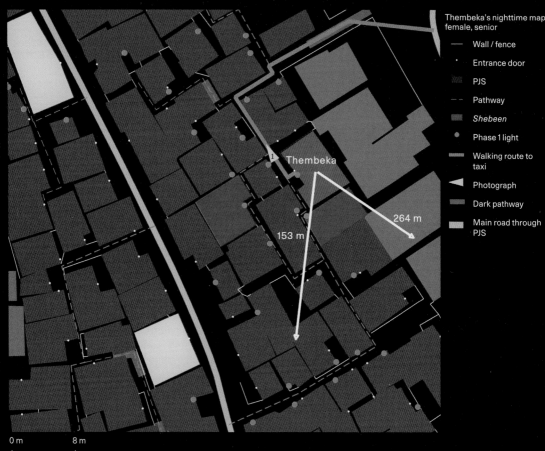

Thembeka's nighttime map
female, senior

— Wall / fence

· Entrance door

PJS

-- Pathway

Shebeen

● Phase 1 light

Walking route to
taxi

◀ Photograph

Dark pathway

Main road through
PJS

Thembeka

264 m

153 m

0 m   8 m

Fig 10   Thembeka's house at night, with a clear view of the pathway from her kitchen window, photograph 1 on **Map 3**

Sibongile: PJS has changed. Because when I am walking at night, at least I can be safer because it's not dark like before. Also, regarding the crime, nothing has changed.

Stephanie: *Is it like Anele said, more gangsterism and less* skollies.

Sibongile: Less *skollies*, now there are bigger *skollies* with guns and stuff.

...

Sibongile: Yes, they are not going to do anything because they have their own things.

Stephanie: *They have bigger fish to fry than the cell phone in your pocket. They are robbing shops.*

Sibongile: Yes.

Stephanie: *Ok, do you agree with that?*

Sibongile: I do. (female, adult, maintenance team focus group, PJS)

The increased gang-related crime was quite evident in recent news stories when six men were shot and killed in a house in PJS (Persens, 2021), and in another incident, a Somalian trader was shot and killed inside his shop in PJS. After the first incident, police started conducting regular armed patrols to reinforce their presence in PJS. None of the interviewees discussed these violent incidents—they seemed more afraid of *skollies* assaulting them in the pathways than increased gang activity.

Interviewees also commented on fewer *skollies* and gangsters walking around at night, saying they saw fewer people and heard less noise at night.

Mr Fata: There was walking around the place, but now they [gangsters] are not walking around.

Stephanie: *Are you walking around at night in PJS?*

Mr Fata: No, I am not walking around, but late at night, there is no noise. (male, elderly, household interview, PJS)

A young female interviewee, Zianda, a senior woman, Thembeka, and Mrs Filifili, an elderly woman, mentioned this as well. Chapter 4 discussed hearing the night. People now heard silence and less rapid walking. They felt that nighttime had improved and was changing for the better.

Zianda: Yes, it's changing a lot because no one is crying outside now. No matter what, going outside at night, I didn't see *skollies* outside. Yes, they are gone. (female, adult, household interview, PJS)

Stephanie: *And when you are walking at eleven thirty at night, what is it like in PJS now?*

Thembeka: During the week, it's quiet; I don't meet anyone. But at the weekend, there are some people going up and down, but I don't get anything. They don't do anything to me. (female, senior, household interview, PJS)

Stephanie: *Why do you think there is less robbery now?*

Mrs Filifili: It's because of the lights, the *skollies* don't like lights because you can recognise a person. It's also quiet now. (female, elderly, household interview, PJS)

Bandla, a senior male who received a light, disagreed that there were fewer *skollies* and commented that he could hear people walking around and taking drugs 24/7 in his section (C-Section). He experienced his section as unsafe and commented that sections differed in safety. Some interviewees, but not all, perceived a shift in the perpetrator type in PJS. Though Bandla was pessimistic about crime in PJS, claiming that it had worsened, he also admitted the lights helped in recognising and reporting perpetrators to "the committee". His reasoning was therefore enabling reporting:

Stephanie: *Why are lights good then?*

Bandla: Even though I don't have the power to fight with you, I know who you are. [It's] to see.

Stephanie: *So that you can do what? Take action? Go to the police?*

Bandla: Yes, yes. If the perpetrator is from PJS, I can go to the committee [leadership] and tell the leadership that this person robbed me, and they can solve it. (male, senior, household interview, PJS)

Interviewees also raised the topic of reporting social conflict. There are two levels of reporting crime. Firstly, most interviewees discussed how they could now identify and describe someone, enabling them to report it to the leadership or the police.

Mveliso: So when I am there [in the pathway], I can be free, even if someone attacks me, I am able to see them, and then I am able to report, and if he robs my phone, then I am able to say, "this one robbed my phone" because I have seen him. (male, young adult, youth focus group, PJS)

The second level is about the leadership experiencing less reporting and the general community experiencing less hearsay. The leaders in the focus group agreed that reporting had decreased, compared with before lights were installed.

Tera:	We didn't get any report.
Stephanie:	*Yes, but before?*
Tera:	Yes, we used to get the reports, yes.
Stephanie:	*Now they don't come anymore?*
Tera:	No.
Mongezi:	Especially in the morning, that's when we always get the report, people who are going to work, especially when it's winter because it's still dark. But now it's less.
	(leadership focus group, PJS)

Xolelwa, a female leader, also noted that she received far fewer reports of house break-ins as a result of the lights:

Stephanie:	*How do you know its [crime] reduced? Do you just feel it?*
Xolelwa:	I know because before there were some reports, more about my house was broken, someone came in my house and took my stuff. But after the lights were installed, there were no reports. **(female, adult, leadership focus group, PJS)**

Mrs Filifili, an elderly woman in PJS, said she heard fewer tales or hearsay about crime incidents and attributed this to the lighting.

Mrs Filifili:	Before, there was a lot of robberies, but now I have not heard any stories of robbery. **(female, elderly, household interview, PJS)**

It seemed that even though interviewees all felt more empowered to report incidents, the leadership had the impression that reporting had decreased drastically. Overall, the ability to recognise people in the light made strangers less of a threat. If robbed, people would have the agency of sight and recognition to report the incident and seek justice. This ability to report seemed to affect the nature of crime. People experienced fewer issues with *skollies* in the now brightly lit pathways at night.

Being outside at night

Some people spent more time outside at night than others. Before, besides *skollies*, who "owned the night", nighttime characters were children, youth and men. Interviewees often regarded these characters as irresponsible for being outside at night. The endline interviews revealed a slight change in the types of characters seen outside, and the length of time spent outside was also extended. The maintenance team all agreed that more people were outside in PJS, and attributed this to the new lights. They argued that they had seen older people socialising outside. Others claimed it was younger people around the same age as the maintenance team. These younger people, late-teens and people in their twenties, were seen outside more often, primarily in new social spots that had developed in brightly lit streets, especially around the *spaza* shop with new WiFi. The maintenance team all emphasised that more children were outside and until much later; other interviewees also mentioned this, some even claiming that children stayed out until 23:00.

Stephanie:	*Are some people sitting outside and not drinking?*
Lucky:	Yes.
Stephanie:	*And what age are they?*
Lucky:	Like me [in their 20s].
Sibongile:	And also old people, they do.
Stephanie:	*Like the gogos [grannies]? Like sitting, chatting to the neighbours?*
Sibongile:	Yes.
Thabile:	Who are the old ladies [in disbelief]?
Stephanie:	*And kids?*
Yamkela:	Yoh, a lot!
All:	A lot!
	(maintenance team focus group, PJS)

PJS seemed to be busier at night until 22:00 or 23:00, but it was quieter later at night or in the early morning. People were no longer hearing noises at night as before. Activity was also concentrated along the pathways, while the main road through PJS was quieter. There may be several reasons for this. People were meeting up in the pathways more often because of the lights, or they preferred to avoid the main road because of routine patrols and lockdown regulations.

I identified one new social hotspot in my fieldwork which everyone was aware of in PJS, a pathway in B-Section. Five houses on the short pathway received lights **(Figures 11 and 12)**. The pathway had a *shebeen* before the lights were installed, but now it was much busier, and the activity had spread throughout that pathway. Residents on the pathway also installed a shade cloth over a section for people to sit under. Leaders commented on the rise in activity, even during the day. Leaders were all aware of the hotspot and agreed that it had only become so popular after the lights were installed.

Thabisa:	We saw you [Tera] at the hotspot there during the night, in that *shebeen*.

Fig 11   New social hotspot, a pathway in BC-Section, where five households received a light

Fig 12   The *shebeen* as part of the new social hotspot, a pathway in BC-Section where five households received a light

Fig 13 Walking through the pathways at night, we found Zianda's and her neighbour's families socialising near their house

Fig 14 Zianda's and her neighbour's families socialising near their house at night, something they did not do before they received lights

Stephanie:	*That* shebeen *was full, full, full.*
Tera:	Oh, that place is always full, there outside because those houses there, one, two, three, four, all got a light. That pathway is clear; I think five houses there got lights.
Stephanie:	*So has it gotten busier, or has it always been busy?*
Tera:	No, it was not busy before. But now it's very busy, even if there are no lights [loadshedding], the solar is always there for them. It's not dark.
Mongezi:	Especially there where you say now.
Xolelwa:	If it is hot during the afternoon, they sit down and chill by those lights.

(leadership focus group, PJS)

Mveliso describes the pathway in B-Section:

Mveliso:	And to those guys who like to party, it is an advantage for them because they can even go to a place, even there, by BB-Section, there is plenty of light there. You can see and hear people partying at night, outside. Because there is one path there which is very light, and you can see people staying outside until twelve o'clock. (male, young adult, youth focus group, PJS)

Some, not all, *shebeens* seemed to have a better reputation than before the lights were installed.

Stephanie:	*Ok, because a lot of people say that they try to avoid the pathways where the she-* beens *are because that is where the trouble is.*
Mveliso:	I think everyone in PJS understands those people [in Figures 11 and 12] because you can see there is a family there, you can see people chatting to one another, going to one another's place.
Yamkela:	Sharing.

(male, youth focus group, PJS)

In an interview, Masi, a teen male, presented a photo of a social space in PJS, saying that lights helped avoid fights escalating around *shebeens*. Although this is not something I focused on during my interviews and have little empirical evidence, alcohol-induced fighting, especially around *shebeens* where lights were installed, may also have reduced or has changed in nature since lights were added.

Stephanie:	*What would be the difference? Is it a good thing if there are lights where people are hanging out and drinking?*

Masi:	Yes, I think so because here, it's dark and they can't see each other. Maybe an incident can happen here. But if there was light and an incident happens, they would see the people who started the problems. But here it's dark, and then they can't see people, maybe they are fighting outside and you don't see them because it's dark. (male, teen, participatory photo interview, PJS)

The nightlife in PJS did seem more active. Most interviewees felt that more people were spending time outside at night, mostly sitting in a circle, drinking alcohol or non-alcoholic beverages as well. Jennifer, one of the maintenance team, had noticed this in her area of PJS, C-Section.

Stephanie:	*Have you noticed a difference in the social life in PJS? Do you see more people chilling outside at night? Do you see a difference?*
Yamkela:	Especially on weekends.
Jennifer:	On my side, I do see it.
Stephanie:	*What is the difference?*
Jennifer:	They are sitting outside.
Stephanie:	*Is it during loadshedding?*
Jennifer:	During the week.
Stephanie:	*In the dark pathways too?*
Jennifer:	Where there is the light.
Stephanie:	*Are they drinking and getting drunk, or are some people just...*
Jennifer:	Drinking.
Stephanie:	*Everyone?*
Jennifer:	No, some of them.
Stephanie:	*And the other people?*
Jennifer:	Just chilling. (female, young adults, maintenance focus group, PJS)

Zianda said her neighbours spent more time outside at night. She joined them during loadshedding and talked to them from her locked patio gate. As shown in **Figures 13 and 14**, I was happy to find her outside her house, socialising with her neighbours and their children one evening. She describes enjoying her neighbours' new practice of sitting outside at night:

Stephanie:	*Are people sitting outside at night?*
Zianda:	Yes, maybe at seven or eight at night. Yes, my neighbours.
Stephanie:	*Do they always sit outside at night?*
Zianda:	No, not always, on weekends.
Stephanie:	*And before the lights were here, were they also sitting outside?*
Zianda:	No.
Stephanie:	*Do you enjoy that?*
Zianda:	Yes! (female, adult, household interview, PJS)

Lenox and Mveliso, both young males, separately discussed how the lights benefited family gatherings in yards at night. Lenox agreed that he had seen more people outside at night. Mveliso thought the lights presented opportunities to attend social events and connect more with neighbours.

Lenox: Sometimes, even if there is a family gathering outside the yard, now it is right because the other households don't have light outside, so their lights are good.

Stephanie: *And have you seen people outside at night?*

Lenox: Yes, now you see people outside at night. (male, young adult, household interview, PJS)

Mveliso: When you see the neighbourhood, you can see they can build a yard so that they can do something in one place because there is light. If someone has a birthday in the yard, they are hosting a party; we can go there even if we are not invited because this is our place. What's happening next door attracts me to go there. So when there is light, you can see, you won't stay inside when you know there are people outside in your yard. (male, young adult, youth focus group, PJS)

Yamkela from the youth focus group talked about developing a social relationship with his neighbour, for they could now share food while sitting outside at night, especially during loadshedding.

Yamkela: I think for me, I see, it's going to change a lot because I have a neighbour; when the loadshedding starts, we take our plates out and share our food. I think that is one thing that is going to change on our side. Because when there is everyone outside, you can taste everyone's food and yeah. (male, young adult, youth focus group, PJS)

With regular loadshedding, certain practices have developed during a power outage, and the combination of loadshedding and the solar lights seems to bring people outdoors. Yamkela and Mveliso commented on the busy streets during loadshedding: due to boredom, people would rather be outside under their solar light than sit inside in the darkness. In their experience, people generally watched TV at home when there was no loadshedding.

Mveliso: No one will see them in the house in the darkness [loadshedding]. Better go outside on the street where many people are.

Yamkela: To add to what is being said. You can also finish your supper outside now, unlike before. If the electricity goes off, you can take your plate and go and finish your plate outside.

Stephanie: *Is that what you are doing?*

Yamkela: I did that yesterday. I even posted it on Facebook. (male, young adult, youth focus group, PJS)

Stephanie: And are there a lot of children playing outside at night?
Sive: When it's loadshedding. I don't know, maybe they like loadshedding, but they like to play outside when it's dark, but it's not safe.

Table 1 In this photo, Sive describes children playing outside during loadshedding (female, teen, PJS)

Yamkela described how people enjoyed sitting outside at night during the festive season (summertime in South Africa). However, before the solar lights were installed, people tended to go inside their houses when there were power outages. With the new solar lights, people preferred to go or stay outside when there were power cuts.

Yamkela:　They sit during the festive time, but when the lights go off [loadshedding], they go inside their houses. But with our solar lights, they sit outside because of the solar, so there is no way that we can go inside. Now at least it's easy now, life. You can have a speaker and put it outside and have a party outside. (male, young adult, youth focus group, PJS)

Sive, a teen living in PJS, pointed out how children seemed to enjoy loadshedding, presenting a photo of children playing outside (Table 1).

Stephanie:　*And are there a lot of children playing outside at night?*
Sive:　When it's loadshedding, maybe they enjoy loadshedding, I don't know, but they like to play outside when it's dark, but they are not safe. (female, teen, participatory photo interview, PJS)

Some interviewees spoke about staying out or going out later at night because of the lights. Zianda now comes back later at night after visiting her mother in another community nearby.

Zianda:　Before the lights, I came inside early. If I'm visiting my mother here in Q-Section, I came early. But now I come past eight, any time.
Stephanie:　*So you come home later now that the lights are installed?*
Zianda:　Yes.
Stephanie:　*Ok, you feel like you can come home later?*
Zianda:　Yes. (female, adult, household interview, PJS)

Mr Fata also mentioned staying out later and that PJS was "nice now" because no bad people were roaming around.

Stephanie:　*What is the latest that you leave your house at nighttime?*
Fata:　At least at ten pm.
Stephanie:　*That's late!*
Fata:　Yes, it's very late, it's nice now!
Stephanie:　*Why is it nice?*
Fata:　I see no people walking around.

Stephanie:　*Those bad people?*
Fata:　Yes. (male, elderly, household interview, PJS)

The new lights changed the nature of everynight life activities on different levels, but ultimately people were going out more and later, developing new social relations and nighttime activities. Sitting outside with a neighbour was now possible, visiting a friend later at night seemed less stressful, and the new solar lights eased the loadshedding burden.

Walking

Walking practices certainly changed for some interviewees, and for others too. The main changes were different walking routes, walking slower and alone at night. Yamkela commented on the nature of walking and how people were not rushing through pathways as before. They sounded more relaxed than before the lights were installed.

Thabile:　You have people walking around until seven in the morning.
Stephanie:　*And the nature of the walking?*
Yamkela:　They are walking freely.
Stephanie:　*People also spoke about hearing people running because they are stressed. Has that changed? Are people more relaxed?*
Yamkela:　Now people are relaxed … (female, maintenance team focus group, PJS)

Mveliso said he found brightly lit routes and changed his own routes accordingly. He felt all youth should do this for their own safety. Yamkela, in the youth focus group, agreed and changed his route to the toilet at night, now using the brighter pathways.

Mveliso:　… so you can walk from P-Section, you can know where is your direction. You can say, "ok, I can pass this light, and I can come back there and there until you reach your home." So you know even the paths that are light. Some people get used to those lights, so they even know which areas they must use when it's dark. (male, young adult, youth focus group, PJS)

The two young brothers interviewed also mentioned changing their routes to the lit paths. Though they were not afraid of walking outside at night, they felt walking along the brighter paths more comfortable and enjoyable.

Stephanie:　*Are you using the other pathways with lights more?*
Siya:　Yes.

Fig 15   Walking in the dark with high-mast lighting in PJS is an uncomfortable experience

Fig 16   Walking more comfortably with the new wall-mounted solar lighting illuminating the flooded street

Stephanie:	*So, do you start to change the way you walk now, to walk on the paths with light?*
Siya:	Yes. (male, young adult, household interview, PJS)

The leaders all agreed that the pathways in PJS were busier early at night than the main road and attributed this change to the lights. Another reason for the busier pathways was to avoid the police patrolling on the main road in PJS during lockdown.

Tera:	No, the pathways are not the same as the main road. There's a lot of people in the pathways.
Stephanie:	*But the main road is quiet?*
Tera:	It's a little bit quiet.
Stephanie:	*And the pathways where people are walking?*
Tera:	They are walking up and down. Because there is light.
Xolelwa:	Because of the light.
Mongezi:	Because there is light. That's why they are using the pathways. (leadership focus group, PJS)

Improved lighting can also positively impact nighttime walking comfort, where there are safety hazards such as sewerage leaks and uneven surfaces. For Masi, a teen male, comfort is the most important element that light brings.

Stephanie:	*And what else would make a difference if you added light here. Besides identifying, how else would light make you feel if you were in this passage?*
Masi:	It [light] would make some people go comfortably because being comfortable passing [walking] in a place is the most important thing. (male, teen, participatory photo interview, PJS)

Den and Thembeka both struggled with their eyesight and said light was important to help them see at night. Den added that the lights did not create too much glare because they were small.

Den:	The lights are good for my eyes because they are not too strong, like the sun, so I can walk around at night. (male, elderly focus group, PJS)
Thembeka:	You see, I am old, so at night I can't see properly. So when there is a light, I can see, I can see "ok" ... . There is a difference, a big difference because that difference helps my eyesight so that I can see. (female, senior, household interview, PJS)

Figures 15 and 16 show two pathways in PJS that flooded due to a blocked stormwater sewer. It is clear that beyond impacting fear of crime, lighting can help people, especially the elderly, in navigating complicated terrains.

Accessing basic services

Baseline fieldwork revealed toilet access was a major concern. This shifted with new practices after the lights were installed. Yamkela, an adult female, told Jennifer, another participant, to her disbelief that she had walked to the toilets at 02:30 by herself without feeling afraid.

Yamkela:	For instance, at the month-end weekend, I woke up at half-past two to go to the toilet.
Jennifer:	Hayibo [no ways]!
Yamkela:	I was not afraid; I woke up freely, went to the toilet by myself and went back. So I was not afraid, like, "Oh, there is probably someone in that passage".
Stephanie:	*And that is because of the lights?*
Yamkela:	It's because of the lights because I can see. (female, maintenance team focus group, PJS)

Zianda also felt more comfortable going to the toilet at night, alone and without using her cell phone for light.

Stephanie:	*And before the lights were here, were you going to the toilet at night?*
Zianda:	Yes, but we are scared. We use our torches on our phones. If I don't have my phone now, I don't have a problem because the lights help us. (female, adult, household interview, PJS)

When asked in a focus group about her general nighttime experiences in PJS, Nonicikelelo, an elderly woman, immediately referred to accessing the toilets — even late at night. She also said she could go to the toilet unaccompanied and without help — something she could not do before the lights were installed.

Nonicikelelo:	The lights are very helpful because I can go to the toilet.
Stephanie:	*Which one? The tall ones?*
Nonicikelelo:	The solar lights. The lights are very good for us because we can go to the toilets. Especially now.
...	
Stephanie:	*Do you feel that you can go to the toilet later at night?*

Fig 17   Imange's photograph showing the dark toilets during loadshedding (female, child, PJS)

Material Change	With light	Without light	TOTAL
Renovations (roof, structure, painting)	65	105	170
Landscaping (planting, shade cloth, fencing, new yard, new compound)	30	28	58
Adding own outdoor light	-	6	6
TOTAL STRUCTURES	85*	112*	197*

*some structures underwent several material changes, e.g., painting and planting

Table 2 Observed material change in PJS ranging from renovations to landscaping and adding a personal outdoor light

Feelings	PJS at night
free, relaxed, comfortable, happy, right, safe, not afraid	less fighting, no noise, quiet, better, changing, less *skollies*, right, different
Social activity	**Lights**
chilling, socialising, busier, drinking, gathering, party, event, nice, benefitting, sharing	bright, right, protecting, helping, loadshedding, like, love

Table 3 Recurring words and phrases used to describe nighttime in PJS under four main themes

Nonicikelelo: Around 10pm I can go. Before not. I couldn't go alone; I needed someone to assist me. (female, elderly focus group, PJS)

In the youth focus group, Yamkela related going to the toilet now, but before he did not use the toilets at nighttime.

Yamkela: ... I also go to the toilet at night now. I can go to the toilet at night. (male, youth focus group, PJS)

Not much had changed for those who didn't get lights around their area—Ukhonaye, a teen female was still negatively impacted by darkness.

Ukhonaye: During the night, it's very dark in AC-Section, I can't even go to the toilet during the night because it's too dark where my house is, and people are getting robbed there.
Stephanie: *And for you, the darkness and nighttime are influencing your life a lot.*
Ukhonaye: Yes. (female, youth focus group, PJS)

Generally, participants who had received lights in their area were more comfortable accessing toilets at night, or they had changed how they went to the toilets. It must be noted that lighting conditions around the toilets are still poor, as Imange, a female child, demonstrated during her participatory photo interview. Her photo was taken during loadshedding and shows dark toilets, pointing to the importance of having brightly lit toilets (Figure 17). As we have learned in this section, it is equally important to have brightly lit routes to walk to the toilets at night.

In one year, at least twenty-six per cent of all PJS structures were materially changed. In my endline fieldwork, I reviewed all structures for observed change, using various categories:

It was challenging to ascertain whether the material changes made in PJS between March 2020 and March 2021 were due to new COVID-19 lockdown distractions or the lighting installations (Figure 18). **Map 4** shows some correlations between households who received a phase 1 light and who made material changes to their environment. Notably, material change often happened in clusters. Although some households that changed their structures did not receive lights, their neighbours may have received a light, which could have influenced the decision to change.

Shifting perceptions of the night

At the time of the baseline fieldwork, interviewees mostly related their nighttime perceptions to fear of crime and not to being able to walk freely. Finally, a change in pride emerging in PJS and the importance of a sense of ownership of the new lights were noticeable, though this had less to do with nighttime perceptions, which had shifted subtly and were slightly less fear-oriented. Though most interviewees still expressed a level of fear of crime at night, they also expressed a new sense of freedom and comfort when going outside. While Thembeka went to is still afraid when going outside at night, with the solar lights she felt reassured because she could identify people.

Thembeka: But now, not that I am not scared, I am still scared ... . At least in light, there is something, "ok, he has got a scar here". You see, there is a big difference. (female, senior, household interview, PJS)

Many interviewees still felt afraid when going outside at night, but they developed a certain sense of courage to confront their nighttime fears, largely because seeing gave them a sense of control.

Map 4 Investigating the correlation between material changes and households who received a light in phase 1

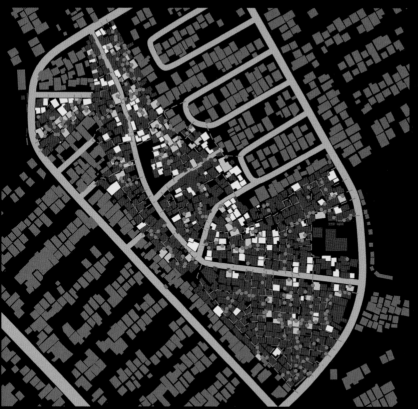

Material change and light

– – Pathway

▨ Material change and no light

▨ Material change and light

• Phase 1 light

26 % of PJS structures underwent material change

57% material change and no light

43% material change and light

30% phase 1 light and material change

0 m ⊢——————————⊣ 100 m

Fig 18 Pathway and house with phase 1 lights and new greenery below the light

Yamkela, a male in the youth focus group, described how the lights help him assess his safety.

Yamkela: [There are] passages that are still dark, but you can see people far from us. But when you are going there, you will see someone is crossing, and you will think "must I go, or must I wait". Then you can decide ok "let me go back" where there is light. (male, youth focus group, PJS)

I started most of my interviews by wanting to know what PJS was like at nighttime after the light installations, then later asked how people felt about walking outside at night. The most common response was that PJS had improved, as Mr Fata says:

Stephanie: *So my first question will be what is PJS like at nighttime at the moment?*

Fata: No, it's better now. (male, elderly, household interview, PJS)

It was challenging for people to express how they felt about nighttime in PJS, but an analysis of endline interviews revealed various repeatedly used words and phrases. The most common word or phrase mentioned during interviews was that the new lights made interviewees feel "free". Some examples:

Mrs Filifili: When it was dark, it was very scary even to go to my neighbours. But now that I have a light, I am free and safe, and I have nothing to be scared of. (female, elderly, household interview, PJS)

Thembeka: But there is a difference to me since I feel free. You see, when you are happy, you don't think of anything else. You just look after your... yeah. (female, senior, household interview, PJS)

Bandla: I feel happy, I feel free when there is light and it's not dark. (male, senior, household interview, PJS)

Zianda: If I am going to the shop at 8 pm, yes. But now I am feeling free when I go out because these lights protect us now. (female, adult, household interview, PJS)

Memory strongly influences perception and changing perceptions can take time. Generally, there has been a shift toward more positive nighttime perceptions in PJS, and after the second phase of lights, I hypothesise this shift will become more apparent.

Performing light: networked change

I conducted my endline fieldwork a year after 283 households had received lights. Due to early fault repairs, by the time I returned to the field, they had been fully functional for six months. Approximately 400 households were still waiting for their light in the second phase. The phased research design and problems with the lights largely impacted the endline findings. Many interviewees said the lighting had no impact since they only lit some pathways and not all. I tried to build a scenario for these interviewees in which every house would receive a light, that all the pathways would be brightly lit. The interviewees generally changed their opinions after considering this and commented that the lights would impact their lives, but there was still some scepticism. Masi, a teen boy, explains:

Stephanie: *Did you see any of the lights in PJS?*

Masi: Yes, I did, they were solar lights, but to me, they didn't make any difference because they were in the place where you could say, "this one, this is the light", but they didn't put it in the place where you could see people pass the most on that corner. You see, maybe they put it here, but people pass a lot here [gesturing]. If there was a light here, then maybe people could even pass on this corner.

Stephanie: *And what if those lights were everywhere?*

Masi: Yes, that could be better cause they are everywhere, but now they are not everywhere, so it sounds like the same thing to me. (male, teen, participatory photo interview, PJS)

This indicates that PJS residents do not only consider their households or pathways when discussing public lighting but instead look at PJS as a network of pathways and consider the overall lighting conditions. Light in front of their house is immaterial if the pathway to access toilets or their friends' houses remains unlit. I am confident that my endline fieldwork results would have been more impactful had it been done after the phase two lighting installation.

The global COVID-19 lockdown regulations imposed by the national government in March 2020 must also be considered in the changes in everynight life. Different alert levels came with varying regulations, but for a full year, bans and restrictions on buying and consuming alcohol had a major impact on nightlife in PJS. Combined with job losses, curfews and school closures, social dynamics in PJS changed. Older interviewees mentioned that it seemed quieter than the previous year, which they associated with safety. When asked why it had seemed quieter, some, such as PJS leader Mongezi, felt it was due to COVID, though others disagreed.

> **Mongezi:** Since the start of the lockdown, there are not so many people out, especially at night, after they can't sell alcohol. After that, we don't have a lot of people. The people are still holding that instruction, and you are not going to find the social people being busy. **(male, leadership focus group, PJS)**

An elderly man in PJS, Mr Fata, initially seemed unsure why he sensed PJS was better than before. In discussion he realised it was because people were not walking around as much anymore. Still, he couldn't determine why they were walking around less, though when I mentioned COVID-19, he appeared to remember this reason and conceded that COVID-19 had "made PJS feel better".

> **Mr Fata:** With the coronavirus, the *shebeens* are closed, and there are less criminals because of this. People were not walking around, they are indoors. **(male, elderly, household interview, PJS)**

Thembeka, a senior PJS resident, mentioned COVID-19 when describing fewer people in PJS's pathways than before. She also said that people's conduct had changed. Before the lights were installed, they tended to rush up and down the pathways, which she clearly associated with *skollies*, but she observed that now people rushed less.

> **Thembeka:** I mean to say that time before, sometimes you see people standing there, you are scared of them. Now, maybe because of COVID or I don't know what, the people are not that rushed like before. **(female, senior, household interview, PJS)**

Mrs Filifili disagreed with this, claiming that no one was afraid of COVID. Her perception was that crime had declined in PJS because of the lighting.

> **Stephanie:** *Why do you think there is less robbery now?*
>
> **Mrs Filifili:** It's because of the lights; the *skollies* don't like lights because you can recognise a person. It's also quiet now.

> **Stephanie:** *Do you think this is because of corona or because of the lights?*
>
> **Mrs Filifili:** No, it's not because of the corona, because people are not scared of corona; they are still walking around. I think it's because of the lights because gangsters come from other sections to come and rob people here. Now that we have lights, they can't do that because they don't know if we are going to shoot them while they are robbing other people. **(female, elderly, household interview, PJS)**

The COVID-19 pandemic likely had an impact on everynight life in PJS. With *shebeens* closed and fewer people drinking alcohol, people were spending less time outside at night. A study by the Institute of Security Studies on lockdown and violence reduction shows a significant decrease in violence, except for gun violence, in South Africa (Faull and Kelly, 2020). In 2020, the South African Police Service also saw a drastic drop in violent crime and attributed this to the alcohol ban (Singh, 2020). With these statistics, my research assistant, Thabisa, mentioned random patrols by armed forces in PJS to enforce lockdown rules. These patrols and shocking news of police brutality to enforce lockdown restrictions certainly instilled fear in many residents, deterring them from venturing out at night. Another important component was the drop in disposable income due to the devastating economic impact of the pandemic. People had less money, so they socialised less.

Since 2019, bouts of nationwide loadshedding significantly influenced everynight life in PJS and piqued residents' interest in the public lighting intervention. Loadshedding resumed during phase one installation, and people showed greater interest in the solar lights. At the time of my endline fieldwork, the same happened—several nights of loadshedding emphasised the value of the solar lights. Loadshedding had a two-fold impact on the research results. The lack of electricity and resulting darkness made the solar lights much more visible and valuable to the community, as Siya, a young male, observed.

> **Siya:** These lights help us a lot, especially during loadshedding. When there is loadshedding, it's very dark, but the lights are on. **(male, young adult, household interview, PJS)**

Loadshedding also increased activity in the streets of PJS, drawing people from their dark homes and increasing nighttime outdoor activity.

The final element in the network of change is the new public WiFi installed in PJS, mid-2019. In March 2021, I discovered iKeja[1], a new start-up company that installed hotspots. They offered 15 minutes per day of free access to individuals and very affordable rates beyond the free availability. Access to WiFi meant that many more people were venturing outdoors at night, drawn to the hotspots. This must be considered part of the network of change in everynight life. iKeja's target market is small businesses, especially *spaza* shops in townships and self-built communities. The two *spaza* shops in PJS acquired iKeja hotspots and have both since become more active social spaces by day and night, as the youth group explained:

Stephanie:	*Has the WiFi made it more active at night? Are people coming at nighttime to use the WiFi at the Somalian [spaza] shop to hang out more, to spend time?*
Mveliso:	They come until the Somalian [*spaza*] closes at ten o'clock.
Stephanie:	*So actually, it has become a social space?*
Mveliso:	Yes. If you can go around the Somalian [*spaza*] shops, you can see four, five people standing around there with their cell phones.
Stephanie:	*So that for you is kind of a hangout area, or not? Girls, do you meet your friends there and spend time there?*
Ukhonaye:	Yes. (youth focus group, PJS)

In a separate interview, Sive, a teen girl living next to a *spaza* shop, also confirmed that the shop had become a social gathering place.

Stephanie:	*[Is the* spaza *shop] much busier?*
Sive:	Yes! A lot of people come and stay there and eat [sic] WiFi. (female, teen, participatory photo interview, PJS)

Before WiFi was added, people did not linger around the shops, but now more people were spending time there, feeling safer because of the increased activity.

Stephanie:	*Do you feel safe now at the* spaza *shop?*
Sive:	Both, they can take your cellphone. But if there are a lot of people, they won't. (female, teen, participatory photo interview, PJS)

In the youth focus group, Mveliso out that said the diversity of people made him feel safer as well.

Mveliso:	Because before those WiFi things, you can see only boys standing by the shop asking for R1, R2. But now you see different genders; you can see girls, boys, you can see everyone.
Stephanie:	*What do you girls say? Do you agree? Has it changed?*
All girls:	[nod and agree] (youth focus group, PJS)

The added WiFi influenced my research because it created a nighttime social activity which did not exist at the start of the research. Nighttime activity increased significantly in PJS since 2019, and the increased activity has also made people feel safer. This must be considered when reviewing the impact of the public lighting intervention. The solar lights could also have increased the nighttime use of the public WiFi due to increased accessibility through lit pathways.

Networked public lighting preferences

Chapter 4 discussed how challenging it was to define public lighting preferences, where many elements played a role in peoples' preferences. Since the residents had been living with wall-mounted lighting for six months, I revisited this question of preferences in my endline interviews, comparing wall-mounted with high-mast lighting. Although preferences were more precise than before the light installations, interviewees' answers were not always straightforward, as described below, where I discuss the positive and negative attributes of wall-mounted lights and high-mast lights.

When asked to choose one or the other, all interviewees preferred wall-mounted lights over high-mast lights. I list below some of the most common themes around people's preferences. Interviewees like Thembeka and Siya mentioned how much the lights help them during loadshedding; some also said that loadshedding no longer made a difference because

---

they had solar lights. Grid independence was the main reason for preferring wall-mounted lights.

Thembeka: So now you don't ask, "oh, the electricity is off?". Now you can just say, "ok, my light is on, it's fine." (female, senior, household interview, PJS)

Siya: These lights help us a lot, especially during loadshedding. When there is loadshedding, it's very dark, but the lights are on.
(male, young adult, household interview, PJS)

Interviewees also observed that high-mast lighting did not light narrow pathways efficiently, casting dark shadows, while the wall-mounted lights lit the narrow pathways well. This was a departure from previous opinions about high-mast lighting. Seniors and elderly interviewees especially noticed the difference between high-mast lighting and wall-mounted lights:

Bandla: The little lights are good for the passages because I can walk through the paths easier. (male, senior, household interview, PJS)

Stephanie: *And what do you like the most about these little lights?*

Fata: It's only because the small lights light clearly; they don't give the shadows.
(male, elderly, household interview, PJS)

Thembeka: Most of the time that [high-mast] light was fine before, and then we are building our hokkies [houses], and then someone builds like this, a double storey, and a double storey can block that light. (female, senior, household interview, PJS)

Den: The high-mast light, yes, it lights all, but there are certain passages where it doesn't light. But these small lights light everywhere. I can see everything.

Nomzamo: I support what Den is saying.
(elderly focus group, PJS)

A common preference for wall-mounted lights was their brightness—the brightness helped people identify perpetrators if they were robbed or assaulted.

Stephanie: *If everyone gets a light now, do you like these high-mast lights more or the small lights more?*

Lenox: Small ones. Because they are going to make PJS bright.

Stephanie: *Why not the high-mast light?*

Siya: The high-mast doesn't brighten all of PJS. (male, young adults, household interview, PJS)

Mrs Filifili: I like the brightness of the light the most because the *skollies* can't reach my house because of this brightness. (female, elderly, household interview, PJS)

We asked if interviewees would oppose the permanent removal of the high-mast lights after all houses received a wall-mounted light. Responses were almost equally divided between those who did not care if the high-mast lights were removed and those who felt high-mast lights were still helpful and should remain. Interviewees who disagreed with removing the high-mast lights felt this way mainly because the high-mast lights lit the streets adjacent to PJS.

Lenox: The high-mast must stay because it lights the main road. The small ones light the passages and directly in front of the houses, but the big one lights like an umbrella, its lights everywhere.
(male, young adult, household interview, PJS)

Stephanie: *Why do you want both of them if the high-mast is just on the roof, then why do you want the high-mast?*

Bandla: Because the high-mast lights the streets where I take the taxi.
(male, senior, household interview, PJS)

Anita: No, because we are going to put solar lights only in PJS, in P-Section, you won't put solar lights. So when I go to P-Section, I depend on the high-mast lights. (female, teen, youth focus group, PJS)

Only Mr Fata, the elderly male interviewee, mentioned the vandal-resistance of high-mast lighting as a reason for not wanting them removed.

Fata: I don't want to high-mast to be switched off because these little lights can easily be destroyed by the criminals, and that high mast is very high, and they can't reach there. (male, elderly, household interview, PJS)

Wall-mounted solar lights are the preferred lighting option for self-built communities due to their high lighting quality and their resilience against power outages. Those who commented that high-mast lights could be removed after all houses in PJS had a solar light cited the unreliability of high-mast lights.

For instance, Mveliso expressed frustration with maintenance issues. Thembeka and Zianda could not depend on the high-mast light because of regular power outages.

Mveliso: The high-mast can leave because it can even go off for three weeks, and there is no one coming to fix it. Even the people around the high-mast make calls, but no one responds. So for me, the high-mast lights can leave as long as I have a light outside my house. (male, youth focus group, PJS)

Thembeka: And then you remove the tall one? No, I won't mind because I have nothing to do there. I don't get anything from them [high-mast lights]. Even when the electricity is off, then it's going to be off, and inside is going to be off, but that one [solar light] won't be off. (female, senior, household interview, PJS)

Zianda: No, I don't care! Even if the electricity is gone [loadshedding], I don't care. (female, adult, household interview, PJS)

The preference for wall-mounted solar lighting was clear in my endline fieldwork, but these lights were rightfully only suitable for the narrow pathways of PJS. Many residents move between there and the surrounding formal areas. The wider formal streets still need public lighting. These streets are currently served by high-mast lights, though they should in fact receive streetlights, like other formal streets in the city. There was definite benefit derived from the lessons learned and new information gained through implementing the project in PJS in terms of understanding lighting preferences and infrastructure management. This evidence provides a vital base for recommendations on lighting technology, community liaison and policy recommendations specific to self-built communities for a feasible, resilient and scalable lighting solution.

Freeing everynight life

Co-producing public lighting infrastructure in PJS produced positive changes in everynight life. Local employment, transparent communication and regular, accurate updates about the project were paramount to the project's success. Residents were also more comfortable reporting issues to leaders or the local maintenance team. The participation process engendered feelings of pride and ownership and minimised vandalism and thefts.

The lights seemed to positively impact social dynamics in PJS, with more people venturing out at night, improved social relations and people feeling less threatened by nighttime crime. *Skollies* who harass people in the pathways late at night are not as common as one year ago. Social relations with strangers in pathways have improved, mainly because people can see and recognise others. Neighbourly relations have also improved. Social conflict seems to have lessened and shifted—the nature of conflict has changed from *skollies* in pathways to organised crime gangsters who leave PJS residents alone. Leaders had fewer reports of incidents, and pathways are quieter late at night. While residents still fear being robbed, the ability to identify the perpetrator provides reassurance.

Nighttime practices also changed and new social hotspots emerged in the pathways where households received lights. The community viewed these hotspots positively. Besides the new hotspots, more people were sitting outside at night, especially during loadshedding. Moreover, PJS is alive with positive nighttime activity until later at night, some people going inside an hour or two later than the 21:00 informal curfew observed before the lights were installed. Some changed their walking practices, using different, newly illuminated pathways, while others were more comfortable walking and pedestrians seemed more relaxed walking at night. An especially positive impact of the light installation was on access to shared sanitation at night. Several interviewees expressed positive changes in this respect. With these changes, nighttime perceptions in PJS shifted subtly, but positively. The most common perception was feeling free at night, offering a certain reassurance and will to confront nighttime fears to venture outside.

The addition of 283 solar lights in PJS highlighted how improved public lighting can foster positive change in everynight life. It was necessary to establish the network of change in which this public lighting intervention is located. With major influencing factors in PJS such as COVID-19, loadshedding, new WiFi access and the phased lighting installation, it is impossible to attribute change only to the lighting intervention. Instead, this chapter deals with changes in everynight life as a dynamic system in constant transition. While everynight life did change, more than 400 households were still awaiting lights—many interviewees had not yet experienced the full impact of the public lighting. Almost all interviewees preferred wall-mounted solar lights over high-mast lights because they could see better in the narrow pathways and the lights worked during loadshedding. However, many found the high-mast lights useful because they lit the wider streets surrounding PJS, again emphasising the networked nature of lighting that must be considered when assessing its impact on everynight life.

Infrastructures of Freedom: Breaking Boundaries with Light

Chapter 7

It is literally and metaphorically appropriate to conclude this book with an extract from Yiftachel's writings on self-built communities as grey space—a position between lightness and darkness:

> The elements of gray space are thus positioned between the 'lightness' of full membership, recognition, permissibility and safety, and the 'darkness' of exclusion, denial, demolition, eviction or death (Yiftachel, 2015, p. 6)

Yiftachel places "full membership, recognition, permissibility and safety" next to lightness, or light. Next to darkness, he relates "exclusion, denial, demolition, eviction and [even] death". My empirical work takes this metaphor and grounds it in the dark self-built communities of Khayelitsha, where literal light and darkness represent the same polarities Yiftachel expresses. Just like the stark boundaries of shadow and light that high-mast lighting produces in PJS, there were many boundaries around everynight life—day and night, inside and outside, safe and dangerous, accessible and inaccessible, trustworthy and untrustworthy. Darkness is a boundary condition that cannot be penetrated to gain equal access to urban life and "the 'bundle' of rights, resources and capabilities enjoyed by urban residents" associated with urban citizenship (Yiftachel, 2015). These rights, resources and capabilities manifest in everyday mundanities. Currently, darkness restricts everyday life (Lefebvre, 1971) in self-built communities and contributes to "marginalised urban citizenship".

Chapter summary: As the closing chapter, Chapter 7 synthesises what it means to be surrounded by light or darkness in self-built communities. The first section looks at how darkness impacts access to urban life and citizenship, where darkness is established as a boundary condition inhibiting access to a safe and dignified everynight life. It elaborates on the specifics that made the public lighting project a success in PJS and establishes light as an example of what I term "infrastructures of freedom". Here, the possible ways of how public lighting could represent citizenship are explored. Later, the chapter discusses the term "everynight life", used throughout the book, as a new term that should be used to refocus research on everyday life to include the night. The chapter, and the book, closes by theorising infrastructures of freedom and relates the concept to the discourse around infrastructure and citizenship. It reaches a broader conclusion on infrastructure provision in self-built communities and asks how the forms of infrastructures of freedom could be generated in self-built communities in South Africa, and globally, with light (and darkness) as the lens.

The technical blind spot in public lighting provision is also a blind spot in the daily lives of residents in self-built communities, where night is a time of challenge rather than a time of peace. This research acknowledged nighttime as a significant and neglected component of everyday life in self-built communities in Cape Town, and specifically in Khayelitsha. Reviewing previous research through *and beyond* light built an understanding that public lighting is about more than reducing crime or making the nocturnal atmosphere more conducive to socialising. It is about improving everynight life. By empirically exploring self-built communities through and beyond light, this work filled a gap in the research, not only on urban lighting but also on everynight life and experiences of darkness. Having light means trusting people. It means feeling acknowledged rather than forgotten; it means visiting a friend rather than being alone. What is considered to be highly technical in government departments is entangled with daily practices, social relations and perceptions on the ground. This research expanded on the entanglement of "the technical" of public lighting infrastructure and "the social" of everynight life. Acknowledging the interaction between the technical and the social is vital in creating infrastructure that recognises people as full urban citizens. As such, the research went beyond light as technical infrastructure to consider light as part of a dynamic network of technical and social infrastructure that, together, comes to represent citizenship.

Collectively, we implemented wall-mounted solar lights in PJS Informal Settlement and revealed the importance of co-producing infrastructure with residents. We heard residents' concerns, worked with them and considered their contributions, using the community's powerful social infrastructure to make the lighting project resilient and viable. Co-producing light extended the performance of infrastructural networks into the night, enabling access to basic services, for example. It further strengthened social networks by day and ensured care and ownership of the public lighting infrastructure.

Each chapter in this book fostered a richer understanding of infrastructure provision in self-built communities and what light really means to people, beyond the dominant narrative of crime prevention.

Chapter 1 established the theoretical basis for the research, looking beyond light and crime and lighting for everyday life, towards lighting infrastructure as a mode of establishing citizenship. The chapter highlighted the value of human-centred and human-scaled light. It also reinforced the importance of lifting human-scale lighting to infrastructural scalability. Chapter 2 contextualised this research by introducing Cape Town's segregated lightscape. It established the case study, Khayelitsha and its self-built communities, as a space of historical resistance to the apartheid regime. This chapter highlighted the deep symbolism present in high-mast lighting infrastructure, reinforcing the importance of infrastructure to represent citizenship in post-apartheid South Africa. Chapter 3 introduced the action research project and focused on the research site, PJS Informal Settlement. It also explored the multi-dimensional nature of studying light in Khayelitsha's self-built communities, elaborating on the mixed methods used to understand everynight life and the impact of public lighting.

The book then moved into three empirical chapters—Chapters 4, 5 and 6—which revealed the struggles of everynight life in dark self-built communities and the inadequacy of high-mast lighting. Chapter 4 elaborated on the lived experiences of high-mast lighting in self-built communities. It concluded that the scale of high-mast lighting is too large for use in self-built communities, and the lived insufficiency of lighting physically and mentally distances people from the infrastructure. This lived insufficiency manifests in a life lived in darkness, detailed in Chapter 5. We learned that darkness traps everynight life, acting as a boundary condition to feeling free. Chapter 6 presented the impact of co-producing wall-mounted solar lighting on everynight life in PJS. The chapter showed that the new public lighting ultimately made people feel free to venture outside and extend or evolve their nighttime practices. Chapters 1 to 6 created a foundation for Chapter 7, the final chapter, that synthesises the work and brings the main themes presented in the Chapters 4, 5 and 6 into conversation with the research discussed in Chapter 2.

Darkness as a boundary

Everyday life in self-built communities features many daily struggles, often related to accessing basic services and opportunities safely, conveniently and in a dignified manner. Darkness amplifies these struggles, adding a layer of fear of social conflict to the struggle of meeting basic needs. The fear of social conflict is greater in the dark—often people do not feel reassured that they can see enough to assess an area's safety, react promptly to social conflict and to report this conflict to the relevant authorities. The study on everynight life in Chapter 5 demonstrated a correlation between darkness and fear of crime or social conflict. In psychosocial terms, darkness negatively affects the social elements of fear (Boomsma and Steg, 2014)— perceived social safety, eyes on the street and determining whether someone is good or bad. If a person cannot be recognised, it is not possible to determine whether their presence provides a sense of safety or threat. In the darkness, people cannot

see the eyes on the street, and nor can the community be adequately surveilled.

Darkness-related fear has a detrimental effect on the psychosocial conditions of most people living in self-built communities. Darkness also exacerbates poor access to basic services in self-built communities and raises more symbolic associations of being left in the dark by government. Many other emotions result from fear of crime, such as loneliness, anger, hopelessness and lack of freedom. These negative perceptions significantly affect everynight practices, leading to onerous and undignified coping mechanisms, furthering negative associations with nighttime. These onerous and undignified nighttime sanitation practices such as using a night pail inside the house links directly with the fear of venturing out at night to access shared sanitation facilities in the dark. As much as it is for any other citizen, living with dignity is vital to residents of self-built communities, and access to adequate sanitation by night needs to improve in these communities, regardless of the availability of adequate facilities by day.

To understand how to improve the everyday life of urban citizens living in self-built communities, darkness needs to be seen as an ever-present and debilitating condition in that environment. This research shows that darkness exacerbates daily struggles, constrains full urban citizenship and is entangled with danger and fear as immediate risks. The restricted access to everynight life results in feelings of exclusion and denial and raises questions around constitutional rights, such as the right to a dignified life. Daily exposure to darkness in self-built communities also results in deeper long-term effects on people's sense of dignity, social justice and access to equal rights. Darkness is therefore experienced both literally—darkness as a material substance— and metaphorically—darkness as being forgotten, excluded and denied full urban citizenship. When an entire component of their lives is not considered in infrastructure provision, it is not surprising that people feel that the state has left them in the dark. Tackling darkness, which comes with so much insecurity and fear, is vital to the improvement of everynight life in self-built communities.

Light as an infrastructure of freedom

The endline results, following the installation of 283 wall-mounted solar lights in PJS, proved that mounting a solar light above or close to each household's front door had a positive impact on psychosocial dynamics at night and on people's practices and perceptions of nighttime. The lights improved outdoor social activities, pedestrian mobility and access to other shared infrastructure such as taps, toilets and public transport. Even though these results were slightly hindered by the phased intervention of the project, discussed later, some broader conclusions can be drawn around wall-mounted solar lights and their role in freeing the night.

Lighting PJS was made possible through a collective effort from the initial site visit, when the community leaders expressed their lighting concerns. The leaders became our project partners. We employed locally and informed everyone of every step in the project. The crucial act of co-producing light with the community and updating all other stakeholders ensured the success *and* impact of the project. Through co-producing light, we could successfully test experiments at the level of everyday life, while simultaneously impacting government policy—a process which Simone and Pieterse refer to as the *double* approach (Simone and Pieterse, 2017). In co-producing, we were required to respect the community governance structures to gain the community's respect and willingness to get involved in the project. This respect included pausing the project while a new leadership was elected and having the leaders decide on and oversee fair hiring processes.

When the local team installed the lights, each household head decided where they would be placed and agreed to lend their structures to light the paths, creating a lightscape that is collectively produced and owned by the community. Residents who received a light were aware that this light benefitted the whole community, yet also felt the light belonged to them and took care of it. As a result of this collective process, remarkably few thefts and acts of vandalism occurred. The lights made sense to the community. This new and collective lightscape threaded through PJS's pathways, creating a resilient mesh of light that ran through and connected both the pathways and residents. Public lighting should be reframed from a technocratic solution of meeting predefined technical standards that must fit into a regulatory framework to a *process* shaped by an array of abstract and concrete societal needs and a *tool* that fosters an improved everynight life in self-built communities. We improved everynight life through co-producing lightweight, decentralised wall-mounted solar lights with the PJS community.

The thickness of darkness thinned with the addition of light. Everynight life boundaries expanded, overlapped and blurred. Daytime extended. People stayed outdoors later and felt less concerned about observing the unwritten 21:00 curfew. Children played outside until later, too,

and daytime socialising extended more seamlessly into the night, with people staying outside after dark. Boundaries between inside and outside also blurred. More people spent time outside at night, extending their personal boundaries to talk with neighbours and perhaps even share food. Extending and blurring inside, outside and personal boundaries happened particularly during loadshedding. During a power outage, the outside became a source of light and sociability, and the inside extended outward from the dark. The lighting blurred what was considered safe and dangerous, especially when accessing basic services. While many still feared getting robbed, it was no longer a debilitating fear that resulted in onerous everynight practices. People spoke about the new lighting related to accessing other infrastructure such as public toilets, taxis, taps and Wi-Fi. Many now felt safer going to the toilet at night, feeling they had a new agency if they were robbed since they would be able to recognise and report the perpetrator. "Reportability" made them feel safe, and this new potential for seeing fostered new notions of trust. Previously, darkness made people unknown, and the unknown was untrustworthy. Now, the light made people known and often trusted. People were able to reconsider who they trusted because they could recognise passers-by; and former strangers in the dark became familiar faces in the light.

The new lightscape created various overlapping, extended and blurred boundaries in a resilient mesh that improved everynight life in PJS, represented socially (meshed social relations), spatially (meshed practices) and materially (meshed lighting). By nature, mesh is built from intersections and gaps, fostering a secure, productive environment for new and unexpected encounters and self-determination. As explained in the diagram below, unexpected encounters occur at the intersections and the gaps provide for self-determination.

Materially, people thought of light at a large scale, like a net extending over space, dissipating in their minds at the point of their destination (i.e. work or a friend's house). After installing the lights, people talked about the surrounding neighbourhood's access to lighting, considering PJS's wall-mounted lights and P-Section's high-mast lights simultaneously and at different scales. These lighting scales should interact. A meshed approach of many decentralised lights stimulated interaction, which is especially important for a population that largely moves between places on foot.

That said, many people in PJS were reluctant to say whether the lighting had improved everynight life

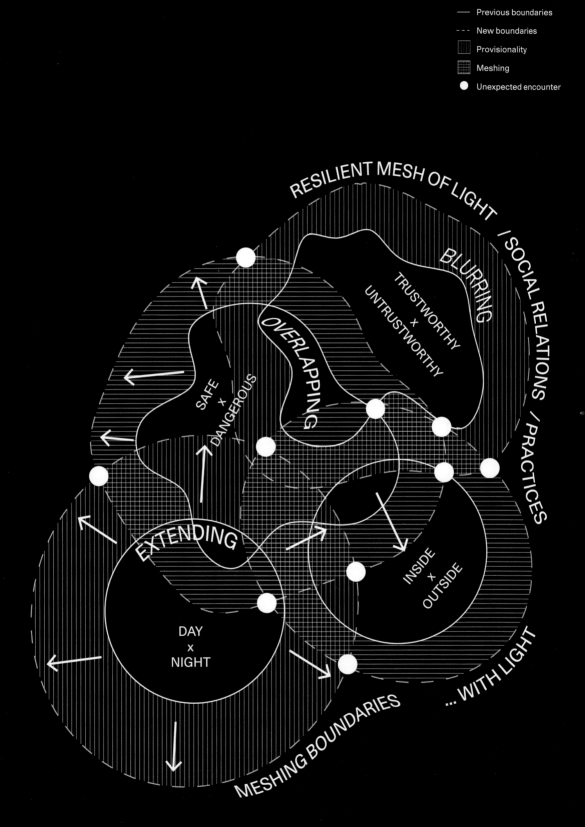

Fig 1   Blurred, extended and overlapping boundaries create a resilient mesh of light, social relations and nighttime practices

or not because not all the houses received a light. The phased approach to the quantitative research design resulted in large holes of darkness, weakening both the mesh of light and the project's impact. To understand the full impact of the lighting project, another round of fieldwork in PJS would be required after the second and final phase of lights is carried out. Although a change in everynight life was observed, more than 400 households still waited for a light, leaving many without the full experience of the new public lighting in PJS. This was raised several times, with people asking about the second phase, sometimes even telling stories of conflict due to the phased intervention. The lesson learned from this is that lighting is experienced at a neighbourhood scale and not at an individual household scale. To fully understand the impact of public lighting in self-built communities, a piecemeal approach is not effective — all the lights should be implemented simultaneously. If a phased approach is necessary, then the impact assessment should happen after all the lights are installed.

With everynight practices in PJS extending, overlapping and interacting with others, new encounters, connections and collisions are formed. A change in practices, such as sitting outside on a summer evening, allowed co-existing practices to reinforce one another and give rise to new practices and social relations. With shifting practices, residents' own boundaries overlap with those of others, sparking new encounters. Over time, this "social mesh" strengthens and transforms nighttime and possibly also daytime social relations. The lighting intervention in PJS created a resilient mesh of light, practices and social relations, with potential for new and unexpected encounters, such as sharing food with a neighbour outside during loadsheddingor greeting strangers previously feared. The provision to self-determine exist within this resilient network of intersections and encounters. The next section elaborates on this provision in more detail.

Not all issues were resolved when light arrived in PJS. Crime still happened and people still feared going out at night, but the heaviness of darkness on everynight life lightened a great deal. The project results showed that decentralised, wall-mounted public lighting made people feel safer than they did under high-mast lighting before the intervention. Lighting in PJS made a difference to everynight life there, but there is an opportunity to consider how public lighting can be improved more broadly. Some research participants in PJS did not want the high-mast lights switched off, despite the presence of the solar lights. They depended on high-mast lighting when venturing beyond PJS. This reveals an area of potential research into the efficacy of high-mast lighting in formal township areas, and perhaps even comparing high-mast lighting with conventional LED street lighting.

Alongside feeling safer, people also reported feeling free — free to walk outside, go to the toilet or to visit a friend after dark. A more secure environment evolved within the mesh of lighting, social relations and practices, and people felt safe enough to act and venture out into the night. The gaps intrinsic to mesh offered provision within this more secure and resilient environment, giving people space to dream, act and self-determine, such as Mveliso, whose dream of hosting shows in PJS at night with his creative youth group seemed more achievable with the new lights. This ability to self-determine is what made people feel free and allowed boundaries to extend, interact and mesh further, producing a self-determined everynight life. Self-determination in everynight life is about self-conception, a co-production of space, creating new forms of citizenship through a sense of belonging to, agency over and ownership of space and, more importantly, the night.

After living with the co-produced lighting in everynight life, it is not surprising that people refer to *freedom* when expressing their experiences. Previously, people were trapped by darkness, setting up thick boundaries. The wall-mounted lights broke the previous boundaries and liberated the night to "the 'lightness' of full membership, recognition, permissibility and safety" (Yiftachel, 2015). This is at the core of infrastructures of freedom — to be able to co-produce an infrastructure intervention and through that, to achieve the freedom of self-determination through lighting infrastructure. The next section elaborates on this concept and places it in the broader debate on infrastructure and citizenship.

Everynight life as a new term

New vocabulary to focus the debate around nighttime — which is remarkably understudied — was an important component and tool to facilitate this research. Understanding light and dark through everyday experiences and how this relates to infrastructure, or lack of infrastructure, was central to this research on public lighting in self-built communities. Graham and McFarlane (2015) emphasise the importance of understanding infrastructure through everyday life as a "powerful means of revealing the rhythms that in large part constitute urban life inequality and change". Here, "rhythm" stands out as the circadian rhythm of day and night which arrives and dissipates each day. They add that understanding infrastructure through every-day experiences, conceptualised as *lived infra-structure*, means understanding infrastructure as "a domain through which practices are regulated and normalised", negotiated and resisted (Graham and McFarlane, 2015). Shaw (2014) also refers to lived infrastructure, specifically focusing on the im-portance of changing policy through understanding everyday public lighting experiences, noting:

> ... practices of developing knowledge in this area of technological change [public light-ing] need to be connected with under-standings of lived experiences of infra-structure. (Shaw, 2014)

Shaw brings the everyday life debate into the policy realm and into the night. Understanding public light-ing infrastructure through everyday experiences can advance the discourse, help to form policies and induce infrastructural change.

These and other authors (Collier, Schnitzler and Mizes, 2016; Davoudian, 2018; Ebbensgaard, 2016) advanced my understanding of everyday infra-structural experiences around public lighting in-frastructure. Yet, in the very essence of the word "everyday", the night is neglected. Creating a new term refocused everyday experiences to nighttime specifically through the new term "everynight life". Nighttime occupies a large portion of our lives. It is a visceral aspect of everyday life in self-built commu-nities. As such, it deserves distinct terminology for study. In addition, everynight life in self-built com-munities often relates to the absence, rather than the present lived experience, of infrastructure. It is notable that even if infrastructure is physically pres-ent during the day (toilets and taps, for example), it is absent in the darkness of everynight life. Through my understanding of everynight life, I found that darkness is a debilitating and layered boundary in self-built communities, restricting very practical needs, compromising dignity and contributing to a sense of marginalised citizenship. This problem de-veloped the investigation into lighting as an infra-structure of freedom—an infrastructure that liber-ates everynight life from debilitating darkness.

Literature on infrastructure and citizenship high-lights the important connection between everyday infrastructural experiences and the ability to articu-late citizenship. This has been done mainly by ana-lysing existing infrastructure, particularly housing (see Lemanski, 2019, 2020; Millstein, 2020), wa-ter (see Wafer, 2012 and von Schnitzler, 2016) and

electricity (see von Schnitzler, 2016). Graham and McFarlane (2015) view infrastructure as lived ex-perience in everyday life, and Shaw (2014) and Ebbensgaard (2016) articulate everyday experi-ences towards lighting, moving the focus from everyday life to *night*. Developing everynight life as a new term facilitated a shift in focus to the night that can support future research too.

Theorising infrastructures of freedom

This research, and most research on infrastructure and citizenship, is located in South Africa but can be generalised to post-colonial territories on a theoret-ical level. In South Africa, infrastructure and its link to citizenship contain a history of non-white popu-lations experiencing the state almost exclusively through infrastructure (von Schnitzler, 2016). As a result, rejection of infrastructure, such as rental boycotts, became the tool to resist the apartheid government's control, leading ultimately to the de-mise of apartheid (von Schnitzler, 2016). Lighting featured in the infrastructural landscape to assert control over the townships in South Africa. These lights were specifically designed to be tall and inde-structible, precisely because of resistance through the destruction of infrastructure (see Chapter 2).

After democracy, the South African government pursued an infrastructure-centric approach to ex-tending citizenship to previously excluded popula-tions (Wafer, 2012), mainly through providing free housing and free basic services (FBS). Lemanski (2020) explores how "citizens' everyday access to, and use of, public infrastructure [explored through housing] in the city affect, and are affected by, their citizenship identity and practices". I build on Wafer and Lemanski, adding that FBS and housing infra-structure was purely about extending an existing in-frastructural language, but the government did not reconceptualise the language of the infrastructure to express citizenship in democratic South Africa.

As much as extending infrastructure to previously excluded populations was important to reinforce a sense of citizenship, the value that embodies infra-structural language is equally important. Collier *et al.* (2016) discuss values embodied in public infra-structures, stating:

> ... infrastructure is contested through claims and counter-claims about the values produced by infrastructure, about the pub-lics those values serve, about the kinds of expert or non-expert knowledge that are

relevant for defining these values, and about the technical means required to realise them. (Collier et al., 2016)

What is important here is the link between embodied values and how those values manifest through infrastructural means, for example, the embodied value of light. Currently, a free government house is valued as "becoming recognised as a 'proper urban citizen' or 'to becoming free', and informality is still associated with being temporary and not recognised wholly as a citizen" (Millstein, 2020). FBS infrastructure, with public lighting as a lens for this argument, currently lacks embodied values of being recognised as a proper urban citizen. A resulting counter-value is produced—the feeling of infrastructure not belonging to a public it is meant to serve, or of infrastructure that disregards a public's needs and dignity. With 16.8%[1] of the country's urban population living in self-built communities, FBS infrastructure in these neighbourhoods must also articulate freedom and recognition of being a proper citizen in South Africa. Infrastructure should embody values that help to articulate citizenship. I argue that the most central value in post-apartheid South Africa should be that of freedom to self-determine.

Through an action research approach, I co-developed and co-implemented decentralised wall-mounted solar lights in PJS Informal Settlement, while simultaneously developing broader understandings around infrastructure provision and citizenship. Scholars of infrastructure and citizenship refer to the important language of citizenship embodied in infrastructure but do not elaborate on what that language should be. Therefore, through the lens of public lighting, the research developed and used the concept of infrastructures of freedom to build on the emerging debate on infrastructure and citizenship. I developed the term to highlight infrastructure's ability to and importance in articulating a sense of freedom. In post-apartheid South Africa this is an important concept used to contrast the previous oppressive apartheid regime. As a conclusion to this research and productive way forward, I discuss and conceptualise the term through the public lighting project and in dialogue with research elaborated on in Chapter 2 and expand this to produce an infrastructural language that successfully articulates citizenship.

The lighting process (design, implementation, maintenance and adaptations) was as important as the tool (wall-mounted solar lights) to achieve resilient public lighting infrastructure that was accepted by the community and addressed their needs and values, improving everynight life. Bordonaro et al. (2018) showed the importance of this process, where they co-designed light using social science methodology, seeing the civic (public) and the domestic (private) as an integral ecology that constitutes the nightscape. To lift this argument higher into conceptualising infrastructures of freedom, I argue that all infrastructure should be both a process that articulates citizenship and a tool for self-determination. Graham and Mcfarlane (2015) support this concept by referring to infrastructure as a "process that enables or disables particular kinds of action in the city". Here they refer more to the lived experiences of the infrastructure as explored through high-mast lighting in Chapter 4. In addition, the infrastructure process consists of a "complex ecology of knowledge producers" (Collier et al., 2016), which is as much part of infrastructure as the material infrastructure is. Collier et al. (2016) call for design thinking in infrastructure, with an array of experts and non-experts co-producing multifunctional infrastructure planning. Haque, Lemanski and Groot (2021) build my argument further in their writings on the acceptance of solar infrastructure in low-income communities. They argue that working with social capital and social norms helps in the acceptance of solar technology. I weave this argument into infrastructure as a process (ibid.). Working with social capital and social norms (Haque et al., 2021) forms a vital part of the "ecology" and process. Regarding infrastructure as a process that works alongside experts and non-experts, social capital and social norms is an important component in further articulating citizenship—not only understanding the values and interests of a local public but by regarding someone as an active agent of infrastructure rather than the passive recipient (Collier et al. 2016). Infrastructures of freedom establish infrastructure both as a process and as a tool for articulating citizenship through self-determination.

Decentralised wall-mounted lighting creates a resilient mesh of lighting that facilitates safe self-built communities. Light becomes performative rather than prescriptive (Ebbensgaard, 2016), giving people agency (Bille and Sørensen, 2007). Ebbensgaard elaborates on performative lighting as "part and parcel of the social practices it aims and intends to shape". With Ebbensgaard's contribution, I further conceptualise the notion of meshing infrastructure, where the process (social) and the tool (light) becomes a resilient mesh of the night. Light as a mesh not only highlights existing social practices but also creates a safe network for self-determination to occur and for new social practices to emerge. Building on this concept, if we see decentralised infrastructure as a mesh, both in the process and as a tool, then we understand that decentralisation is intrinsic for self-determination to occur. The meshed nature of decentralised infrastructure offers simultaneous regularity and provisionality (Simon, 2004). Simon elaborates further, referring to the multiple possibilities to act other than in what is specified by "domains of power" (provisionality), but acting as if one operates only within the domains of power (regularity) (ibid.). Taking this concept of "multiple connotations" within the domains of power, the notion of mesh allows for multiple possibilities within a safe and resilient environment.

Self-determination can occur within this meshed process and tool of lighting, social capital and social norm; and the act of self-determination fosters a feeling of freedom so central to articulating citizenship in a democratic country such as South Africa. Infrastructure and the link to citizenship has been a growing topic in recent years (Lemanski, 2019, 2020; Millstein, 2020; Palmer, Moodley and Parnell, 2017; Parnell and Pieterse, 2010; Swilling, 2006; von Schnitzler, 2016; Wafer, 2012). This research builds on this scholarship, taking the next step and conceptualising how and which infrastructure can successfully embody a sense of citizenship and belonging. The term infrastructures of freedom exercises this concept to successfully articulate a full sense of citizenship, at the centre of which should be the freedom to self-determine.

I conceptualised infrastructures of freedom as a process and a tool for self-determination, building on Graham and Mcfarlane (2015) and adding to Lemanski's (2021) suggestion that all infrastructure should work with social capital and social norms, which is part and parcel of the process of infrastructure. Simone (2004), Ebbensgaard (2016) and Bille and Sørensen (2007) helped to build the argument that infrastructures of freedom form a mesh and active agent, alongside giving people agency to self-determine. Finally, I add to Collier *et al.*'s (2016) text on the importance of values embodied in infrastructure and how those values are co-produced. My contribution here is that by embodying the correct values in infrastructure, the opportunity for infrastructure to articulate citizenship emerges. Infrastructures of freedom is understood as a decentralised process and a tool in which citizens are the active agents and recipients of infrastructure. Such infrastructure must offer a mesh of regularity and provisionality for citizens to self-determine

their everyday or everynight life. Finally, infrastructures of freedom must embody values co-produced by the public it serves; the central value should be that of freedom which manifests in self-determination. The concept of infrastructures of freedom unifies these valuable pieces of literature on infrastructure, everyday life and citizenship to envision a holistic approach to collectively developing infrastructure that articulates citizenship.

Epilogue

"I went to PJS on Wednesday evening. Then around half-past six, loadshedding started. The work you did in PJS is useful because even people from other sections went to PJS for social networking and also the taverns are full, business is growing."

Thabisa Mfubesi, 1 July 2022

Since writing *Infrastructures of Freedom* in August 2021, first as a doctoral thesis, then preparing to publish the work as a book, the project itself has made significant progress.

This epilogue elaborates on the ongoing developments around the PJS project and other projects emerging.

The PJS project was initiated in 2017. The CoCT noticed the project in about December 2020. It released a request for information (RFI) for innovative off-grid public lighting solutions in self-built communities. One could speculate that this request resulted from our and the Social Justice Coalition's advocacy efforts for more effective public lighting in self-built communities. Our response to the RFI was well received as the only built example to address the RFI criteria.

The second phase of lighting was completed in September 2021. Most lights still shine brightly in PJS today—so brightly that surrounding communities have approached PJS leaders to learn more. Similarly, organisations have approached my research partner and I to learn more about our work, and several spin-off projects have emerged. These contribute to a growing evidence base and present an opportunity to learn more lessons, iron out issues in our initial project and to continue advocating to CoCT for improved public lighting in self-built communities.

Between September 2021 and February 2022 we worked with the CoCT, answering questions, coordinating site visits and advising them on applications to fund their own pilot project. The City went further, initiating a cost-benefit analysis of the project with GreenCape, an NGO focused on building the green economy, who continues to show interest in the project. In February 2022, supported by the City, GreenCape made a short documentary about the project to showcase successful alternative service delivery models in self-built communities. In 2023, the City hopes to replicate the project in five different communities if GreenCape's cost-benefit analysis shows that the solution is viable and scalable.

In another spin-off, four surrounding communities set out to learn more about how to install the lighting in their neighbourhoods. Working with an NGO, People's Environmental Planning (PEP), they initiated their own projects based on the process we followed in PJS. In collaboration with the University of Cape Town, PEP and the four communities of about 40 households each, initiated an enumeration of their neighbourhoods and collectively chose to pursue solar lighting as a development that would yield the most benefits for their community. As it stands today, these four self-built communities aim to collectively install wall-mounted solar lighting by April 2023. The lighting technology, donated by a company, differs slightly from the technology installed in PJS. Projects of this kind need to accept different technologies, given their limited resources. PEP gladly accepted the generous donation.

In September 2022, the University of Exeter in the United Kingdom showed an interest in the project, expressing desire to implement the same solution in Qandu Qandu, a large self-built community of over 4,000 households in Khayelitsha. With a limited budget to install 400 wall-mounted solar lights, the project had to delve deep into the design process to co-create a public lighting solution that would benefit the entire community. The first step was to nominate a project steering committee. From October 2022 we held regular meetings with the Project Steering Committee (PSC), the ward councillor, and the general community. A series of workshops are planned with an elected team of twenty-six representatives from each of the thirteen sections. Through these workshops we hope to find a strategic solution in its approach to lighting areas that would benefit everyone. The lighting installation is planned to take place in April or May 2023 before the rainy winter arrives in Cape Town.

PJS project's elephant in the room

Although the project in PJS attracted much positive attention, the short and intense project period running from 2018 to 2021 offered little time to address a vital component of infrastructure—maintenance. After the phase 2 installation, the project funded a maintenance period. The maintenance thereafter fell on the PJS community. The primary maintenance was premature battery replacement. The batteries in the phase 1 lights did not fulfill the supplier's quality promise and the batteries died well before their three-year warranty—an important lesson learned about finding a trusted technology supplier. The supplier also absconded, so our warranty was meaningless. It was our responsibility to install a better battery in the phase 1 lights. Thankfully, we had built a trusting relationship with a South African company who led the phase 2 lighting installation and who could source replacement batteries through a trusted Chinese supplier. My research partner's research unit had budget for the batteries. In all, 150 phase 1 batteries were replaced and an additional twenty-two batteries where replaced in December 2022. All batteries were used. After a routine check, the maintenance team counted 49 lights that were no longer working and needed battery replacements.

Earlier in 2022, the maintenance team met the PJS community to discuss how to cover battery replacement costs, suggesting that each household could pay for their own replacement battery. This was not well received. Each battery costs R320 ($18) to replace, not including the maintenance team's wages. Because of the failed warranty, we felt responsible to pay to replace the phase 1 batteries. We self-funded an order of fifty batteries to finally have all the remaining phase 1 lights repaired. However, a plan is needed not only to keep the lights on in PJS, but also for the many projects arising using PJS as an example.

The meeting between the PJS maintenance team and leaders showed that single households could not afford the battery replacement costs. This removes the collective element of the public lighting project, which is essential to this project. The project was co-created; it needs to be co-maintained too. We are exploring a stokvel, or a collective savings scheme, as a potential approach for future maintenance issues. For example, if each of the 768 households in PJS had donated R10-R20 per month ($1.50), we could have replaced twenty batteries per month. Under a community savings scheme, and with the three-year warranty, enough money could be collected to replace all the batteries in an area, using a locally trained team supported by a trusted supplier of a reliable stream of batteries—such as the phase 2 supplier.

As described, there are issues that arise beyond a project's funded timeline. We have now entered a new post-project phase of learning, tackling these issues and collectively resolving vital elements with drivers of other new projects.

The 'LightUp' community of practice

Out of necessity, with other projects approaching us for advice and with our own maintenance challenges, we decided to form a community of practice around off-grid public lighting in self-built communities. All projects are working towards the same objective: to advocate for more effective and off-grid public lighting, implemented in a bottom-up approach by self-built communities themselves. Since December 2022, a group of about ten people from five organisations, companies and communities meet monthly to discuss the different projects. At the time of writing, the group is co-creating a memorandum of understanding that addresses the components to our collective mission, laid out here:

Improving public lighting in informal settlements over the long term, through:

- Community-driven approach: alternative to "top-down" provision, repair the broken social compact between the urban poor and the state

- Upliftment: job creation, skills development in each community

- Technically efficient: off-grid technology development, smooth-running, proper manufacturing, vandal-proof and durable

- Scalable solution: incremental improvements, shared learning by doing, build institutions/mechanisms that scale grounded practice

- Policy: evidence-based policy that would affect the CoCT's decision-making around alternative modes of infrastructure provision in self-built communities

This epilogue serves as a snapshot in time in an ongoing process and does not aim to be a final conclusion. After two meetings, we have already seen increased collaboration between the different parties as a result of these interactions. A community of practice seems to be an effective tool to address the unexpected and real-world challenges described above. I look forward to seeing the benefits unfold.

Appendix

Timeline of segregated Cape Town

1865	Census reveals that black people lived in Papendorp (Woodstock today)
1865–1881	Calls for commitment to providing segregated housing
1890s	Cecil John Rhodes introduces the Bill for Africa to create separate land reserves for black Africans across the Cape colony
1900	Stanford Commission Report recommends separating natives as far as possible from Europeans
1901	Bubonic Plague allows governor to evict black Africans from the city centre
1901	Governor imposes residential segregation and sets up Ndabeni
1902	Native Reserve Location Act No. 40, the first act that spatially segregated races
1902	Land five kilometres from Ndabeni designated for Langa, the first township designated for black Africans
1923	The development of Langa begins
1925	Langa is built
1928	Township's board report features words like "barriers", "buffers" and zones for "European", "Coloured" and "Natives"
1930	Langa's population is approximately 10,000
1934	Slums Act of 1934, easing the eviction of black Africans living in Cape Town's centre
1939	Squatter population estimated at 50,000 in Cape Town
1945	Urban Areas Act designates independent homelands to different tribes
1946	Land eight kilometres SE of Langa designated for Nyanga's site and service scheme as labour demand booms in Cape Town
1948	National Party comes into power, apartheid legally recognized
1950	Group Areas Act, segregating urban areas for different races as classified by the apartheid government
1950	Population Registration Act
1952	Black Laws Amendment Act, limiting the category of black Africans who have the right to permanent residence in urban areas
1955	W.H. Eiselen, Secretary of Native Affairs, announces Coloured Labour Preference Policy (CLPP) or the Eiselen Plan: Cape Town becomes an area that takes preference of employing "coloured" people over black Africans
1953	Reservation of Separate Amenities, enforcing the use of separate amenities by different racial groups
1955	Clearing of the largest squatter camp, Windermere, begins; out of 2,500 families surveyed, 750 qualified to stay under the Urban Areas Act of 1945
1956	Construction of Gugulethu, the second township for black Africans in Cape Town; people are moved into the area in 1959
1962	Eiselen Plan in full force
1962	General Law Amendment Act (Sabotage Act): It widens the definition of sabotage to include strikes, trade union activity, and writing slogans on walls
1964	Bantu Labour Act prohibits Africans from seeking work in towns or employers from taking them on unless they were channelled through the state labour bureaux
1965	Black Labour Regulation Act amendment: Labour officers can deny work permits to African labour in Western Cape if coloured labour is available
1966	The black African population is frozen in Cape Town to reduce the Black population by five per cent each year
1968	Bantu Labour Regulation Act: Black Africans are allowed a maximum contract of twelve months, after which the contract worker has to return to his homeland to renew the contract
1969	The start of the demise of the Eiselen Plan as black Africans continue to settle in Cape Town regardless of continuous "deportation"
1970s	Economic boom and increased demand for cheap labour leads to population increase and increase in squatter camps in Cape Town
1973	Bantu Affairs Administration Boards (BAAB) take over township administration, townships see rental increases
1974–1978	Black squatter camps continuously raided, many eventually destroyed completely
1974	KTC Emergency Camp (in the Crossroads complex) built for "legal" families on the housing waiting list
1975	Central government takes control of black residential areas through the BAAB (Act 45 of 1971)
1975	Re-introduction of leasehold rights for black Africans in cities
1975	Crossroads squatter settlement expands as other settlements are demolished around Cape Town

1976	Soweto Uprising in Johannesburg marks a turning point in apartheid resistance
1976	Family housing for Africans frozen until this point, with the exception of 3,686 houses in Gugulethu
1976	Crossroads declared a "legal" emergency camp after much community resistance
1976, 1977, 1980	Amendments to the Prevention of Illegal Squatting Act
1977	Community Councils Act of 1977 includes new township regulations
1978	99-year leasehold introduced and black Africans can stay more permanently in South African cities
1979	Housing shortage reaches crisis proportion in Cape Town; 2,575 houses are erected between Nyanga and Gugulethu
1979	Koornhof "deal" promises a new era for housing Africans in urban areas
1982	Black Local Authorities Act to establish town and village councils in black townships
1981	Only 1,731 of 2,575 houses built in New Crossroads
1981	Eviction of 600 people from Langa barracks, attracting public attention
1982	Western Cape Development Board reports a 1.5 million pound deficit and housing backlog is growing
March 1983	Khayelitsha announced: Dr Piet Koornhof announces development of a satellite city for black Africans forty kilometres away from Cape Town city centre to house 250,000 people
1983	Phase 2 of New Crossroads is scrapped after the Khayelitsha announcement
July 1983	First residents move to Khayelitsha, 200 residents from KTC "squatter camp" in Crossroads
1983	Photographic evidence of high-mast lighting in Khayelitsha with no houses built
1983	Western Cape Development Board reports 2.4 million pound deficit
1983-1984	Internal conflict over whether or not to move to Khayelitsha reaches crisis point in Crossroads
1984	National state of emergency declared
1984	The South African Defence Force deploys military troops to the townships
1984	Black Communities Development Act provides for the purposeful development of Black communities outside the national states
1986	Government imposed a series of states of emergency
1987	Archive notes record of tenders for high-mast lighting for Khayelitsha
1987	Railway built in Khayelitsha, with three stations
1990	F.W. de Klerk announces the end of apartheid, caused largely by nationwide rental boycotts in townships
1994	First democratic election in South Africa: African National Congress takes power

Abbreviations and terms

ANC	African National Congress
BAAB	Bantu Affairs Administration Boards
CoCT	City of Cape Town
CLPP	Coloured Labour Preferential Policy of 1955
DoE	Department of Energy
EDG	Energy Directorate
ESKOM	South Africa's state-owned energy utility
ISSP	Informal Settlement Support Programme
ISTP	Institute of Science, Technology and Policy
RFI	Request for Information
SADF	South African Defence Force
SAPS	South African Police Service
SJC	Social Justice Coalition
USDG	Urban Settlement Development Grant
URI	Urban Research Incubator
WHAM	Winning of Hearts and Minds infrastructure upgrading programme

Amapara-para	see "skollie"
Basic services	water, sanitation, refuse removal and electricity
Blacks	people of African descent as classified by the apartheid government
Coloureds	people of mixed-race or African descent from the Khoisan tribes as classified by the apartheid government
High-mast light	a forty-metre tall sodium vapour floodlight
Indians	people of Indian descent as classified by the apartheid government
Informal settlement	the official term used by the South African government for self-built communities
Pota-pota	a bucket that is used as a toilet in a house and emptied out daily
Shebeen	an unlicensed establishment or private house selling alcohol
Skollie	a petty criminal, a naughty or ill-mannered child or young adult
Spaza shop	an informal convenience shop
Squatter camp	term used during apartheid for areas of self-built housing

Township areas that were designated under apartheid legislation for exclusive occupation by people classified as blacks, coloureds and Indians

Whites people of Caucasian descent as classified by the apartheid government

Credits: figures

Introduction

Opener: The central *spaza* shop in PJS Informal Settlement at night, author, 2019, p. 10
Figure 1: Author, 2021, p. 15
Figure 2: Author, 2021, p. 15

Chapter 1:
Reading Through and Beyond Light

Opener: PJS Informal Settlement at night with wall-mounted lighting and high-mast lighting, author, 2019, p. 18
Figure 1: Author, 2021, p. 20
Figure 2: Mihinjac and Saville, 2019, p. 24
Figure 3: Rob Atherton, 2022, p. 28
Figure 4: *Scientific America* 46 (11), March 18, 1882, p. 28
Figure 5: Author, 2019, p. 29
Figure 6: Mathieu Young, 2013, p. 29
Figure 7: Matteo Ferroni, 2011, p. 32/33

Chapter 2:
Cape Town's Segregated Lightscape

Opener: Aerial view of high-mast lighting in Johannesburg, author, 2019, p. 38
Figure 1: Doug Hurley, 2020, p. 41
Figure 2: Author, 2019, p. 42
Figure 3: Data: StatsSA, 2019; CoCT, 2015, p. 42
Figure 4: Nic Coetzer, 2013, p. 44
Figure 5: RJ Davies, 1981, p. 45
Figure 6: Josette Cole collection, 1984, p. 49
Figure 7: *Independent News Paper*, p. 49
Figure 8: David Goldblatt, 1987, courtesy the Goldblatt Legacy Foundation and Goodman Gallery, 1987, p. 50
Figure 9: *Cape Argus*, 2019, p. 52
Figure 10: Author, 2021, p. 52
Figure 11: Author, 2020, p. 54
Figure 12: Author, 2018, p. 55
Figure 13: CoCT Energy and Climate Change, 2019 (the information derived from the interviews and data analysis are not regarded as official CCT policy), p. 55
Figure 14: CoCT Energy and Climate Change, 2019, (the information derived from the interviews and data analysis are not regarded as official CCT policy), p. 55

Chapter 3:
Endeavours of Studying Khayelitsha's Lighting

Opener: PJS community meeting before phase 1 of the solar lighting installation, author, 2019, p. 64
Figure 1: Author, 2021, p. 67
Figure 2: CoCT, Open Data Portal, 2018, p. 68
Figure 3: Social Justice Coalition, 2018, p. 73
Figure 4: Author, 2017, p. 76
Figure 5: Author, 2017, p. 76
Figure 6: Author, 2020, p. 76
Figure 7: Author, 2020, p. 77
Figure 8: Author, 2020, p. 77
Figure 9: Author, 2020, p. 77
Figure 10: Author, 2019, p. 82/83
Figure 11: Author, 2021, p. 87
Figure 12: Author, 2021, p. 87
Figure 13: Author, 2018, p. 90

Everynight Life Screenplay

Opener: Lizwi, the main character, anxiously waiting for his mom to get home from work as it gets darker outside, Stephanie Briers and Ilze Myburgh, p. 94
Figure 1: Stephanie Briers and Ilze Myburgh, 2022, p. 96
Figure 2: Stephanie Briers and Ilze Myburgh, 2022, p. 97
Figure 3: Stephanie Briers and Ilze Myburgh, 2022, p. 98
Figure 4: Stephanie Briers and Ilze Myburgh, 2022, p. 98
Figure 5: Stephanie Briers and Ilze Myburgh, 2022, p. 99
Figure 6: Stephanie Briers and Ilze Myburgh, 2022, p. 100
Figure 7: Stephanie Briers and Ilze Myburgh, 2022, p. 100
Figure 8: Stephanie Briers and Ilze Myburgh, 2022, p. 101

Credits: maps

Credits: graphs

Chapter 2:
Cape Town's Segregated Lightscape

Graph 1: Statistics South Africa, 2018, p. 61

Chapter 3:
Endeavours of Studying Khayelitsha's Lighting

Graph 1: Yael Borofsky and Stephanie Briers, 2019, p. 71

Chapter 4:
Life in the Shadows of Area Lighting

Graph 1: Yael Borofsky and Stephanie Briers, 2019, p. 105
Graph 2: Yael Borofsky and Stephanie Briers, 2019, p. 105
Graph 3: Yael Borofsky and Stephanie Briers, 2019, p. 106
Graph 4: Stephanie Briers and Michael Walczak, 2019, p. 126
Graph 5: Stephanie Briers and Michael Walczak, 2019, p. 126
Graph 6: Stephanie Briers and Michael Walczak, 2019, p. 126
Graph 7: Stephanie Briers and Michael Walczak, 2019, p. 128

Chapter 5:
Trapped by Darkness

Graph 1: Yael Borofsky and Stephanie Briers, 2019, p. 137
Graph 2: Yael Borofsky and Stephanie Briers, 2019, p. 137
Graph 3: Yael Borofsky and Stephanie Briers, 2019, p. 137
Graph 4: Yael Borofsky and Stephanie Briers, 2019, p. 148
Graph 5: Yael Borofsky and Stephanie Briers, 2019, p. 151
Graph 6: Yael Borofsky and Stephanie Briers, 2019, p. 156
Graph 7: Yael Borofsky and Stephanie Briers, 2019, p. 158

Bibliography

Anderson, B., Wylie, J. (2009): On geography and materiality. In *Environment and Planning A* 41, pp. 318–335.

Armitage, R. (2016): Crime Prevention through Environmental Design. In *Environmental Criminology and Crime Analysis Crime Science Series*, 2nd edition, pp. 259–285.

Atkins, S.; Husain, S.; Storey, A. (1991): The influence of street lighting on crime and fear of crime. In Gloria Laycock (Ed.): *Crime Prevention Unit*. London. Available online at http://www.popcenter.org/library/scp/pdf/07-Atkins_Husain_Storey.pdf, accessed on 7/2/2018.

Atkinson, R. (2004): The evidence on the impact of gentrification: new lessons for the urban renaissance? In *European Journal of Housing Policy* 4 (1), pp. 107–131. DOI: 10.1080/1461671042000215479.

Atmodiwirjo, P.; Johanes, M.; Yatmo Yandi, A. (2019): Mapping stories: representing urban everyday narratives and operations. In *Urban Des Int* 24 (4), pp. 225–240. DOI: 10.1057/s41289-019-00100-x.

Bafna, S. (2003): Space Syntax. In *Environment and Behavior* 35 (1), pp. 17–29. DOI: 10.1177/0013916502238863.

Bell, S. (2009): Mental Maps. In N. J. Thrift, Rob Kitchin (Eds.): *International encyclopedia of human geography*. Amsterdam, London, Oxford: Elsevier.

Bille, M. (2015): Lighting up cosy atmospheres in Denmark. In *Emotion, Space and Society* 15, pp. 56–63. DOI: 10.1016/j.emospa.2013.12.008.

Bille, M.; Sørensen, T.F. (2007): An Anthropology of Luminosity. In *Journal of Material Culture* 12 (3), pp. 263–284. DOI: 10.1177/1359183507081894.

Bittle, J.; Craven, J. (2018): Do NYCHA's $80 Million Crime-Reducing Lights Actually Reduce Crime? In *Gothamist*, 5/14/2018. Available online at https://gothamist.com/news/do-nychas-80-million-crime-reducing-lights-actually-reduce-crime, accessed on 2/4/2021.

Bollens, S. (2012): *City and Soul in Divided Societies*. London: Routledge.

Bond, P.; Dugard, J. (2008): The case of Johannesburg water: What really happened at the pre-paid 'Parish pump'. In *Law, Democracy and Development* 12 (1), pp. 1–28. DOI: 10.4314/ldd.v12i1.52878.

Fisher, Bonnie S., Nasar, Jack L. (1992): Fear of Crime in Relation to Three Exterior Site Features. Prospect, Refuge, Escape. In *Environment and Behavior* 24 (1), pp. 35–65.

Boomsma, C.; Steg, L. (2014): Feeling Safe in the Dark. In *Environment and Behavior* 46 (2), pp. 193–212. DOI: 10.1177/0013916512453838.

Boraine, A. (1989): Security management upgrading in the black townships. In *Transformations* 8.

Bordonaro, E.; Entwistle, J.; Slater, D. (2018): The Social Study of Urban Lighting. In Navaz Davoudian (Ed.): *Urban lighting for people. Evidence-based lighting design for the built environment.* [S.l.]: RIBA PUBLISHING.

Borofsky, Y.; Briers, S. (2019): [Unpublished raw data on nighttime experiences in PJS Informal Settlement]. ETH Zurich.

Borofsky, Y. (2022): Night in the Informal City: How Limited Public Infrastructure Shapes Life After Dark in Informal Settlements. Dissertation. ETH Zurich. DOI: 10.3929/ethz-b-000531758.

Boyce, P.R.; Eklund, N.H.; Hamilton, B. J.; Bruno, L. D. (2000): Perceptions of safety at night in different lighting conditions. In *International Journal of Lighting Research and Technology* 32 (2), pp. 79–91. Available online at https://journals.sagepub.com/doi/pdf/10.1177/096032710003200205, accessed on 12/16/2020.

Breetzke, G.D.; Cohn, E.G. (2012): Seasonal Assault and Neighborhood Deprivation in South Africa. In *Environment and Behavior* 44 (5), pp. 641–667. DOI: 10.1177/0013916510397758.

Briers, S. (2/28/2019): *High-mast lighting and the late apartheid counter insurgent strategies.* Interview with A. Boraine. Cape Town.

Brooklyn Eagle (2018): *High-tech lights at NYCHA projects: The jury's still out.* Available online at https://brooklyneagle.com/articles/2018/05/15/high-tech-lights-at-nycha-projects-the-jurys-still-out/, updated on 2/4/2021, accessed on 2/4/2021.

Brown-Luthango, M.; Reyes, E.; Gubevu, M. (2017): Informal settlement upgrading and safety: experiences from Cape Town, South Africa. In *Journal of Housing and the Built Environment* 32 (3), pp. 471–493. DOI: 10.1007/s10901-016-9523-4.

Bruyns, G.; Graafland, A. (2012): *African perspectives, [South] Africa. City, society, space, literature, and architecture.* Rotterdam: 010 Publishers (Delft School of Design series on architecture and urbanism, 7).

Calitz, J. R.; Wright, J. G. (2021): *Statistics of utility-scale power generation in South Africa in 2020.* The Council for Scientific and Industrial Research. http://hdl.handle.net/10204/11865.

Callon, M.; Lascoumes, P.; Barthe, Y. (2009): *Acting in an uncertain world. An essay on technical democracy.* Cambridge, Mass.: MIT Press (Inside technology).

Chalfin, A.; Hansen, B.; Lerner, J.; Parker, L. (2022): Reducing Crime Through Environmental Design: Evidence from a Randomized Experiment of Street Lighting in New York City. In *Journal of Quantitative Criminology* 38, pp. 127–157. DOI: 10.1007/s10940-020-09490-6.

Charles, M. (2019): Township left in the dark. Khayelitsha won't get a cent from R62.5m City budget. In *Cape Argus*, 3/12/2019. Available online at https://www.iol.co.za/capeargus/news/khayelitsha-wont-get-a-cent-from-citys-r625m-budget-for-public-lighting-19816319, accessed on 4/12/2019.

Chipkin, I. (2003): 'Functional' and 'Dysfunctional' Communities: The Making of National Citizens. In *Journal of Southern African Studies* 29 (1), pp. 63–82. DOI: 10.1080/0305707032000060520.

City of Cape Town (2014): Design and Management Guidelines for a Safer City. Best practice guidelines for the creation of sustainable, safe and lively neighbourhoods in Cape Town.

City of Cape Town, Department of Informal Settlements (2015): Matrix Version 3.0. 22/8/2015. [Microsoft Excel spreadsheet]. Cape Town.

City of Cape Town Open Data Portal (2017a): Public Lighting: City of Cape Town Open Data Portal. Available online at http://web1.capetown.gov. za/web1/opendataportal/AllDatasets, accessed on 5/2/2018.

City of Cape Town Open Data Portal (2017b): Public Lighting. [data set].

City of Cape Town, Department of Informal Settlements (2019): Informal Settlement Boundaries. [data set]. Cape Town.

Cock, J.; Nathan, L. (Eds.) (1989): *Society at war. The militarisation of South Africa.* New York: St. Martin's Press.

CoCT Energy and Climate Change (2019): ECC 13/08/19: Khayelitsha Lighting Master Plan. The City of Cape Town. https://www.capetown.gov. za/, accessed on 10/21/2019.

Coetzer, N. (2013): *Building apartheid. On architecture and order in imperial Cape Town.* Farnham: Ashgate (Ashgate studies in architecture).

Cole, J. (2013): *The Making and Re-imagining of Khayelitsha.* Report for the Commission of Inquiry into Allegations of Police Inefficiency in Khayelitsha and a Breakdown in Relations between the Community and the Police in Khayelitsha. https://s3-eu-west-1.amazonaws. com/s3.sourceafrica.net/documents/14375/5-b-j-cole-affidavit.pdf, accessed on 8/4/2020.

Collier, S. J.; Schnitzler, Antina von; Mizes, J. C. (2016): Preface: Public Infrastructures / Infrastructural Publics. In *limn* (7). Available online at https://limn.it/articles/preface-public-infrastructures-infrastructural-publics/, accessed on 5/8/2018.

Cook, G. P. (1986): Khayelitsha: Policy Change or Crisis Response? *In Transactions of the Institute of British Geographers* 11 (1), p. 57. DOI: 10.2307/622070.

Cross, J. (2013): The 100th object: Solar lighting technology and humanitarian goods. In *Journal of Material Culture* 18 (4), pp. 367–387. DOI: 10.1177/1359183513498959.

Area Lighting Guideline, 2013: CTEG 001 Area Lighting Guideline.

Davoudian, N. (2018): Introduction to urban lighting and evidence-based lighting design. In Navaz Davoudian (Ed.): *Urban lighting for people. Evidence-based lighting design for the built environment.* [S.l.]: RIBA PUBLISHING.

Department of Human Settlements (2020): FAQ. Republic of South Africa, Department of Human Settlements. Available online at http://www.dhs.gov.za/content/faq, updated on 10/26/2020, accessed on 10/26/2020.

Desai, A. (2002): *We are the poors. Community struggles in post-apartheid South Africa.* New York, NY: Monthly Review Press. ISBN 978-1-58367-050-7.

Dewar, D.; Watson, V. (1984): *The concept of Khayelitsha. A planning perspective.* Cape Town: Urban Problems Research Unit University of Cape Town (Project report, no. 18).

Drewett, M.(2019): Music and Fear in Night-Time Apartheid. In Geoff Stahl, Giacomo Bottà (Eds.): *Nocturnes. Popular music and the night.* Cham, Switzerland: Palgrave Macmillan (Pop music, culture and identity).

Duff, C. (2010) On the Role of Affect and Practice in the Production of Place. In *Environment and Planning D: Society and Space*, 28(5), pp. 881–895. DOI: 10.1068/d16209.

Dunn, N.; Edensor, T. (Eds.) (2020): *Rethinking darkness. Cultures, histories, practices,* 1st ed. London: Routledge (Ambiances, atmospheres and sensory experiences of spaces).

Ebbensgaard, C. L. (2016): *Rethinking urban lighting. Geographies of artificial lighting in everyday life.* Dissertation. Queen Mary University of London; Roskilde University.

Edensor, T. (2012): Illuminated Atmospheres: Anticipating and Reproducing the Flow of Affective Experience in Blackpool. In *Environment and Planning D: Society and Space* 30 (6), pp. 1103–1122. DOI: 10.1068/d12211.

Edensor, T. (2013): Reconnecting with darkness: gloomy landscapes, lightless places. In *Social and Cultural Geography* 14 (4), pp. 446–465. DOI: 10.1080/14649365.2013.790992.

Edensor, T. (2017): *From Light to Dark. Daylight, Illumination, and Gloom*. Minneapolis: University of Minnesota Press. ISBN 978-0-8166-9443-3.

Elliason, O. (2016): *Why art has the power to change the world*. Available online at https://www.sobtell.com/images/questions/1496517194-20170521071935untitled_2.pdf, accessed on 13/04/2019

Entwistle, J.; Slater, D. (2019): Making space for 'the social': connecting sociology and professional practices in urban lighting design. In *The British journal of sociology* 70 (5), pp. 2020–2041. DOI: 10.1111/1468-4446.12657.

Entwistle, J.; Slater, D.R. (under review): *The Material Politics of Light: Urban Lighting and Masterplanning in a Municipal Regeneration Process*.

Evans, J. (2020): 260 lockdown 'land invasions' and counting for City of Cape Town. In *news24*, 8/3/2020. Available online at https://www.news24.com/news24/southafrica/news/260-lockdown-land-invasions-and-counting-for-city-of-cape-town-20200803, accessed on 3/16/2021.

Fainstein, S.S. (2000): New Directions in Planning Theory. In *Urban Affairs Review* 35 (4), pp. 451–478. Available online at http://journals.sagepub.com/doi/pdf/10.1177/107808740003500401, accessed on 6/19/2018.

Farral, S.; Bannister, J.; Ditton, J.; Gilchrist, E. (1997): Questioning the measurement of 'fear of crime'. Findings from a Major Methodological Study. In *The British Journal of Criminology* 37 (4). Available online at http://www.jstor.org/stable/23638681, accessed on 4/2/2021.

Farrington, DP.; Welsh, B. C. (2002): *Effects of improved street lighting on crime: a systematic review*. DOI: 10.4073/csr.2008.13

Faull, A.; Kelly, J. (2020): *Lockdown lessons on violence and policing in South Africa*. Institute for Security Studies. Cape Town. Available online at https://issafrica.org/iss-today/lockdown-lessons-on-violence-and-policing-in-south-africa, accessed on 4/22/2021.

Foucault, M.; Rabinow, P. (1984): *The Foucault reader*. 1st ed. New York: Pantheon Books.

Frasch, T. (2012). Tracks in the City: Technology, Mobility, and Society in Colonial Rangoon and Singapore. In *Modern Asian Studies* 46 (1), pp. 97–118.

Gallaher, C. (Ed.) (2009): *Key concepts in political geography*. London, Los Angeles: SAGE (Key concepts in human geography).

Gandy, M. (2007): Planning, Anti-Planning, and the Infrastructure Crisis Facing Metropolitan Lagos. In Martin J. Murray, Garth A. Myers (Eds.): *Cities in Contemporary Africa*. Basingstoke: Palgrave Macmillan, pp. 247–264.

Gandy, M. (2017a): Negative Luminescence. In *Annals of the American Association of Geographers* 107 (5), pp. 1090–1107. DOI: 10.1080/24694452.2017.1308767.

Gandy, M. (2017b): Urban atmospheres. In *Cultural geographies* 24 (3), pp. 353–374. DOI: 10.1177/1474474017712995.

Gibson, V. (2016): *Third Generation CPTED? Rethinking the Basis for Crime Prevention Strategies*. Dissertation. Northumbria University, Newcastle. Available online at http://nrl.northumbria.ac.uk/27318/, accessed on 8/2/2021.

Graham, S.; McFarlane, C. (Eds.) (2015): *Infrastructural lives. Urban infrastructure in context*. London: Routledge.

Guide plan committee for the Cape Metropolitan Area (1984): Cape Metropolitan Area: Draft Guide Plan. City of Cape Town Spatial Planning.

Hall, A., Konate, B., Kulkarni, A. (Eds.) (2012): Foroba Yelen. Portable Solar Lighting and Sustainable Strategies for Remote Villages in Malian Villages. International Conference of Engineering and Product Design Education. Artesis University College, Antwerp, Belgium, 6–7 September 2012. Available online at http://researchonline.rca.ac.uk/1041/1/Hall_Foroba_Yelen_2012.pdf, accessed on 10/1/2018.

Haque, A.N., Lemanski, C.; Groot, J. (2021): Why do low-income urban dwellers reject energy technologies? Exploring the socio-cultural acceptance of solar adoption in Mumbai and Cape Town. In *Energy Research and Social Science* 74, p. 101954. DOI: 10.1016/j.erss.2021.101954.

Harrison, P. (2014): Making planning theory real. In *Planning Theory* 13 (1), pp. 65–81. DOI: 10.1177/1473095213484144.

Hasse, J. (2012): *Atmosphären der Stadt. Aufgespürte Räume.* Berlin: Jovis Verlag.

Hölscher, C. (2017): *Evidence-Based Design. Methods and Tools for Evaluating Architectural Design.* Chair of Cognitive Science, ETH Zurich, 2017. Available online at https://cog.ethz.ch/teaching/evidence-based-design.html, accessed on 7/20/2020.

Houssay-Holzschuch, M. (2010): *Crossing boundaries: vivre ensemble dans l'Afrique du Sud post-apartheid.* Dissertation. Université de Paris I Panthéon-Sorbonne, Paris, p. 94.

Jacobs, J. (1992): *The death and life of great American cities.* New York: Vintage Books.

Jeffery, C. Ray (1971): Crime Prevention Through Environmental Design. In *American Behavioral Scientist* 14 (4), p. 598. DOI: 10.1177/000276427101400409.

Kumar, A. (2015): Cultures of lights. In *Geoforum* 65, pp. 59–68. DOI: 10.1016/j.geoforum.2015.07.012.

Lancaster, L. (2018): Unpacking Discontent: Where and why protest happens in South Africa. In *South African Crime Quarterly* 64, pp. 29–44. DOI: 10.17159/2413-3108/2018/v0n64a3031.

Lange, E., Young, S. (2019): Gender-based violence as difficult knowledge: pedagogies for rebalancing the masculine and the feminine. In *International Journal of Lifelong Education* 38 (3), pp. 301–326. DOI: 10.1080/02601370.2019.1597932.

Lefebvre, H. (1971): *Everyday life in the modern world.* Reprint. New York: Harper and Row (Harper torchbooks, TB1608, 1608).

Lefebvre, H. (1991): *The production of space.* Malden, Oxford, Carlton-Melbourne: Blackwell publishing.

Lemanski, C. (Ed.) (2019): *Citizenship and infrastructure. Practices and identities of citizens and the state.* 1st ed. London: Routledge (Routledge studies in urbanism and the city).

Lemanski, C. (2020): Infrastructural citizenship: The everyday citizenships of adapting and/or destroying public infrastructure in Cape Town, South Africa. In *Transactions of the Institute of British Geographers* 45 (3), pp. 589–605. DOI: 10.1111/tran.12370.

Lynch, K. (1960): *The image of the city.* Cambridge Mass: MIT Press (Publications of the Joint Center for Urban Studies).

Maslow, A.H., Frager, R. (1987): *Motivation and personality.* 3rd ed. New York, London: Harper and Row.

Mbembe, A. (2003): Necropolitics. In *Public Culture* 15 (1), pp. 11–40.

McFarlane, C., Rutherford, J. (2008): Political Infrastructures: Governing and Experiencing the Fabric of the City. In *International Journal of Urban and Regional Research* 32 (2), pp. 363–374. DOI: 10.1111/j.1468-2427.2008.00792.x.

Mcleod, SA. (2018): *Maslow's Hierarchy of Needs. Simply Psychology.* Available online at https://www.simplypsychology.org/maslow.html, accessed on 8/2/2021.

Meyer, D. (2020): City of Cape Town demolishes 60 000 structures in three months. In *The South African*, 9/4/2020. Available online at https://www.thesouthafrican.com/news/city-of-cape-town-demolishes-60-000-structures-land-invasions-friday-4-september/, accessed on 3/16/2021.

Mihinjac, M., Saville, G. (2019): Third-Generation Crime Prevention Through Environmental Design (CPTED). In *Social Sciences* 8 (6), p. 182. DOI: 10.3390/socsci8060182.

Millstein, M. (2020): 'If I Had My House, I'd Feel Free': Housing and the (Re)Productions of Citizenship in Cape Town, South Africa. In *Urban Forum* 31 (3), pp. 289–309. DOI: 10.1007/s12132-020-09397-2.

Miraftab, F. (2009): Insurgent Planning: Situating Radical Planning in the Global South. In *Planning Theory* 8 (1), pp. 32–50. DOI: 10.1177/1473095208099297.

Miraftab, F., Wills, S. (2005): Insurgency and Spaces of Active Citizenship. In *Journal of Planning Education and Research* 25 (2), pp. 200–217. DOI: 10.1177/0739456X05282182.

Mitchell, T. (1999): State, Economy, and the State Effect. In George Steinmetz (Ed.) *State/Culture: State-Formation after the Cultural Turn*. Ithaca, NY: Cornell University Press, pp. 76–97.

Morton, F. (2009): Performance, Research as. In N. J. Thrift, Rob Kitchin (Eds.): *International encyclopedia of human geography*. Amsterdam, London, Oxford: Elsevier, pp. 120–125.

Mtembu, N. (2017): Poor lighting and inaccessibility in Khayelitsha . In *IOL*, 5/21/2017. Available online at http://www.iol.co.za/weekend-argus/poor-lighting-and-inaccessibility-in-khayelitsha-9245298, accessed on 5/22/2017.

Muanda, C.; Goldin, J.; Haldenwang, R. (2020): Factors and impacts of informal settlements residents' sanitation practices on access and sustainability of sanitation services in the policy context of Free Basic Sanitation. In *Journal of Water, Sanitation and Hygiene for Development* 10 (2), pp. 238–248. DOI: 10.2166/washdev.2020.123.

Mutyambizi, C.; Mokhele, T.; Ndinda, C.; Hongoro, C. (2020): Access to and Satisfaction with Basic Services in Informal Settlements: Results from a Baseline Assessment Survey. In *International journal of environmental research and public health* 17(12): p. 4400. DOI: 10.3390/ijerph17124400.

Nasar, J.L.; Bokharaei, S. (2017a): Impressions of Lighting in Public Squares After Dark. In *Environment and Behavior* 49 (3), pp. 227–254. DOI: 10.1177/0013916515626546.

Nasar, J.L.; Bokharaei, S. (2017b): Lighting modes and their effects on impressions of public squares. In *Journal of Environmental Psychology* 49, pp. 96–105. DOI: 10.1016/j.jenvp.2016.12.007.

Neumann, D. (2002): *Architectural illumination since World War II*. New York: Prestel.

Nye, D.E. (2019): *American Illuminations. Urban Lighting, 1800-1920*. Cambridge: MIT Press.

Oldfield, S., Greyling, S. (2015): Waiting for the state: a politics of housing in South Africa. In *Environment and Planning A* 47 (5), pp. 1100–1112. DOI: 10.1177/0308518X15592309.

Orbann, C. (1984): *South African defense policy*. Monterey, California. Naval Postgraduate School.

Otter, C. (2008): *The Victorian eye. A political history of light and vision in Britain, 1800-1910*. 3rd ed. Chicago, London: University of Chicago Press. ISBN: 9780226640761.

Painter, K. (1991b): The West Park Estate Survey: Evaluation of public lighting as a crime prevention strategy. In *Security Journal*, 5(3), pp. 116–124.

Painter, K. (1994): The impact of street lighting on crime, fear, and pedestrian street use. In *Security Journal* 4 (3). Available online at https://popcenter.asu.edu/sites/default/files/137-painter-the_impact_of_street_lighting_on_crime_fear_an.pdf, accessed on 31/03/2019

Painter, K. (1996): The influence of street lighting improvements on crime, fear and pedestrian street use, after dark. In *Landscape and Urban Planning* 35, pp. 193–201, accessed on 10/24/2019.

Palmer, I.; Moodley, N.; Parnell, S. (2017): *Building a capable state. Service delivery in post-apartheid South Africa*. London: Zed.

Pareek, S. (2015): A Plastic Bottle Is All You Need To Light Up A Home In The Most Amazing Way. In *The Better India*, 3/6/2015. Available online at https://www.thebetterindia.com/19986/a-plastic-bottle-provide-light-in-a-low-income-home-liter-of-light/, accessed on 2/19/2021.

Parikh, P., Bisaga, I., Loggia, C., Georgiadou, M.C., Ojo-Aromokudu, J. (2020): Barriers and opportunities for participatory environmental upgrading: Case study of Havelock informal settlement, Durban. In *City and Environment Interactions* 5, p. 100041. DOI: 10.1016/j.cacint.2020.100041.

Parnell, S., Pieterse, E. (2010): The 'Right to the City': Institutional Imperatives of a Developmental State. In *International Journal of Urban and Regional Research* 34 (1), pp. 146–162. DOI: 10.1111/j.1468-2427.2010.00954.x.

Patel, L. (2008): Getting it Right and Wrong: An Overview of a Decade of Post-Apartheid Social Welfare. In *Practice* 20 (2), pp. 71–81. DOI: 10.1080/09503150802058822.

Patel, L. (2012): Developmental Social Policy, Social Welfare Services and the Non-profit Sector in South Africa. In *Social Policy and Administration* 46 (6), pp. 603–618. DOI: 10.1111/j.1467-9515.2012.00858.x.

Pease, K. (1999): A review of street lighting evaluations. In *Crime Prevention Studies* 10, pp. 47–76. Available online at https://popcenter.asu.edu/sites/default/files/library/crimeprevention/volume_10/03-PeaseLighting.pdf, accessed on 3/2/2021.

Peña-García, A., Hurtado, A., Aguilar-Luzón, MC. (2015): Impact of public lighting on pedestrians' perception of safety and well-being. In *Safety Science* 78, pp. 142–148. DOI: 10.1016/j.ssci.2015.04.009.

Persens, L. (2021): Six men killed in brazen shooting in Khayelitsha. In *Eyewitness News,* 4/26/2021. Available online at https://ewn.co.za/2021/01/31/six-men-killed-in-brazen-shooting-in-khayelitsha, accessed on 4/26/2021.

Polk, M. (2014): Achieving the promise of transdisciplinarity: a critical exploration of the relationship between transdisciplinary research and societal problem solving. In *Sustainainability Science* 9 (4), pp. 439–451. DOI: 10.1007/s11625-014-0247-7.

Prieto Curiel, R., Bishop, S. (2017): Modelling the fear of crime. In *Proceedings. Mathematical, physical, and engineering sciences* 473 (2203), p. 20170156. DOI: 10.1098/rspa.2017.0156.

Ramsay, M., Newton, R. (1991): *The effect of better street lighting on crime and fear: a review.* Home Office Crime Prevention Unit. ISBN 9780862526702.

Republic of South Africa (1996): The Constitution of the Republic of South Africa. As adopted on 8 May 1996 and amended on 11 October 1996 by the Constituent Assembly. Pretoria: Department of Justice and Constitutional Development.

Rowana GL (2019): 24SUB: 24/03/2019. Statement by the City's Mayoral Committee member for Energy and Climate Change, councillor Phindule Maxiti. City of Cape Town, accessed on 1/4/2021.

Sanyal, B. (2002): Globalization, Ethical Compromise and Planning Theory. In *Planning Theory* 1 (2), pp. 116–123. DOI: 10.1177/147309520200100202.

Schmid, C. (2008): Henri Lefebvre's theory of the production of space. Towards a three-dimensional dialectic. In K. Goonewardena, S. Kipfer, R. Milgrom, C. Schmid (Eds.): *Space, Difference, Everyday Life. Reading Henri Lefebvre.* London, New York: Routledge, pp. 27–45.

Semmens, N. (2002): Preliminary Findings on Seasonality and the Fear of Crime. A Research Note. In *British Journal of Criminology* 42 (4), pp. 798–806. DOI: 10.1093/bjc/42.4.798.

Shaw, R. (2014): Street lighting in England and Wales: New Technologies and Uncertainty in the Assemblage of Street lighting Infrastructure. In *Environment and Planning A* 46 (9), pp. 2228–2242. DOI: 10.1068/a130313p.

Simone, A. (2004): People as Infrastructure: Intersecting Fragments in Johannesburg. In *Public Culture* 16 (3), pp. 407–429. DOI: 10.1215/08992363-16-3-407.

Simone, A., Pieterse, E. (2017): *New urban worlds. Inhabiting dissonant times.* Cambridge, UK, Medford, MA, USA: Polity.

Singh, K. (2020): Murder cases down by 72%. Cele attributes drop to alcohol ban, increased patrols and lockdown. In *news24,* 4/22/2020. Available online at https://www.news24.com/news24/southafrica/news/murder-down-by-1-110-cases-cele-attributes-drop-to-alcohol-ban-increased-patrols-and-lockdown-20200422, accessed on 4/22/2021.

Sinwell, L. (2010): Conceptualizing Direct Action as a Form of Participation in Development: A South African Case. In *Politikon* 37 (1), pp. 67–83. DOI: 10.1080/02589346.2010.492150.

Slater, D.; Entwistle, J. (2018): Light as material/lighting as practice: urban lighting and energy. In *Science Museum Group Journal* 9 (9). DOI: 10.15180/180906.

Sloane, M.; Slater, D.; Entwistle, J. (2016): Tackling Social Inequalities in Public Lighting. Configuring Light: Staging the Social. London. Available online at http://www.configuringlight.org/wp-content/uploads/2019/03/CL-Round-Tables-Report-reduced-size.pdf, accessed on 10/2/2021.

Smith, D.M. (Ed.) (2005): *The Apartheid City and Beyond. Urbanization and Social Change in South Africa*. 1st ed. Abingdon, Oxon: Taylor and Francis.

Social Justice Coalition (2018): *Effective Public Lighting*. Available online at https://sjc.org.za/campaigns/publiclighting, updated on 11/27/2018, assessed on 3/16/2021.

Social Justice Coalition (2020): social justice coalition. Cape Town. Available online at http://www.sjc.org.za/, accessed on 5/22/2017.

Somekh, B. (2008): Action Research. In Lisa M. Given (Ed.): *The Sage Encyclopedia of Qualitative Research Methods*. Los Angeles, London: SAGE, pp. 4–7.

Star, S. L. (1999): The Ethnography of Infrastructure. In *American Behavioral Scientist* 43 (3), pp. 377–391. DOI: 10.1177/00027649921955326.

Statistics South Africa (2018): Statistical release. General Household Survey 2017. P0318. Statistics South Africa. Pretoria. Available online at http://www.statssa.gov.za/publications/P0318/P03182017.pdf#page=51, accessed on 10/14/2020.

Surplus People Project South Africa (1984): Khayelitsha: new home - old story. Cape Town: The Project.

Swilling, M. (2006): Sustainability and infrastructure planning in South Africa: a Cape Town case study. In *Environment and Urbanization* 18 (1), pp. 23–50. DOI: 10.1177/0956247806063939.

Swilling, M.; Annecke, E. (2006): Building sustainable neighbourhoods in South Africa: learning from the Lynedoch case. In *Environment and Urbanization* 18 (2), pp. 315–332. DOI: 10.1177/0956247806069606.

Thibaud, J. (2011): The Sensory Fabric of Urban Ambiances. In *The Senses and Society* 6 (2), pp. 203–215. DOI: 10.2752/174589311X12961584845846.

Truth and Reconciliation Commission (1998a): Truth and Reconciliation Commission of South Africa.

Truth and Reconciliation Commission (1998b): Truth and Reconciliation Commission of South Africa report.

UN-Habitat (2012): *State of the world's cities 2012-2013. Prosperity of cities*. Nairobi: United Nations Human Settlements Programme (UN-HABITAT).

Unwin, J. (2018): Lighting for Reassurance. In Navaz Davoudian (Ed.): *Urban lighting for people. Evidence-based lighting design for the built environment*. [S.l.]: RIBA PUBLISHING, pp. 56–74.

Urban Research Incubator (2020): Urban Research Incubator. Institute of Science Technology and Policy, ETH Zurich. Available online at https://istp.ethz.ch/research/uri.html, updated on 07/30/2020 09:57:58, accessed on 7/30/2020.

Vertigans, S.; Gibson, N. (2020): Resilience and social cohesion through the lens of residents in a Kenyan informal settlement. In *Community Development Journal* 55 (4), pp. 624–644. DOI: 10.1093/cdj/bsz012.

von Schnitzler, A. (2008): Citizenship Prepaid. Water, Calculability, and Techno-Politics in South Africa*. In *Journal of Southern African Studies* 34 (4), pp. 899–917. DOI: 10.1080/03057070802456821.

von Schnitzler, A. (2016): *Democracy's infrastructure. Techno-politics and citizenship after apartheid*. Princeton: Princeton University Press.

Wafer, A. (2012): Discourses of Infrastructure and Citizenship in Post-Apartheid Soweto. In *Urban Forum* 23 (2), pp. 233–243. DOI: 10.1007/s12132-012-9146-0.

Wainwright, O. (2014): Apartheid ended 20 years ago, so why is Cape Town still 'a paradise for the few'? In *The Guardian*. Available online at https://www.theguardian.com/cities/2014/apr/30/cape-town-apartheid-ended-still-paradise-few-south-africa, accessed on 6/8/2018.

Watson, V. (2013): Planning and the 'stubborn realities' of global south-east cities: Some emerging ideas. In *Planning Theory* 12 (1), pp. 81–100. DOI: 10.1177/1473095212446301.

Weizman, E.; Tavares, P.; Schuppli, S.; Situ Studio (2010): Forensic Architecture. In *Architectural Design* 80 (5), pp. 58–63. DOI: 10.1002/ad.1134.

Welsh, B.C.; Farrington, D.P. (2008): Effects of Improved Street Lighting on Crime. In *Campbell Systematic Reviews* 4 (1), pp. 1–51. DOI: 10.4073/csr.2008.13.

Western Cape Department of Human Settlements (2018): Questionnaire. Standard questionnaire fields to be included in enumerations and profiling for projects undertaken by the Western Cape Government Department of Human Settlements. Western Cape Department of Human Settlements, accessed on 7/28/2020.

Western Cape Development Board (1986): Tenders. South African National Archive, 8/4/8/1986/wk34. Formal tenders; aquisition and performance; building works; Crossroads electrical reticulation phase 1, supply and installation of high-mast lighting.

Western Cape Development Board (1987a): Tenders. South African National Archive, 8/4/8/1986/wk40. Formal tenders; acquisition and performance; building works; Khayelitsha Phase, Street Lighting, Town 2, Part 1.

Western Cape Development Board (1987b): Tenders. South African National Archive, 8/4/8/1987/wk11. Formal tenders; acquisition and performance; building works; Khayelitsha Electrification, Town 2, Village 3, high mast lighting.

Western Cape Development Board (1987c): Tenders. South African National Archive, 8/4/8/1987/wk13. Formal tenders; acquisition and performance; building works; Khayelitsha Electrification, Stage 2, Town 2, Primary HV Electrical Reticulation.

Weyers, D. (2019): OPINIONISTA: Streetlights and ward allocations. Discrimination on the basis of race and poverty in the City of Cape Town. In *Daily Maverick*, 3/8/2019. Available online at https://www.dailymaverick.co.za/opinionista/2019-03-08-street-lights-and-ward-allocations-discrimination-on-the-basis-of-race-and-poverty-in-the-city-of-cape-town/, accessed on 3/24/2019.

Wilson, J.Q.; Kelling, G.L. (1982): Broken Windows. The police and neighbourhood safety. In *The Atlantic Monthly* (March 1982). Available online at https://www.theatlantic.com/magazine/archive/1982/03/broken-windows/304465/, accessed on 5/2/2021.

Winther, T. (2008). *The Impact of Electricity: Development, Desires, and Dilemmas*. Oxford: Berghahn.

WNYC (2014): *Spotlight on Safety in Public Housing*. New York Public Radio. New York. Available online at https://www.wnyc.org/story/spotlight-safety-housing-projects/, updated on 2/4/2021, accessed on 2/4/2021.

World Health Organization (2018): *Global status report on alcohol and health 2018*. Geneva: World Health Organization.

Yiftachel, O. (2009): Critical theory and 'gray space': Mobilization of the colonized. In *City* 13 (2–3), pp. 246–263. DOI: 10.1080/13604810902982227.

Yiftachel, O. (2015): Epilogue-from 'Gray Space' to Equal 'Metrozenship'? Reflections On Urban Citizenship. In *International Journal of Urban and Regional Research* 39 (4), pp. 726–737. DOI: 10.1111/1468-2427.12263.

Zielinska-Dabkowska, K.M. (2018): Urban lighting masterplan. Origins, methodologies, and collaborations. In Navaz Davoudian (Ed.): *Urban lighting for people. Evidence-based lighting design for the built environment*. [S.l.]: RIBA PUBLISHING, pp. 18–41.

The open access publication of this book has been published with the support of the Swiss National Science Foundation.

© 2023 author; published by jovis Verlag GmbH, Berlin

This publication is available as an open access publication via www.degruyter.com.

Copy editing: **Hilary Alexander**
Proofreading: **Bianca Murphy**
Cover and design concept: **jovis Verlag**
Layout: **Stephanie Briers**
Printed in the European Union.

Bibliographic information published by the Deutsche Nationalbibliothek
The Deutsche Nationalbibliothek lists this publication in the Deutsche Nationalbibliografie; detailed bibliographic data are available on the Internet at http://dnb.d-nb.de

jovis Verlag GmbH
Lützowstraße 33
10785 Berlin

www.jovis.de

jovis books are available worldwide in select bookstores. Please contact your nearest bookseller or visit www.jovis.de for information concerning your local distribution.

ISBN 978-3-86859-776-9 (softcover)
ISBN 978-3-86859-780-6 (e-book)
DOI 10.1515/9783868597806